# THE SOVIET FAR EAST
# MILITARY BUILDUP

*A SeCAP Publication*

# THE SOVIET FAR EAST MILITARY BUILDUP

*Nuclear Dilemmas and Asian Security*

Edited by

**RICHARD H. SOLOMON**
*The Rand Corporation*

**MASATAKA KOSAKA**
*Kyoto University*

**𝒜uburn House Publishing Company**
Dover, Massachusetts

*Library of Congress Cataloging in Publication Data*

Main entry under title:

The Soviet Far East military buildup.

Includes bibliographies and index.
1. East Asia—National security—Addresses,
essays, lectures. 2. Soviet Union—Military relations—
East Asia—Addresses, essays, lectures. 3. East Asia—
Military relations—Soviet Union—Addresses, essays,
lectures. 4. Soviet Union—Military policy—Addresses,
essays, lectures. I. Solomon, Richard H., 1937–
II. Kosaka, Masataka, 1934–
UA830.S69   1986        355'.03305        85-30664
ISBN 0-86569-140-1

Printed in the United States of America

*This volume is dedicated to Dr. Masamichi Inoki, distinguished educator, scholar, and strategic thinker who has made a singular contribution as founder and president of the Research Institute for Peace and Security and as Chairman of the Japanese organizing committee of the Security Conference on Asia and the Pacific (SeCAP).*

# ACKNOWLEDGMENTS

The authors want to express their appreciation for the invaluable support and assistance provided by a number of institutions and individuals in the publication of this volume.

Financial support for the April 1984 SeCAP conference on "Reducing Nuclear Threats in Asia," which was the initial source of the papers in this volume, was provided by grants from the Ford Foundation, the Rockefeller Foundation, and the U.S.-Japan Foundation.

In preparing the manuscript, Brigadier (ret.) Kenneth Hunt provided timely and important editorial assistance. Ms. Dorothy Diamond, Secretary of SeCAP/U.S., played the primary role in organizing and producing the manuscript. The authors are particularly indebted to her and her associate Pamela Christensen for invaluable care in preparation of the manuscript, and Patricia Wood for logistical support. They are also indebted to Anna Sun Wynston and Mary Yanokawa for research assistance and additional logistical support.

Major support was provided SeCAP/Japan, in coordinating with the U.S. editorial and production group, in producing the Japanese-language version of this volume by Seiichiro Onishi, Executive Director, Research Institute for Peace and Security, Professor Masashi Nishihara, National Defense Academy, and Akihiko Tanaka, also of the Research Institute for Peace and Security. This version of the book has also been published by Ningen-no-Kagaku Sha.

# PREFACE

In 1978 a group of American and Japanese specialists in defense and foreign policy issues convened in Honolulu to discuss ways of improving communication between the two countries on matters affecting their shared security interests. The result of their deliberations was the formation of SeCAP—the Security Conference on Asia and the Pacific.* In its nearly eight years of activity, SeCAP has convened seven working conferences of U.S. and Japanese experts and published four studies dealing with the energy crisis as it affects the economic security of the two countries, and the ever-growing Soviet military presence in the Asia-Pacific region.† The culmination of this first phase of SeCAP was publication of a joint policy statement, *The U.S.–Japan Relationship in the 1980s: Achievements, Challenges, and Opportunities* (January 1983), which assessed major issues affecting the future of the relationship. This statement was presented to senior officials in both governments just prior to Prime Minister Nakasone's meeting with President Reagan in Washington in January 1983.

During 1984, after conclusion of the initial series of SeCAP conferences and publications, the organizers decided to expand the scope of the Japanese-American dialogue to include defense and foreign policy specialists from a number of countries in the Asia-Pacific region, and to address one of the major security problems jointly facing them—the growing nuclearization of the Soviet military presence in the Far East. Consequently, SeCAP convened a workshop on the subject of "Reducing Nuclear Threats in Asia" in San Diego, California, that brought together specialists from the People's Republic of China, the Republic of Korea, the Philippines, Australia, England, and the Federal Republic of Germany, as well as from Japan and the United States.

---

*In Japan, SeCAP is organized under the auspices of the Research Institute for Peace and Security (RIPS).
†The SeCAP publications are listed on p. xiv.

vii

This volume is an outgrowth of the San Diego conference. The issue of the growing Soviet nuclear presence in Asia—especially Moscow's deployment of SS-20 intermediate-range "theater" missiles and long-range *Backfire* bombers—was viewed as sufficiently important to warrant publication of this unique collection of analytical papers by a multinational group of defense and foreign policy experts. At a time when the SS-20 issue and Intermediate-Range Nuclear Force (INF) modernization is being widely discussed among American and NATO defense experts, and when public anxiety about the spread of nuclear weapons is especially intense, we believe it is both timely and important to make this contribution to a more informed and reasoned debate on the INF issue as it affects allied and friendly states in the Asia-Pacific region—especially those that share concern with the growing Soviet nuclear threat to regional security.

*Richard L. Sneider*
*Chairman, SeCAP/United States*
*Adjunct Professor, Columbia University,*
*New York City*

*Masamichi Inoki*
*Chairman, SeCAP/Japan*
*President, Research Institute for*
*Peace and Security, Tokyo*

# CONTENTS

# LIST OF ILLUSTRATIONS

# LIST OF TABLES

# SeCAP PUBLICATIONS

*How the West Should Protect Persian Gulf Oil: And Insure Against Its Loss,* by Henry S. Rowen (August 1982).

*The U.S.–Japan Relationship in the 1980s: Achievements, Challenges, and Opportunities* (January 1983).

*Soviet Expansionism in Asia and the Sino-Soviet–U.S. Triangle,* by Harry Gelman (March 1983).

*U.S.–Japan Economic Problems,* by Shinichi Ichimura (April 1983).

*Power Balance and Security in Indochina,* by Evelyn Colbert (April 1983).

# SeCAP DIRECTORS

## United States

President: Richard Sneider
Adjunct Professor
Columbia University
New York, New York

Vice-President: Albert Wohlstetter
Director of Research
Pan Heuristics
Marina del Rey,
California

Fred S. Hoffman, Director, Pan Heuristics, Marina del Rey, California

Henry S. Rowen, Graduate School of Business, Stanford University, Stanford, California

Robert Scalapino, Director, Institute of East Asian Studies, University of California, Berkeley, California

Richard H. Solomon, Head, Political Science Department, The Rand Corporation, Santa Monica, California

## Japan

Chairman: Masamichi Inoki
Director, Research
Institute for Peace
and Security
Tokyo

President: Masataka Kosaka
Faculty of Law
Kyoto University
Kyoto

Fuji Kamiya, Keio University, Tokyo
Masashi Nishihara, National Defense Academy, Yokosuka
Kiichi Saeki, Director, Nomura Research Institute, Kamakura

*Chapter 1*

# NUCLEAR DILEMMAS AND ASIAN SECURITY: PROBLEMS OF COALITION DEFENSE IN THE NUCLEAR ERA

*by Richard H. Solomon and Masataka Kosaka*

## Introduction: The Dilemma of Deterring the Soviet Union

This volume is an assessment, from the diverse perspectives of an international group of defense and foreign policy analysts, of one of the major military buildups of recent decades: the expansion of the Soviet Union's ground, naval, and air forces in the Asia-Pacific region, and the nuclearization of the Soviet military presence to a point that now threatens all the countries of East Asia that are allied to or have friendly relations with the United States.

This introduction and the chapters of Part One, seek to evaluate the meaning of Moscow's military buildup in the global context of Soviet (and American) concerns about confronting a two-front, or multi-front, security challenge—in Europe (and/or the Middle East) as well as in the Asia-Pacific region.

In Part Two, five authors from major states of East Asia describe from differing perspectives how the Soviet military buildup affects the security of the People's Republic of China (PRC), Japan, the

1

Republic of Korea (ROK), the states of ASEAN (the Association of Southeast Asian Nations),[1] Australia, and New Zealand.

The Soviet military buildup interacts in substantial measure with the two major unresolved regional conflicts in East Asia—that between North and South Korea and the continuing rivalry for control of the Indochina Peninsula. Part Three assesses recent developments on the Korean Peninsula and in Indochina as they enmesh the nuclear powers in these regional conflicts.

Part Four attempts to draw lessons from the experience of Western Europe in responding to the expansion of Soviet "theater" or intermediate-range nuclear forces (INF) for the defense of Asia. It also seeks to assess the linkages between the security of the states of Europe and the security of the Asia-Pacific region as both areas confront, from different quarters of the Eurasian landmass, the Soviet Union's seemingly inexorable expansion of its military power.

Despite the varied, and sometimes conflicting, perspectives of this diverse group of authors in assessing the Soviet military threat, all agree that the United States should not overreact to Moscow's nuclearization of its military presence in the Asia-Pacific region. This policy assessment, however, poses a major security dilemma for the United States and its allies in East Asia. On the one hand, effective defense against the Soviet military buildup requires a coalition of efforts. No one country, not even the United States, is capable by itself of countervailing Moscow's extensive military capabilities. The United States needs the use of foreign bases and the collaboration of regional allies if it is to effectively deter Soviet expansionism. At the same time, the states of East Asia require America's global military capabilities, including its nuclear deterrent, to countervail Moscow's forces deployed in the Soviet Far East, in the Western Pacific, and in the various bases the Soviets are establishing in Vietnam, Japan's Northern Territories, Afghanistan, and Mongolia. On the other hand, an increase in U.S. military capabilities, even though lagging behind the growth of Soviet forces—especially nuclear forces—would likely generate indigenous political reactions that would strain the alliance relationships necessary to sustain an effective defense against the Soviets.

Moscow can be expected to play on popular fears of nuclear war in Asia, as it has done in Europe, in an effort to break up the alliances its post–World War II expansionism has provoked. The challenge to the United States and its Asian allies is to assemble a sufficiently robust defense capability to deter Moscow from opportunistic adventures in the region—such as those taken in recent years in Afghanistan, in Indochina (via support for its ally Vietnam), and in Japan's Northern Territories—without, in the process, giving the Soviets the opportunity to exert political influence through popular fears of a nuclear arms race between the superpowers.

The contributors to this volume largely agree that the nature of the Soviet military challenge in the East Asia-Pacific region is such that the United States need not maintain an exact equivalence in types and numbers of weapons with the various systems deployed by Moscow to effectively deter Soviet aggression. Specifically, Moscow's troops, naval units, nuclear-capable missiles, and aircraft need not be matched on a one-for-one basis to maintain a credible deterrent. The structure of the region, with the Soviet ground force threat largely limited to China (which deters Moscow with the threat of a draining "people's war") and with naval, air, and missile forces the predominant threat in a geographically dispersed area, provides the United States and its allies with the potential to exploit their technological superiority in order to deploy a conventional defense force at a level that will deter Moscow from nonnuclear military adventures. (See Figure 1–1.)

At the same time, the United States, by virtue of its ability to sustain a low-profile nuclear deterrent at sea, in rear areas, and in the continental United States, should be able to maintain an effective "coupling" between its own security interests in the region and those of its allies—a strategic nuclear force combined with an offshore nuclear capability of theater range sufficient to deter Moscow without putting allied territories as visibly at risk as would land-based theater nuclear forces.

U.S. and allied security interests inevitably diverge on the assessment of whether the Soviet Union is effectively deterred by a purely defensive counterforce deployed on a regional basis, or whether a more offensive capability deployed in coordination with forces in other theaters—so as to present Moscow with a multifront security challenge—would most effectively constrain the Soviet Union's expansionist inclinations. The countries of East Asia will naturally tend to evaluate their security interests on a local or regional basis, whereas the United States, as a power with worldwide commitments and concerned about a two-front military threat, will approach the Soviet challenge on a global basis.

## The Soviet Union's Asian Military Buildup: Seeking Security on the Far Eastern Frontier

Securing lightly populated yet resource-rich Siberian and Far Eastern provinces has been a concern of Russian leaders from the

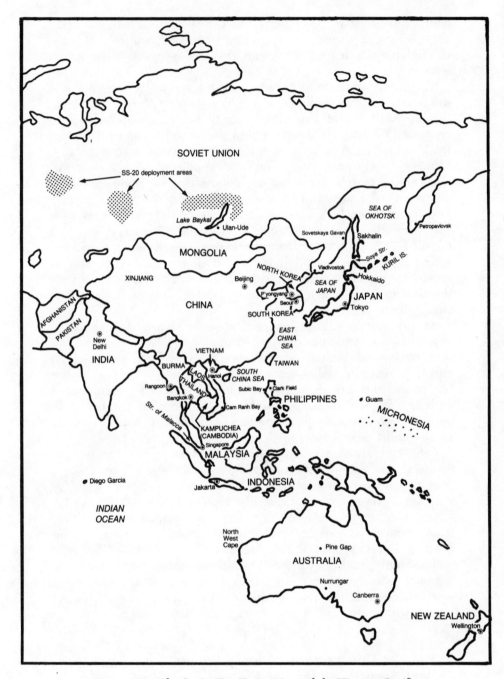

**Figure 1–1  The Soviet Far East, Asia, and the Western Pacific**

time of the Mongol invasion of Europe through Russia's defeat at the hands of the Japanese navy in 1905. Seeing their Asian frontier as but one vulnerable front of a multi-front challenge has been a preoccupation of Soviet leaders from the days of the Bolshevik Revolution, when the British led international interventions against Lenin's new government at Archangel on the White Sea and Vladivostok on the Pacific Coast, through World War II, when Imperial Japan allied itself to Nazi Germany.[2]

The Communist victory in China's civil war in 1949 seemed to resolve Moscow's two-front security problem. The Sino-Soviet alliance of 1950 created a friendly "buffer" state for the USSR in the Far East—and a new two-front security challenge for the United States. The breakdown of the alliance in the summer of 1960, however, and China's subsequent raising of border issues along the 4,650-mile Sino-Soviet frontier as part of a broader political challenge to Soviet influence in Asia, reopened Moscow's concerns about the security of its Far Eastern provinces. It was in this context that the Brezhnev leadership in 1965 initiated the first phase of its Asian military buildup, increasing its ground force divisions in the Siberian, Transbaykal, and Far East military districts from less than 20 to more than 50 today.

Military clashes along the disputed Sino-Soviet frontier in 1969 further deepened the Moscow-Beijing feud, ultimately impelling the Chinese leadership to improve relations with the United States, Japan, and Western Europe to avoid international isolation and to build political counterpressures against the mounting Soviet threat. This militarization of the Sino-Soviet political feud, in concert with Moscow's anticipation of China's normalization of relations with the United States and Japan, led the Soviets to initiate a second phase in their Asian military buildup in 1977. This phase was designed not only to encircle China but also to prepare for the possible formation of a coalition of U.S., Chinese, and Japanese forces against the Soviet Union. Thus, in 1978 Moscow created an independent theater command for its Far East forces at Ulan Ude in the Siberian Military District. Simultaneously, it accelerated the expansion of its Pacific fleet (now the largest of the four Soviet fleets) and began to deploy its most modern aircraft and armor to the Far East. Hanoi's victory in the Vietnamese civil war in 1975 and the rapid deterioration in Sino-Vietnamese relations enabled Moscow to acquire use of the former American naval and air bases at Cam Ranh Bay, thus furthering the military encirclement of China and enabling Moscow to project its air and naval forces south from Vladivostok to the Straits of Malacca and into the Indian Ocean.

This second phase of the Soviet Asia-Pacific military buildup has also involved the nuclearization of Moscow's military forces. With its initial deployment of the SS-20 intermediate-range "theater" missile in 1977 and deployment of the medium-range *Backfire* bomber in early 1980, Moscow significantly altered the character of its military presence in the region, creating a qualitatively new threat to the U.S. Seventh Fleet, to U.S. bases in Japan, South Korea, and the Philippines, and to a broad range of military and economic targets in China and other states throughout the Western Pacific.[3]

Moscow's Far Eastern nuclear buildup presents as much a political as a military challenge to the Asian region. A Soviet nuclear threat has existed since the 1960s—in ICBMs, in the short-range SS-4 FROG and SS-5 SCUD missiles deployed against China, and in the Tu-16 *Badger* bombers and tactical strike aircraft also deployed along the Sino-Soviet frontier. The new, longer-range and more accurate mobile nuclear missiles and aircraft now targeted throughout the region seem designed as much for political intimidation as for deterring attacks on the Soviet Union's still lightly populated Far Eastern territories.[4] As demonstrated by Moscow's concurrent SS-20 missile buildup in the European theater, the heightening of a visible nuclear threat has been used by Soviet leaders—in conjunction with indigenous peace movements—to raise fears among America's allies about the "decoupling" of the U.S. strategic deterrent from the defense of Europe, to stimulate public anxieties about the possibility of nuclear conflict as a means of undermining the political foundations of the NATO alliance, and to build pressures on the United States to enter into disadvantageous arms control agreements.[5]

Moscow seems to be pursuing a similar strategy in Asia. Its unabated military buildup has been paralleled by a series of political initiatives designed to focus public anxieties about a regional arms buildup on its adversaries: (1) Leonid Brezhnev's 1969 proposal for an Asian Collective Security organization—now refurbished in a 1985 call for an all-Asian security conference; (2) a series of proposals to the Chinese for nonaggression treaties; and (3) a range of proposals for nuclear-free zones, confidence-building measures, and agreements for the no-first-use of the nuclear weapons it has been deploying to the region.

As Hiroshi Kimura and Masataka Kosaka note in Chapters 6 and 7 of this volume, the Soviets have been less successful in Asia than in Europe in building public pressures against American and allied responses to its military buildup, partly because of Moscow's blatant use or encouragement of military force in Indochina,

Afghanistan, and Japan's Northern Territories, and partly because of the restrained response of the United States. Yet antinuclear sentiments persist throughout the region, as is evident in New Zealand's formal opposition to port visits by nuclear-powered or armed ships of the U.S. Seventh Fleet, in Australia's unease about American military facilities on Australian territory, and in the August 1985 effort by the South Pacific Forum states, in drafting the Treaty of Raratonga, to create a nuclear-free zone in the Southwest Pacific.[6]

The objective of this volume is to assess as straightforwardly as possible the character of the Soviet military buildup, especially its nuclear dimensions, in order to provide the basis for measured and effective U.S. and allied responses that will sustain an effective deterrent against Moscow's expansionist inclinations and reassure allies and friends about America's security role in Asia, while not playing into Moscow's hands politically.

## Regional Reactions to the Soviet Military Buildup in Asia

The United States responded slowly, and only with the prodding of its NATO allies, to Moscow's deployment in the late-1970s of the SS-20 "theater" nuclear missile in Europe. Yet even though the American reaction was belated relative to Moscow's initiative and was based on close consultations with its NATO allies, the strong public reaction it generated nearly undermined NATO's intermediate-range nuclear force (INF) modernization decision.[7] In East Asia, pressures on the United States from allied governments to respond to Moscow's nuclearization of its military presence do not exist, although both the Japanese and Chinese governments protested Moscow's expanding deployments in the context of the INF negotiations in Geneva. The SS-20, with its capacity for mobile deployment in either the European or Asian theaters, has brought home to Asian leaders and defense specialists the linkage between security developments on either side of the Eurasian landmass and the manner in which arms control negotiations between the United States and the Soviet Union affect Asian as well as European security.[8]

Asian reactions to the Soviet military buildup have been remarkably diverse. They reflect the political and geographical diversity of the region. After two decades of confrontation under Mao Zedong's leadership, the Chinese, whose dispute with the Soviets initially stimulated Moscow's military buildup in the mid-1960s, have now adopted a policy of using political means to try to defuse the Soviet military buildup, even as they maintain a modest nuclear deterrent of their own. As late as 1980, Deng Xiaoping called for a "united front" of the countries threatened by Moscow's force buildup to resist Soviet "hegemony." But today, as Yao Wenbin details in Chapter 5, Chinese leaders have abandoned the policy of political confrontation and call on Moscow to remove the "three big obstacles" of military encirclement of the PRC as the basis for normalizing Sino-Soviet relations. The Chinese have thus given Moscow a major opportunity to use political rather than military means to project its influence into the Asia-Pacific region.

It is not clear whether the new Soviet leadership under Mikhail Gorbachev will have the flexibility to respond positively to this change in Chinese policy. As Harry Gelman observes in Chapter 3, the Soviets, by long tradition, believe military power and intimidation to be the most reliable approaches to guaranteeing their security. Moreover, the civilian leadership in Moscow may not have sufficient control over the Soviet military to modify well-established defense policies and deployments. How the Chinese would eventually respond to inflexibility on Moscow's part is also not clear. If China's leaders were once again to feel an imminent threat from the Soviet military presence on their borders, they might again seek common cause with the United States and other countries threatened by Moscow's military power. In the absence of heightened pressures, however, China may well accommodate to the encircling Soviet military presence—which, Moscow will assert to Beijing, is directed against the United States and Japan— and sustain its current policy of "independence" and alignment with the Third World.

Japan has responded to Moscow's military pressures with slow but steady increases in its conventional defense capabilities and with heightened military cooperation with the United States. As Hiroshi Kimura describes in Chapter 6, Moscow's militarization of the islands of Etorofu and Shikotan in the Northern Territories, its invasion of Afghanistan, and the shooting down of an unarmed Korean Air Lines plane in 1983 have significantly shifted public opinion in Japan against the Soviet Union and in favor of more active defense cooperation with the United States. And while this gradual modification of public opinion and defense activity has not significantly reduced Japan's "nuclear allergy," the government's three nonnuclear principles are now being applied more flexibly, with some greater tolerance of port calls and maritime passage in Japanese waters of nuclear-powered and possibly nuclear-armed ships of the U.S. Seventh Fleet. Thus, as Kimura's analysis concludes, one effect of Moscow's military buildup has been to make Japan a more stalwart security partner of the West.

The Republic of Korea, South Korea, is in its fourth decade of intense military confrontation with North Korea (formally called the Democratic People's Republic of Korea). And while the North is currently showing some interest in political discussions with the South (as described by Fuji Kamiya in Chapter 10), its persistent use of violence—most notable in its bombing of the South Korean leadership in Rangoon, Burma, in 1983—presents, at best, a highly ambiguous impression of its intentions. Since the warfare of the early 1950s, South Korea has depended for its security on a combination of its own military forces and the U.S. defense commitment, as manifested by the current deployment of some 40,000 American troops and various aircraft on South Korean territory.[9] The intensity of North Korean hostility, the substantially larger and offensive military posture of the North, and occasional doubts about the reliability of the U.S. security commitment give the South some incentive to develop nuclear weapons of its own. Indeed, the impulse to proliferate is probably mirrored in North Korea by its own nuclear research program.

Each Korean state has attempted to weaken international backing for the other by political approaches to its adversary's supporters. The South has succeeded in recent years in establishing informal cultural contacts with the Soviet Union and China, and a significant, if indirect, Sino-South Korean trade has now developed. Moreover, the ROK has gained substantial international recognition as symbolized by recent decisions allowing it to host a meeting of the International Parliamentary Union, the Asian Games in 1986, and the 1988 Olympics. The North has been less successful in diversifying its international contacts, in part because of its own rather isolationist foreign policy, in part because of its policy of economic autarky—which has restricted the development of foreign trading relationships—and because of the distrust its aggressive behavior has generated abroad.

Contemporary signs of heightened economic and defense cooperation between North Korea and the Soviet Union hold uncertain implications for the future of the military balance on the Korean Peninsula, but it is widely assumed that none of the major powers with concerns in Northeast Asia—China, the Soviet Union, Japan, and the United States—have any interest in another Korean war. Yet, the intensity of the North-South confrontation, together with Pyongyang's aggressive political and military posture toward Seoul, sustains the concern about renewed warfare on the peninsula. Given the backing of the Soviet Union and China on the one hand, and the United States on the other, for the two Korean antagonists, the possibility exists of a nuclear confrontation among the major powers growing from a new Korean war. As J. J. Martin notes in Chapter 4, however, the interests of the Soviet Union and the United States in Korea are not such as to warrant risking nuclear escalation even if the two superpowers did become embroiled in a new Korean conflict. Nonetheless, the implications of war in Korea for security in Northeast Asia remain ominous and have direct relevance for management of nuclear issues.

Any weakening of defense support for the two Korean states by their major power backers will heighten incentives in Pyongyang and Seoul for nuclear proliferation. This danger locks the United States, on the one hand, and China and the Soviet Union on the other, into an ongoing stabilizing role on the peninsula. In terms of the balance of theater nuclear forces of the major powers in Northeast Asia, the ground deployment of Soviet SS-20 missiles in the Soviet Far East might lead to some inclination on the part of the United States to seek a countervailing deployment of ground-based nuclear forces in East Asia; and the most hospitable location for a deployment of either *Pershing II* missiles, ground-launched cruise missiles, or long-range nuclear-capable aircraft would be South Korea. Such an action, however, despite the Soviet buildup of theater nuclear forces, would be viewed widely as provocative and unsettling to regional security. It would be exactly the type of response that the Soviets would seek to turn against the United States by playing on antinuclear sentiments in Japan and elsewhere in the region.

Nuclear issues are not a matter of immediate concern to most of the states of ASEAN. Proliferation is not thought to be an active problem in the region at this time;[10] the major ASEAN concern has been to limit great-power involvement in the disputes of Southeast Asia, primarily the unending warfare in Indochina. Thus ZOPFAN—the creation of a zone of peace, freedom, and neutrality—has been an ASEAN ideal since the concept was first proposed in 1971. Unfortunately, the reality is that major power intervention in Southeast Asia is, if anything, increasing.

For a few years following the end of American involvement in the Vietnam War in 1973, it appeared that there might be some respite from the interaction between local conflicts and great-power involvements that had persisted in Southeast Asia since the nineteenth-century European colonial interventions in Indochina. But with the Khmer Rouge victory in Cambodia in April 1975, and Hanoi's subsequent conquest of South Vietnam, it took only three years for the Sino-Soviet rivalry to replace the Sino-American confrontation as the great-power overlay to the Vietnamese and Cambodian communist rivalry for control of Indochina. In November 1978, Hanoi and Moscow signed a friendship and cooperation treaty—a precursor to the Vietnamese invasion of Cambodia in December—and within five months Soviet air force and naval units began making use of the vacated American base facilities at Cam Ranh Bay. And while the Soviet-Vietnamese treaty and Moscow's expanded military presence were not enough to deter China from its "lesson teaching" war with Hanoi in February 1979, the heightened Soviet involvement was no doubt a constraining factor in China's tutelary military action against its former Vietnamese ally.

The current, third phase of the post–World War II Indochina conflict now deepens—as Karl Jackson details in Chapter 11—with the great irony that China has replaced the United States as the power restraining Vietnamese regional hegemony. Despite occasional "peace offensives" by Hanoi in its efforts to divide ASEAN and regain some of the international support it lost with its invasion of Cambodia, war seems to be endemic to Indochina. As with Korea, the Indochina Peninsula suffers from the intersection of too many great-power interests. The primary contemporary effect of the unending conflict is to provide the Soviet Union with a context within which it can establish itself as a major military presence in the area. As long as Hanoi feels threatened by China, which is determined to thwart Vietnam's ambition of establishing an Indochina federation under its control, it will need the protection of the Soviet Union. And the price of that protection is use of the military facilities at Cam Ranh Bay, which enables Moscow to threaten China's southern frontier and project naval and air power more than 2,200 miles south from the Soviet maritime provinces into the East and South China Seas, and through the Straits of Malacca into the Indian Ocean.

Among the naval and air units the Soviets now stage through or base at Cam Ranh Bay are nuclear-capable Tu-16 *Badger* bombers and nuclear-powered and presumably nuclear-armed naval units. *Backfire* bombers could also be deployed to the base on short notice.

One of the rationales invoked by the Vietnamese for hosting the Soviet military presence on their territory is an asserted "threat" from the American bases at Clark Field and Subic Bay in the Philippines. The ultimate impact of the growing political crisis in Manila on American use of the Philippine bases remains to be seen; but no one should expect the Vietnamese to invite the Soviets to vacate Cam Ranh Bay if the United States loses its access to the Philippine bases. The Soviet Union will retain use of the Vietnamese facilities as long as Hanoi perceives a threat to its security from China; and it would not be prudent to anticipate a Sino-Vietnamese reconciliation in the near future.

Concern with embroilment in the rivalry of the nuclear superpowers has been a contentious political issue for some years in the ANZUS states of Australia and New Zealand. As Tom Millar describes in Chapter 9, despite concern with the growing Soviet military presence in Southeast Asia and generally positive attitudes toward the United States, popular fears of nuclear conflict have led New Zealand's Labor government to exclude American nuclear-armed or nuclear-powered naval vessels from its waters—thus calling into question the viability of the ANZUS alliance—and to press for establishment of a nuclear-free zone in the South Pacific. While such sentiments are less intense in Australia, concern with becoming the target of a Soviet nuclear strike has generated political pressures against the American military communications facilities at Northwest Cape, Pine Gap, and Nurrungar.

The overall effect of these regional trends is not an encouraging prospect for limiting the nuclear dilemmas facing the United States and its Asian allies. The Soviet Union shows no restraint in its drive to extend its military reach from Northeast to Southeast Asia and to nuclearize the threat to the United States, its allies, and China. The persisting conflicts in Korea and Indochina give Moscow the political access it needs to extend its influence. China, which in years past was a firm political opponent of the Soviet Union's hegemonic impulses, and which still maintains both nuclear and conventional forces sufficient to deter a direct Soviet attack, has at least temporarily offered Moscow the alternative of political normalization if it will reduce the military threat now encircling the PRC. It is generally assumed that the Soviets will attempt to gain the benefits of an improvement in bilateral relations with the Chinese *without* any diminution in their military presence in Asia. To discourage PRC military cooperation with the West, Moscow will claim to Beijing that its forces are directed only against the United States and its allies. Whether the Chinese will ultimately accommodate to an unyielding Soviet military presence in the region or return to a more active policy of confronting Soviet expansionism will become known only as the decade runs its course.

For the United States and its allies, the Asian security environment, while still relatively favorable, is clouded with growing uncertainties. The overt conflicts of the region are still largely confined to the Communist states, and the Soviet Union has had only minor success in translating its inexorable military expansion into political influence. Yet this situation may be changing, as indicated by China's less confrontational policy toward Moscow and North Korea's new receptivity to cooperation with the USSR. Economic trends certainly favor South Korea; and ASEAN continues to benefit from Hanoi's entrapment in its regional ambitions—a situation that cripples the Vietnamese economy and burdens it with military pressure from China and dependence on Soviet assistance and protection. Yet the loose coalition of bilateral alliances that has structured the American security role in the Asia-Pacific region for three decades is increasingly troubled by (1) domestic political disarray (in the Philippines, and perhaps later in the decade in South Korea), (2) bilateral trade tensions that threaten to compromise positive political and security relations (especially in the U.S.-Japan relationship, and perhaps eventually with the U.S.-South Korean tie), and (3) antinuclear sentiments (most notably in New Zealand and the island states of the South Pacific, and perhaps eventually in Australia as well) that threaten the viability of the ANZUS alliance.

## U.S. and Allied Responses to the Growing Soviet Nuclear Threat in Asia

How should the United States and its Asian allies and friends respond to Moscow's inexorable expansion of its military presence in the Asia-Pacific region, especially the deployment of theater-range nuclear missile forces and nuclear-capable bombers? If there is one dominant lesson to be drawn from the European experience in dealing with the INF issue, it is that Moscow's deployment of the SS-20 missile and *Backfire* bomber presents more of a political challenge than a military problem for the United States and its allies. It would be unnecessary in military terms, and counterproductive politically, to overreact to these deployments by rushing to field "equivalent" weapons systems—and thereby stir up public anxieties about a presumed heightened nuclear threat. One of the dilemmas of dealing with the nuclear issue is that a response of deploying equivalent military systems would doubly play into Soviet hands: It would advertise Moscow's enhanced nuclear deployments, thus facilitating Soviet efforts to intimidate potential adversaries; it would also stimulate antinuclear political pressures in allied countries that the Soviets would work to exploit through "peace" campaigns and the public disinformation activities that are a major component of their approach to managing arms control negotiations.[11]

An appropriate response by the United States and its allies must involve a combination of low-key but appropriate military measures (detailed below) and assiduous efforts to build a political consensus among allied and friendly governments, reinforced by public information about the Soviet threat. Effective political management of this issue is likely to be the most difficult aspect of the response, for as John Roper and Yukio Satoh conclude in Chapter 14, the United States has not always effectively consulted with allied governments in building a consensus for its defense initiatives. Yet even where detailed consultations have been undertaken, as James Thomson recounts in Chapter 13, in assessing NATO's response to the growing Soviet INF threat, the European governments that pressed the United States to modernize alliance theater nuclear forces came to face determined resistance from their own publics, which made even consensual decisions difficult to implement.

The one saving grace of this situation for the United States and its allies is that the Soviets have a well-established record of eventually undercutting their own positions, either by overplaying their hands politically (as through overt threats which turn public opinion against them) or through military actions on their part which demonstrate the real threat they pose. In Asia, as numerous contributors to this assessment attest, Moscow's recent use or encouragement of force in Indochina, in Afghanistan, in Japan's Northern Territories, and against Korean Air Lines Flight 007 (not to mention episodes of aggressive action in years past along the Sino-Soviet frontier and in Eastern Europe) has established widespread distrust of Soviet intentions among Asian leaders and publics.

Military responses to Moscow's theater nuclear force buildup must begin with recognition that it would serve neither American nor allied interests to initiate first use of nuclear weapons in the Asia-Pacific theater. The human and material targets in the region—cities and economic infrastructures, as well as military installations—are of central value to the United States and its allies, in contrast to the largely undeveloped and underpopulated Far Eastern provinces of the Soviet Union. Thus, the primary defense tasks for the United States and its Asian security partners are to deter Soviet first use of its nuclear forces and to counter Moscow's efforts at political and military intimidation. To this end, the following military responses to the Soviet INF buildup seem appropriate:

1. The United States should *maintain an effective but low-visibility nuclear retaliatory force* in the region, composed of submarine-launched ballistic missiles and cruise missiles and nuclear-capable aircraft—buttressed by intercontinental nuclear forces based in the United States—to deter Soviet nuclear initiatives and to assure allied governments that there is an effective "coupling" between American defense capabilities and their own security. Given the geographical structure of the region, in which Soviet air and naval forces are the primary threat (except for China, which faces Soviet ground forces along the extensive Sino-Soviet frontier), the United States can maintain its retaliatory forces largely at sea, in rear areas, and at home where they are less obtrusive to allied states than a land-based theater force would be. An equivalent or symmetrical deployment of land-based retaliatory forces is not necessary to exercise effective deterrence; indeed, to deploy such a force would only heighten political tensions in the region, to Moscow's benefit.

2. The United States and allied governments can undertake a variety of relatively passive measures to *ensure the survivability of the American retaliatory nuclear force*, such as securing command, control, and communications systems and developing effective early-warning capabilities for surveillance of Soviet aircraft movements (especially to counter the *Backfire* bomber threat) and naval deployments. Cooperation between the United States and its allies in the areas of air defense, sea surveillance, and antisubmarine warfare are of particular importance. Such measures do not directly involve nuclear force operations, so they are politically nonprovocative, yet they can help bind the alliance together, limiting the tendency—commented on by Masataka Kosaka in Chapter 7—for totally passive allies to become "politically irresponsible" because of their lack of direct involvement in alliance defenses.

3. America's allies should *maintain sufficiently robust conventional forces* to counter nonnuclear threats by the Soviet Union and its allies. Ground forces on Japan's Hokkaido should be strengthened to counter Soviet air- and ground-force deployments in the Northern Territories; naval forces should be enhanced to make good on the commitment to a 1,000-mile sea lane defense; and South Korean forces should be maintained at a level that will deter the North Korean threat. Such conventional forces will diminish the need for early nuclear use—as *has* been the case for many years in Europe, where NATO's conventional defenses have been vulnerable relative to the Warsaw Pact threat, thus requiring the likely early employment of nuclear weapons to thwart a Soviet

invasion. Such conventional forces would also be reassuring to Japan and South Korea should U.S. forces deployed in Northeast Asia be required for use in a Southeast or Southwest Asian contingency.

4. *Arms control negotiations* should be one aspect of a comprehensive response to the Soviet nuclear challenge. As James Thomson concludes in Chapter 13, however, the European INF experience brought home to NATO the danger of directly linking modernization of the alliance's conventional and nuclear forces to progress in arms control negotiations. Such a linkage enables the Soviets to constrain allied defense modernization programs through manipulation of the highly visible and politically charged negotiating process. This was the lesson of the Soviet-American INF negotiations at Geneva in the period 1980 to 1983, leading up to the Soviet walkout from the talks,[12] and the highly contentious but ultimately successful effort to modernize NATO's theater nuclear forces in the face of Moscow's SS-20 buildup.

The European INF experience also made visible the interaction between developments in the European theater and those in the Far East. At one point in the negotiations, the Soviets offered to "solve" the Europeans' concern with the SS-20 by redeploying the missiles east of the Urals—to the obvious detriment of America's Asian allies. Ultimately, a negotiating position stressing the need for a "global ceiling" on numbers of SS-20s was worked out among the United States, Japan, China, and the Europeans, thus thwarting Moscow's efforts to play the Europeans against the Asians. But the experience highlighted the need for ongoing consultations between the United States and its European and Asian security partners to develop responses to the Soviet Union on arms control issues, if not the need for something broader than a regional forum for conducting such negotiations.[13]

Nuclear arms control talks for Asia, if held at all, would face a political context and problems quite different from such negotiations in Europe. The absence of clear East-West demarcation lines in Asia, with the exception of the confrontation across the 38th parallel on the Korean Peninsula, would make it difficult to compute what might constitute a balanced reduction of arms. How should China's nuclear arms be treated, given Beijing's stress on an independent foreign policy? And as most of the U.S. nuclear arms in the Asia-Pacific region, which are deployed on surface ships and submarines, are mobile, as are the Soviet land-based SS-20s, regional arms control talks are almost meaningless. Any arms control measures for Asia must be worked out in a global context.

What should be done if the Soviet Union is unwilling to moderate or reduce its Far Eastern buildup through arms control talks, or even to respond to China's offer of political reconciliation in return for a reduction in the military threat that surrounds it? The simple answer is to continue to rely on coalition defenses and sufficient conventional and nuclear deployments to deter Moscow from further expansionism in the Asia-Pacific region. Such a response, however, ignores the complexities of maintaining a security coalition in the nuclear age. Will allied governments be willing and politically able to sustain the forms of military cooperation—port calls, base usage, maintenance of communications and early warning facilities, and their own defense contributions—that are essential to constructing an effective deterrent? How will allies react in a crisis situation to Soviet threats and warnings to desist from cooperation with the United States? Ultimately, a considerable element of luck, as well as careful management, will be required to make a voluntary security coalition work: domestic politics in key allied states must remain politically stable and supportive of the alliance; bilateral tensions—such as those related to trade—must remain within manageable limits; and allied publics must come to understand their own security interests despite the anxieties of coalition defense in the nuclear age.

## Endnotes

1. The member states of ASEAN are Brunei, Malaysia, Indonesia, the Philippines, Singapore, and Thailand.
2. This point is developed by Robert Scalapino in Chapter 2 of this volume, and in John J. Stephan, "Asia in the Soviet Conception," in Donald S. Zagoria, *Soviet Policy in East Asia* (New Haven: Yale University Press, 1982), pp. 29–56.
3. The character and significance of Soviet nuclear forces in the Far East for regional security are explored in Chapter 4 of this volume, "Thinking About the Nuclear Balance in Asia" by J. J. Martin.
4. This point is stressed by Harry Gelman in Chapter 3, "The Soviet Far East Military Buildup: Motives and Prospects."
5. See Chapter 13 by James A. Thomson, "The European Theater Nuclear Force Deployment Decision, 1975–1979: Implications for U.S.-Alliance Relations" and Chapter 14 by John Roper and Yukio Satoh, "Public Debate Over INF Modernization: European and Japanese Public Debate Over Lessons for the Future of Western Security Cooperation."
6. See Chapter 9 by Tom Millar, "ANZAC Perspectives on Soviet Power in the Pacific."
7. This history is documented in Chapter 13 by James A. Thomson, "The

European Theater Nuclear Force Deployment Decision, 1975–1979: Implications for U.S.-Alliance Relations."

8. See Strobe Talbott, *Deadly Gambits* (New York: Alfred Knopf, 1984), especially pp. 68–69.

9. See the assessment of the military balance on the Korean Peninsula in Chapter 8 by Young-sun Ha, "The Soviet Military Buildup in the Far East: Implications for the Security of South Korea."

10. See Lewis A. Dunn, *Controlling the Bomb: Nuclear Proliferation in the 1980s* (New Haven: Yale University Press, 1982).

11. See Alexander R. Alexiev, *The Soviet Campaign Against INF: Strategy, Tactics, Means,* N-2280-AF (Santa Monica: The Rand Corporation, February 1985).

12. For a detailed history of these negotiations, see Talbott, *Deadly Gambits*.

13. This issue was called to public attention again in the fall of 1985 when the new Soviet leader, Mikhail Gorbachev, called for a freeze in SS-20 missiles at 243 (the aggregate number of British and French nuclear forces), and asserted that Soviet missiles over that number would soon be rendered "inactive"—in order to appeal to the Dutch to forego deployment of U.S. theater nuclear systems on their territory. Gorbachev's public proposal left unclear the status and future of the SS-20 missile force deployed in the Far East. Would it, too, be "frozen?" Or would Moscow's "European" missiles be moved eastward into the Asian theater? Such issues highlighted the need to coordinate arms control positions as they affect U.S., European, and Asian allies. See, "Soviet Arms Bid Interests U.S., Adviser Reports," *New York Times,* October 24, 1985.

*Part One*

# THE SOVIET MILITARY BUILDUP IN THE ASIA-PACIFIC REGION

*Chapter 2*

# ASIA IN A GLOBAL CONTEXT: STRATEGIC ISSUES FOR THE SOVIET UNION

*by Robert A. Scalapino*

## The Soviet Union's Two-Front Security Problem

In approaching issues of security and power, the Soviet Union sustains certain views deeply imbedded in Russian history and culture, adjusting and supplementing these in an effort to come abreast of the rapidly changing strategic conditions created by the most profound scientific-technological revolution mankind has known. For the most part, the Soviet Union has been a follower, not a leader, in the "modernization" of strategic doctrine. In the development of both doctrine and weaponry, it has advanced in the wake of American innovation, and while certain important distinctions have been maintained, the Russians have generally viewed the United States as a strategic guide and model. Moscow's posture has been that of reaction to and pursuit of U.S. capabilities, thus giving a continuing sense of both defensiveness and fierce competitiveness to its defense and foreign policies. These qualities culminated in the late 1970s in an insistence on being accepted as a global power, at least co-equal to the United States.[1]

For Americans, the psychologically wrenching process involved in losing strategic superiority and entering an age vaguely defined as that of "essential equivalence" with the Soviet Union has been made all the more difficult because in the absence of mutual trust, and with incidents of Soviet assertiveness accumulating, there has been only intermittent and unbalanced slackening of the race with the Soviets to advance to new military levels, both quantitative and qualitative. In this race, the Soviet Union has lagged in technological innovation, and it has attempted to compensate for qualitative deficiencies by making major strides quantitatively. When SALT negotiations first commenced in November 1969, the United States had a commanding numerical lead in intercontinental ballistic missiles (ICBMs), submarine-launched ballistic missiles (SLBMs), and heavy bombers; but the Soviet Union already had a sufficient quantity of delivery vehicles under construction to equal and surpass those of the United States. By the time the SALT I Treaty was signed in 1972, the Soviet Union had slightly more missile launchers than did the U.S., but as it reached parity in delivery vehicles, the United States advanced a buildup in warheads, first introducing Multiple Independently Targetable Reentry Vehicles (MIRVs) in 1970. The Russians entered the MIRV contest in the years 1975 to 1978.

NATO military statistics, which rely heavily on recently revised figures of the U.S. Central Intelligence Agency (CIA), indicate that Soviet military expenditures reached a high point, in terms of percentage of gross national product (GNP), in the early and mid-1970s. Subsequently, this expenditure rate was reduced somewhat. Meanwhile, the U.S.-Soviet arms competition has become increasingly qualitative in character, with issues of warhead accuracy, timing, and operational variables assuming key importance.[2] In the most general terms, this trend has been part of an increasing globalization of strategic planning and doctrine. However, issues of regional force "balance" or "imbalance" between the United States and the Soviet Union continue to have a strong psychological impact on Soviet and American defense analysts as well as on regional powers, affecting the degree to which local actions on the part of each of the two "superpowers" and other states are encouraged or inhibited. Regional conditions thus remain important in their own right, even though increasingly such considerations are integrated in the minds of American and Soviet strategic planners into a global perspective, thereby adding both political and strategic complexities to issues of regional security.

While the Soviet Union is being drawn rapidly into a global conceptualization of strategy, Soviet strategic thinking still focuses heavily on the traditional security problems involved in the defense of a Eurasian empire recently constructed, not wholly assimilated, and thus containing elements of fragility, especially on its peripheries. It is natural, therefore, that the old fear of a two-front war, in which the empire would be simultaneously assaulted from

West and East, remains strong, together with the special concern for control over potentially restive border states and ethnic groups in Central Asia, the Far East, and especially Eastern Europe. The primacy of the European theater in the minds of Soviet leaders derives from a mix of strategic, political, economic, and psychological factors. European Russia is still the empire's heartland, economically and politically. The costly buffer-state system established in Eastern Europe continues to be regarded as critical by Moscow, despite its substantial economic and political costs and its increasing obsolescence as a strategic barrier.

In Europe, therefore, the USSR and its allies maintain 164 divisions to confront 69 NATO divisions, with about one-half of the Warsaw Pact divisions in Category 1 (75 to 100 percent strength). This includes about 30 Soviet divisions comprising some 565,000 soldiers in Central and Eastern Europe, with the bulk of these in East Germany (approximately 380,000 men) and 65 USSR divisions in the military districts of European Russia, together with an additional 16 divisions in the central strategic reserve. Warsaw Pact forces outnumber NATO forces in aircraft over two to one, and in tanks by almost two to one, with the numerical balance over the past 20 years having moved slowly but steadily in favor of the Warsaw Pact states.[3]

Nonetheless, certain qualified analysts have reached the conclusion that when all quantitative and qualitative factors are taken into account, NATO can preclude Soviet-led forces from achieving rapid victory in an all-out conventional attack.[4] This judgment, moreover, does not weigh seriously the major political risks for the Soviet Union involved in drawing East Europeans into any such conflict. It is perhaps understandable, therefore, that Soviet leaders reacted so sharply to the NATO decision to deploy *Pershing II* IRBMs and ground-launched cruise missiles in Western Europe. Prior to these deployments, the combination of Soviet SS-20s and quantitatively larger conventional forces gave Moscow a feeling of assured superiority in any conventional or "limited" nuclear conflict in Europe (while Soviet doctrine denies the possibility of the latter eventuality, Soviet practice does not). European theater deterrence has thus tilted in the Soviet direction, and the Russians—like many Europeans—doubt that the United States will risk intercontinental nuclear war in the event of a "limited" regional conflict. The deployment of the new U.S. missiles, however, has had both psychological and strategic implications for Moscow's military planners, and the Soviet Union has proclaimed the *global* as well as the European theater nuclear balance to have been disrupted. They have seen the move as an effort by the

United States to obtain a first-strike capacity against targets in the USSR from NATO bases in Europe, a capability they see related to the development of an American antimissile space program designed to thwart a retaliatory Soviet strike—a combination which they assert represents a dire peril for the security of the USSR.[5]

The initial Soviet response to these U.S. theater nuclear deployments in Western Europe, in addition to withdrawing from the Geneva talks in late November 1983, was to press forward deployment of Soviet medium-range nuclear weapons in East Germany and Czechoslovakia and to announce that Soviet nuclear weaponry would also be forward deployed in the oceans neighboring the United States "equal to the threat of U.S. missiles in Europe for us and our allies." The latter action does not represent a new development, since Soviet submarines have long patrolled close to American shores. But taken as a whole, recent NATO and Soviet actions serve to further connect the regional and global strategies of the two superpowers, thereby adding to the political as well as the strategic complexities of the U.S.-Soviet confrontation. One vital element in the unabated rivalry, therefore, will be continuing efforts by both Moscow and Washington to influence the politics of Europe. It is ironic that while the political proclivities of Europe— both West and East—are generally in the direction of very selective international involvement and heightened stress on national interest—the strategic trends favor increased internationalization. In this paradox lies the political uncertainties accompanying both U.S. and Soviet defense strategies.

Current developments will probably force the Soviet Union to devote primary attention to Europe even more strongly than in the recent past, coupling this with actions designed to improve its global surge capacities on the seas, in the air, and in outer space. At the same time, Moscow must remain alert to political and military developments, single state or regional in nature, that may challenge the Soviet Union on its more vulnerable frontiers. There is bound to be heightened concern about developments in Southwest Asia, given the volatile character of the situation in Iran and the protracted effort to pacify Afghanistan, not to mention the ferment throughout the Arab world. Some observers see in this situation an opportunity for heightened Soviet influence. To date, however, Moscow's policies in the region have been marked by caution and uncertainty, with gains—strategic or otherwise—more minimal than might have been expected, particularly in view of the singular lack of success of American policies in this part of the world.

Clearly, the Middle East does not represent a zero-sum game

between the United States and the Soviet Union; and Soviet caution seems warranted, both because the indigenous political forces through which the USSR might operate are very weak at present, and because the threat to the USSR from most developments that might occur is minimal. Conversely, the risks stemming from heightened Soviet involvement are appreciable. Increased Soviet activities in the Middle East in the near term, therefore, are likely to be directed more toward global rather than regional considerations. We are likely to see some effort to exploit current basing operations, and an attempt to strengthen what is still a slender strategic line of communication (via facilities in South Yemen and Ethiopia) into the Indian Ocean and beyond.

If Soviet leaders perceive the Middle East to represent a limited threat (and a limited opportunity as well), the Pacific-Asian region presents a more complex picture. The eastern reaches of the Soviet empire have long been seen as vulnerable to external penetration. Populating Central Asia with European Russians has not been easy, although over the decades some gains have been made. The Central Asians, however, are a largely static population, with a high birthrate. It has been estimated that by the end of the century, one-third of the soldiers of the Soviet Army will be non-Russian speakers, the majority of them Soviet Asians.[6] While there is no basis for characterizing contemporary race relations in the region as bad, Moscow's policies have led to separateness rather than integration; and sooner or later it is likely that the Asians will demand heightened political and social status to accompany their improved economic conditions.

Siberia represents another challenge. In the nineteenth and early twentieth centuries, hundreds of thousands of Koreans flooded into this region, especially after the Japanese annexation of Korea. Other Asians—Buriats, Mongols, and Chinese—also made their homes in the vast, underpopulated areas of Russia's Far East. Moscow's leaders came to regard many of these national minority groups, especially the Koreans, as a potential security threat, and took the occasion of rising tension with the Japanese in the late 1930s to transfer the Koreans to Central Asia. Had the Germans defeated the Russians in the course of World War II, there is little doubt that the Japanese empire would have been extended into Russian-held territory, directly or indirectly through puppet states like Manchukuo, a potentiality that present Soviet leaders have not forgotten.

In recent times, however, the more serious security concern in the Soviet Far East has related to China. Occasional statements by Mao Zedong and other Chinese leaders have alerted the Russians to the fact that the Chinese still regard the seizure of hundreds of thousands of square miles of territory by Czarist Russia, including the region encompassing Vladivostok, as illegal. Nor has the independence of Outer Mongolia—formalized by the Soviet agreement with the Nationalist Chinese government of Chiang Kai-shek in 1945—ever been fully accepted by Beijing. The Chinese, to be sure, have taken the position that if only the Russians would acknowledge the illegality of past territorial seizures, they would magnanimously set the issue aside, with border negotiations confined to minor areas of dispute along the Ussuri River. The provocative manner in which the Chinese have posed the territorial issue, however, seems calculated to make the Russians both defensive and nervous.

It will be recalled that when the Sino-Soviet border controversy erupted in bloodshed in 1969, the Russians gave every evidence of contemplating a serious war with China. Soviet officials let it be known that in such an eventuality they would not limit themselves to the use of conventional weapons. Against this background, it is natural that Soviet leaders would become concerned over the warming of Sino-American relations, a development they had anticipated prior to its unfolding. For a time, in the mid-1970s, the Russians appeared to accept a situation in which the United States was improving relations with both Moscow and Beijing, thereby occupying the enviable "swing" position in the "strategic triangle." Even in this period, however, Moscow warned that "certain forces" wished to turn the Sino-American relationship into an anti-Soviet alliance.

## Moscow's Far East Military Buildup and the China Challenge

By the end of the 1970s, Deng Xiaoping's call for a global united front against Soviet hegemonism, issued in the context of the Soviet invasion of Afghanistan and the Sino-Vietnamese conflict, brought U.S.-Soviet and Sino-Soviet relations to low points. The Russians became convinced that a two-front pincer movement against them was under way, with NATO in the West and an evolving American-Chinese-Japanese entente in the East. The Soviet military buildup in the Far East, first initiated in the mid-1960s against China, took on new dimensions after 1977. Moscow's military planners moved to establish an autonomous theater command in the Far East and reinforce their growing conventional ground, air, and naval forces with strategic weapons that would ultimately challenge American dominance of the Pacific and pose a two-front threat to the United States itself.

The scale and pace of this buildup is set out in some detail in subsequent chapters. It is sufficient to say here that the Soviet ground forces stationed in the four military districts that are subordinated to the theater command at Ulan Ude now represent about one-fourth of the total Soviet ground forces, numbering some half a million men in 53 divisions. The Soviet Pacific fleet is now the largest of the four Soviet fleets, with around 90 major surface combatants, 135 submarines, a naval infantry division, and amphibious shipping. And one-fourth of the Soviet air force is also in the Far East, with about 2,200 combat aircraft. Both naval and airforce *Backfire* bombers have been deployed to the region, along with the other modern aircraft, including Tu-16 bombers deployed at Cam Ranh Bay in Vietnam. And there has been steady modernization of equipment throughout the forces.[7]

As indicated, however, the most significant development in recent years has been a substantial increase in Soviet strategic forces in the Asia-Pacific region. These forces fall into two broad categories, namely, those applicable to use within Asia, and those designed with American targets in mind. In the former category are more than 170 SS-20 intermediate-range ballistic missiles (IRBMs) deployed in the Far East (as of late 1985), mainly near the northern Mongolian border, and capable of reaching China, Japan, and much of Southeast Asia. In the latter category are submarine launched ballistic missiles (SLBMs). Some 30 percent of all Soviet SLBMs are on submarines in the Pacific. According to one source, approximately 35 to 40 percent of the Soviet ICBM force and over 30 percent of its strategic bombers are now deployed east of the Urals.[8]

From these facts, the following conclusions can be drawn. First, Soviet forces currently in the Far East would be far from sufficient to fight a successful conventional war against the People's Republic of China, and there is no indication that Soviet leaders have any such intention. The purpose of these forces, however, is not wholly that of defending Soviet territory. They also serve to restrain Chinese actions against third parties, notably Vietnam. At the time of the Chinese border war with Vietnam in 1979, Soviet maneuvers on the Manchurian border caused China to increase its troop strength in the north. The limited character of the Chinese military operations against Vietnam, and the clear signals sent in advance that the incursion would be limited, seem to testify to the effectiveness of Soviet deterrence.

Using augmented conventional forces, the Soviet Union could

undoubtedly penetrate Chinese territory deeply from either Central Asia or Mongolia and Siberia. Given the importance of China's Northeast or Manchurian area to the country's energy supply and industrial strength, this possibility may be influencing Beijing's current thinking about defense policy, as will be noted shortly. Yet any effort by the Soviets to hold Chinese territory would produce a combined guerrilla-conventional response that would make Afghanistan pale into insignificance. Moreover, the Soviet Union could never be certain that China would not take the risks of a limited nuclear response despite the lopsided nuclear balance between the two countries.

It has been suggested that Soviet strategy might be to drive quickly to Beijing and then to set up a "friendly" Chinese government. Under present conditions, this is a highly unrealistic scenario, as the political base for such a regime is totally lacking. A Soviet incursion, purely punitive in nature, followed by withdrawal—similar to that conducted by China against Vietnam—has also been advanced as a possibility, but it is difficult to perceive the rationale for such an attack. In the case of Vietnam, the Chinese objective was to prevent a consolidation of Vietnamese power in Cambodia by forcing the Vietnamese to divert resources indefinitely to extensive northern frontier defenses. But China already has between 800,000 and 1.5 million troops on its northern and western frontiers. A Soviet punitive expedition would accomplish little except to leave in its wake a sea of hatred, and it would carry the risk of disruptive Chinese actions within Soviet territory.

Despite statements by Soviet leaders disclaiming any first use of nuclear weapons, it is difficult to believe that the Soviet Union—if drawn into serious conflict with China—would confine itself to conventional weaponry alone. It must be emphasized that Moscow is likely to do everything possible to avoid a war of any type with China because the effect of a Sino-Soviet conflict upon such high priority Soviet objectives as maintaining global strategic parity with the United States and a position of strength in Europe would be disastrous. If war came, however, the Soviet Union would certainly want to avoid a protracted, limited conflict of the type now under way in Afghanistan. Thus, a resort to nuclear weapons would be very tempting.

In this context, the present thrust of Chinese strategic planning must be of special interest—and growing concern—to Soviet leaders despite the reduction of tension between the PRC and the USSR now taking place.[9] Available data suggest that China is placing high priority on the expansion and diversification of its nuclear force while accepting a lengthy, stretched-out process of modernizing its ground forces. China conducted its first ICBM test in the spring of 1980. In October 1982, an SLBM was successfully test-fired. Meanwhile, in the previous June, PLA units conducted maneuvers under conditions of simulated tactical nuclear warfare.

Chinese leaders are well aware that their nuclear forces at present are both limited and relatively primitive, and extremely vulnerable to Soviet attack. In timing, accuracy, command, control, and communications ($C^3$), Chinese nuclear capacities are woefully deficient, as are their options for ballistic missile defense. It appears that China has focused on developing an SLBM force as well as dispersing ICBMs and deploying them deceptively in relatively secure underground sites. There is also the possibility that Beijing is considering the development of tactical nuclear weapons, with the idea of challenging border intrusions rather than the previous reliance on a "people's war" strategy of drawing the enemy in deep.

If this should be the direction of evolution of Chinese strategic policy, it would represent a movement beyond Beijing's previous nuclear posture of minimal deterrence. It would also involve substantial risks for China. Apart from having pledged no first use of nuclear weapons, Beijing can scarcely contemplate with equanimity the prospects of a massive Soviet nuclear retaliation in the event of even a limited Chinese nuclear strike, or the escalatory risks involved in the use of tactical nuclear weapons. Nonetheless, the present Chinese course might be considered a logical extension of earlier deterrent policies, especially if the costs of upgrading China's conventional forces make rapid progress on this front possible. Various estimates hold that a viable Chinese SLBM force could be developed for some $6.7 billion, whereas the conventional force modernization of the PLA would cost in the range of $41 to $235 billion.[10] No doubt PLA modernization will continue to be a goal, but it will be pursued at a modest pace and largely through the efforts of the Chinese themselves, applying technology obtained from abroad where possible.

If the foregoing assessment of Chinese strategic plans is roughly correct, it will have an ever-growing impact on Soviet policies. The Soviet leaders will be forced to concern themselves with an expanding Chinese nuclear threat, and this issue will make itself increasingly felt in all arms limitations talks. In the broader sense, military developments in the Asia-Pacific region will be increasingly suffused with global strategic considerations. China and Japan, for example, have evinced a concern that the United States and the USSR might reach an agreement on the deployment of SS-20s that would permit the Soviet Union to shift additional missiles to Asia in exchange for a commitment to a global limit.

If China moves to augment and diversify its nuclear arsenal, moreover, the impact on other Asian countries could be significant, especially if China were to develop tactical nuclear weapons. For some states, such as India, the pressure to move into the nuclear field might increase; for others, like Vietnam, the interest in obtaining Soviet nuclear protection might emerge (similar to that which the United States affords South Korea), especially if the perceived threat from China remains high. Thus, Chinese strategic decisions are likely to have both regional and global consequences, and similarly, strategic decisions of a global nature can affect China. In this connection, U.S.-Soviet negotiations over the Strategic Defense Initiative (SDI) are certain to be watched carefully by the PRC, which has already come out against research, testing, or deployment of space weapons. Potentially, SDI could cancel out the PRC's modest strategic retaliatory capacity.

## Trends in Northeast Asian Politico-Military Relations

Meanwhile, is the expressed Soviet concern over Japanese "militarism" a genuinely felt worry, or is Moscow's alarmism primarily political, or at most an effort to deter further Japanese defense efforts? As noted earlier, in the late 1970s Soviet leaders had reason to be apprehensive about the emergence of a loose strategic entente among the United States, China, and Japan. Deng Xiaoping's call for a united front against Soviet "hegemony" clearly pointed in this direction, although Japan evinced considerable reluctance to be drawn into such an arrangement from the outset. With the more recent turn of Chinese foreign policy toward nonalignment and the opening of Sino-Soviet normalization talks, Moscow's immediate attention has turned to the prospects of an American-South Korean-Japanese military entente, with the Reagan visit to the latter two countries in 1984 serving as an illustration of the potential danger to Soviet security interests.[11]

In point of fact, knowledgeable Soviet experts must realize that Japanese military power will grow only incrementally, with no major military buildup on the offing. A host of factors, including the deep divisions within both the Japanese public and elite groups, inhibit Japan from making dramatic changes in its foreign policies in general or its defense policies in particular. Such advances in political and strategic posture as take place will be within the parameters of the Japanese constitution and supplementary to the predominant role of the United States in Japan's defense. Nevertheless, as the 1980s advance, Japan will gradually assume a more important political and strategic role, both within the region and in selective other areas. This will not take place without protracted, intensive domestic debate. The proponents of an "omnidirectional" foreign policy will urge the retention of a low-cost, low-risk policy emphasizing economic rather than security priorities, and geared to extensive reliance on the United States for protection. Gradually, however, Japan will play a role of signifi-cance in the "soft regionalism" involving South Korea and China that is emerging in Northeast Asia.[12] Prime Minister Nakasone has pointed the way with his cultivation of Seoul and the consultations also undertaken with such Chinese leaders as Hu Yaobang. Taiwan, moreover, is being encompassed in a sphere of Japanese economic and cultural interest, albeit without any great warmth on the part of Taipei's key political figures.

For China, the key decision is whether—within the parameters of a nonaligned foreign policy—Beijing will add low-level strategic ties to its economic and cultural relations with Japan and the West (i.e., the United States), while confining its efforts at normalization of Sino-Soviet relations to the nonstrategic realm. To date, the Chinese have indicated that theirs is not a policy of equidistance despite trenchant criticism of many aspects of American policies, foreign and domestic.[13] The Soviet Union remains identified as the primary threat. If the tilt toward Japan and the West persists, Japan could play a critical role in the unfolding of a greater sense of regionalism encompassing economic, political, and strategic com-ponents within Northeast Asia.

Soviet concern over such a development is understandable, yet the nonmilitary instruments available to Moscow to counter it are weak. Only one of the three Communist states of the region is aligned with the Soviet Union—the Mongolian People's Republic. And this backward and sparsely populated country is scarcely an asset except as a Soviet-manned military buffer. Nor is there any prospect of restoring the political-strategic alliances with China and North Korea (the DPRK) in their earlier forms. The DPRK, dependent though it is upon the Soviet Union for economic and military assistance, will probably continue to tilt toward China, although North Korean-Soviet relations have recently improved. In any case, Pyongyang's strategy will be to feint first in one direction, then in the other, as its interests dictate. In Japan, the Soviet Union has even lost the support of the Japanese Communist Party and must be content with the backing of a small segment of the Japan Socialists, together with a few special interest groups.[14]

Theoretically, Siberia's vast resources should constitute a power-ful lure to Japanese investors, and some Soviet experts have advanced the thesis that as economic relations with the United States and Europe become more troubled, Japan can be wooed by the prospect of playing a major role in the development of the Soviet Far East without any need on Moscow's part to make political or strategic concessions. Possibly, but to date a combination of political, economic, and strategic considerations have inhibited such a trend. In addition to the issues of the four Northern Islands and concern over American and Chinese reactions to any large-scale Japanese involvement in Siberia, Japanese entrepreneurs have not been attracted in substantial numbers to the economic opportunities offered by the Russians. As to the future, it has been argued that the direction now being taken by Japanese industry will gradually diminish the need for the types of resources available in Siberia.[15] In any case, up to this point Moscow's economic carrot has not been sufficiently large to outweigh the effects of its military stick.

Logically, Sino-Soviet trade should increase significantly from recent abnormally low levels, especially with the reduction of political tension that is now taking place. Yet various barriers, economic as well as political, will remain. Nor is the Soviet Union likely to be able—or willing—to tap China's vast labor force for developmental purposes. Even North Korean workers, once imported in significant numbers, no longer go to the Soviet Union. The Vietnamese serve as substitutes, but without adaptability to the Siberian climate. Another potential source of economic interaction, South Korea (the ROK), is ruled out for political reasons (although nonrecognition has not inhibited China from economic intercourse with the ROK).

If political and economic conditions in Northeast Asia are not propitious for the Soviet Union, the cultural gap is equally discouraging. In virtually every respect, Russia remains very foreign to the peoples of this region. Language, food, etiquette, life style—all pose problems of communication and mutual appreciation, notwithstanding the existence of a small group of Soviet Asian specialists who are well trained in the required languages, history, and culture.

## Limits and Vulnerabilities to the Soviet Position in Asia

Thus, unless Soviet leaders are prepared to make major policy alterations, they can only counter what they perceive to be highly adverse political-security trends in this region by a heavy reliance on military responses. And as has been noted, the Soviet military buildup has been sustained for two decades, with the recent emphasis on naval expansion and nuclear force augmentation and improvement. First priority must be given to the defense of Soviet territory against any threat of border states singly or in combination, including those in alignment with the United States. This requires a mix of conventional and strategic power sufficient to meet the threat of a multi-front war, and to counter levels of violence from border skirmishes to intercontinental nuclear strikes, whether commencing in Asia or elsewhere.

The first priority flows naturally into a second, namely, the capacity to confront the United States itself with a two-front threat by developing Soviet strategic strength in the Asia-Pacific region, both on land (to counter U.S. bases in South Korea, Japan, the Philippines and the ANZUS states, and the Seventh Fleet) and at sea (to bring U.S. continental targets within range). A third priority is closely related: to influence and bring pressure on Asian adversaries (and, in some instances, neutral or aligned states), while remaining secure in the possession of a range of conventional and strategic deterrents that serve as a shield against countermeasures.

Having outlined these objectives, however, one must guard against the assumption that the Soviet Union has achieved a position of military superiority in the Pacific or in the neighboring regions intimately connected—namely, the Indian Ocean and Southwest Asia. Soviet political and military leaders continue to speak defensively about their position in the Asia-Pacific area, and with good reason.[16] Soviet land-based forces in the Far East provinces of the USSR are formidable, although as has been noted, they are not sufficient to undertake a successful conventional war with China—or with any other major Asian state. Soviet land-based air strength and submarine power in Northeast Asia are also superior to the regional strength of the United States, but they are limited in their outreach. The United States could not operate near Soviet bases in the event of war, nor conduct effective antisubmarine warfare (ASW) or air operations from Japanese or Korean bases or waters against the USSR except at great cost. The Soviet intention is to make their northwest Pacific holdings (especially the Sea of Okhotsk) into a ballistic missile submarine bastion, in which close-in enemy operations would be thwarted by naval—and naval air—power, thus enabling Soviet forces to conduct their own short-, intermediate-, and long-range operations in the region and beyond, as necessary.

The very geographic position of the Soviet Union, however,

provides structural limitations on its military operations. The Soviet Pacific fleet is based essentially in the areas of Sovetskaya Gavan and Nakhodka-Vladivostok on the Siberian coast and Petropavlosk on the peninsula. Much of this fleet must pass through three choke points—the Tsushima, Soya, and Tsugaru straits—making fleet operations extremely vulnerable. Lacking significant carrier-based aircraft or substantial sea-lift capacity, and lacking also the base structure available to the United States, Soviet forces are far inferior to those of the United States in projection capability—outreach and mobility. Moreover, limitations in command, control, communications, and intelligence capabilities are a major constraint, with the United States holding an equally strong position with respect to ASW capabilities. Since the current U.S.-Soviet arms competition has shifted largely to qualitative considerations, the Soviet Union has ample reason for concern. Within the next few years, the United States will deploy into the Pacific the 2,500 nautical mile-range *Tomahawk* sea-launched cruise missile and the *Trident II* submarine, with missiles of a 6,000 nautical mile range. For the Soviet Union to contemplate turning a conventional war in Asia into a nuclear conflict would represent an extraordinarily high risk if there were a reasonable chance that the United States would become involved.

From a Soviet standpoint, moreover, its successful efforts to encircle China with substantial military power are currently mirrored by the U.S. "encirclement" of the Soviet Union by strategic and conventional forces ranging from those located in South Korea, Micronesia, the Philippines, and the Seventh Fleet, to the bases stretching into South Asia and the Indian Ocean (Diego Garcia), West Asia (Oman, Saudi Arabia), and the Horn of Africa (Somalia and Kenya), thence to Europe—south, west, and north. Moscow's own foreign base structure, while having grown in recent years, remains comparatively sparse. The bases at Cam Ranh in Vietnam and Ream in Kampuchea give substantially greater outreach to Soviet reconnaissance and ASW operations as well as attack capabilities against South China and U.S. bases in the Philippines. In the event of any war involving the United States, however, these bases and their exposed supply lines would be quickly eliminated. To the west, reliance is essentially on shaky regimes in South Yemen and Ethiopia. Only in Europe can Soviet power be considered preeminent (yet, in Soviet eyes, this is now threatened by the American theater nuclear buildup).

As is well known, the political and economic position of the Soviet Union in Southeast Asia is a mixture of gains and losses, with the balance a negative one.[17] Soviet access to the region on a more sustained basis has been achieved via the alliance with Vietnam. Yet this alliance has proven costly to Moscow. Soviet aid totals approximately $1 billion per year. In addition, the Soviet-Vietnamese alliance serves to estrange the states comprising ASEAN and constitutes a primary obstacle to any significant improvement in Sino-Soviet relations. Moreover, Moscow knows that for Hanoi, the alliance is a marriage of convenience, not of love. It is therefore subject to change at some point, particularly as, sooner or later, Vietnam will have to reach an accommodation with China unless it chooses to remain a permanently mobilized society, with all of the economic and political disadvantges this entails.

The Soviet position in South Asia is better, largely because of the continuing strong ties with India. Here, the Soviet Union has shown considerable sophistication in managing relations with New Delhi, having come to play an important role through industrial and military assistance without having been widely accused of interference in India's internal affairs. At the same time, in fact, the Soviet Union was very helpful to Mrs. Gandhi in keeping the Communist Party of India and certain other "left" elements in line. In contrast to the United States, which has virtually no leverage in Indian politics, the Soviet Union could harm or help Mrs. Gandhi, a fact that did not escape her; and Moscow can do the same for Rajiv Gandhi. Thus, the Soviet-Indian relationship survived the Afghanistan invasion, although India has toyed with the idea of diversifying its weapons purchases, and has even condescended to wink at the United States once or twice in recent times. (Despite Indian interest in European arms, the Soviet Union evidently countered with an offer New Delhi decided to accept.) Will Rajiv follow the same international course as his mother? His personal sentiments seem devoid of Indira's anti-Americanism; and he is supportive of a strong private sector in the Indian economy. Moreover, India's increasing interest in high technology makes enhanced U.S.-Indian economic relations attractive to New Delhi. Yet for a variety of reasons, India is not likely to make any abrupt shift from its ties with Moscow, although the Russians have some apprehensions about Rajiv's intentions.

With Pakistan, despite major differences, especially over Afghanistan, the Soviet Union is seeking to avoid a widening cleavage and is currently suggesting that economic relations can be advanced without the need for agreement on other matters. Yet the problem of Afghanistan continues to be a heavy burden on Soviet relations with the subcontinent. A private, nonideological Soviet explanation of the decision to go into Afghanistan and the subsequent actions taken there can be phrased succinctly as follows:

> We Soviets realized that the situation in Kabul was untenable and
> that a Marxist government friendly to the Soviet Union could not
> survive without our direct involvement. The alternative was an
> Islamic fundamentalist government, anti-Soviet and probably aided
> by the United States. We had more than sufficient hostility and
> threats on our borders with other countries of the region. We knew
> that there would be political and military costs to intervention, and
> the decision was neither easily nor painlessly reached. We may have
> underestimated those costs, but we do not intend to make the
> mistakes which the United States made in Vietnam. We will keep our
> ground forces at around the 100,000 man level, sufficient to control
> the main cities and primary arteries of communication, but we will
> not abandon our commitment to sustain a friendly government in
> Kabul. If it takes eight, ten years or even longer to achieve an
> Afghan administration capable of governing, we shall stay the
> course.

This evaluation—advanced several years ago—may be accurate
or inaccurate as a prediction of Moscow's future policy. There can
be little doubt now that the Soviet Union did underestimate the
costs. If affairs in Afghanistan show limited progress, Soviet casualties mount, and the hostility of the Islamic world remains high,
some effort to change course may be undertaken, although there
are no signs at present that the Soviet leadership finds the current
balance sheet in Afghanistan intolerable. In any case, continuing
involvement there places a substantial constraint on any direct
Soviet intervention in another conventional conflict at present.[18]

In conclusion, the following generalizations appear to summarize the Soviet strategic position at present. First, the Soviet
Union, like the United States, has discovered that the costs and
risks of achieving and maintaining the status of a global power are
extensive. With its internal economic situation less than satisfactory, its political system lacking in dynamism or external appeal,
and its imperial problems entering a new phase, the Soviet Union
finds its security challenged anew on its Western front. Its Southern front is rendered complex by the force of Islam in sundry
manifestations. And its Eastern front is threatened by new coali-
tions imperfect yet not without military importance. In Asia,
moreover, the specter of an ever more powerful China friendly to
Japan and the United States—however overdrawn or distant as a
prospect—disturbs virtually every Russian.[19]

Under these conditions, an acceleration of the race with the
United States for qualitative advances in strategic and conventional

weaponry, and in this context the advance toward new arenas such as space, with the strategic balance achieved by the Soviet Union threatened at each turn, is an awesome prospect.[20] It probably is this generally unfavorable context that has brought the Soviet Union back to the bargaining table at Geneva, although the extent to which a heightened will exists (on both sides) to reach agreements on arms limitations remains to be seen. Meanwhile, the United States and other nations of the Asia-Pacific region await with great interest any new initiatives by the Gorbachev leadership in Moscow. Some observers anticipate the development of more flexible and attractive Soviet economic and political policies toward the region designed to correct past deficiencies and make the USSR a more effective competitor for political influence. To be truly effective, however, such policies must at some point be accompanied by steps to meet the security concerns of the Asia-Pacific states. Are Soviet leaders prepared to reduce the formidable conventional and nuclear forces that now encircle China, press against Japan, and threaten other nations, including the United States—and under what conditions?

## Endnotes

1. A stimulating assessment of basic Soviet objectives is presented by George W. Breslauer in the introduction to his monograph, *The Dynamics of Soviet Policy Toward the Arab-Israeli Conflict: Lessons of the Brezhnev Era* (Working Paper No. 8, October 1983, The Center for Foreign Policy Development, Brown University, Providence). See also the fine article by Robert Legvold, "The Nature of Soviet Power," *Foreign Affairs* (October 1977) for an earlier evaluation.
2. For a review of these developments, see Raymond L. Garthoff, *Perspectives on the Strategic Balance* (Washington, D.C.: Brookings Institution, 1983).
3. See *The Military Balance 1983-1984* (London: International Institute for Strategic Studies, 1983); *Asian Security 1983* (Tokyo: Research Institute for Peace and Security, August 1983); and RUSI and Brassey's *Defence Yearbook—1983* (London: Royal United Services Institute for Defence Studies, 1983) for basic data. For an article that succinctly summarizes the current balance in Europe, see Otto P. Chaney, Jr., "The Soviet Threat to Europe—Prospects for the 1980s," *Parameters,* vol. 13, no. 3 (September 1983), pp. 2-22.
4. See John J. Mearsheimer, "Why the Soviets Can't Win Quickly in Central Europe," *International Security,* no. 7 (Summer 1982), pp. 3-39.
5. The new missile deployment provides significant NATO gains in timing and accuracy, placing the Soviet Union in more imminent risk, at least in theory. For a typical Soviet reaction, see Lt. General D. A. Volkogonov, "The Logic

of Countermeasures," *Komsomolskaya Pravda* (Moscow), pp. 1, 3, (translated in Foreign Broadcast Information Service (FBIS), *Daily Report—Soviet Union,* 19 December 1983, pp. AA 1–5). See also, the December 5, 1983, Moscow press conference of Marshal N. V. Ogarkov, then chief of the USSR Armed Forces General Staff.

6. *The Military Balance 1983–1984,* p. 12.

7. For two assessments of Soviet military forces in Asia, see G. Jacobs, "Soviet Forces and the Pacific Basin," *Jane's Defense Review,* vol. 4, no. 2 (1983), pp. 131–141, and Anthony H. Cordesman, "The Military Balance in Northeast Asia," *Armed Forces Journal International* (November 1983), pp. 80–109. See also, *Asian Security 1984* (Tokyo: Research Institute for Peace and Security, August 1984) and *The Military Balance 1984–85* (London: International Institute for Strategic Studies, 1984).

8. See William T. Tow, "Nuclear Security Problems in the Far East," *Asia-Pacific Community* (Winter 1983), pp. 52–71. This is a well-researched, excellent article.

9. For several insightful papers from which I have drawn extensively in the section that follows, see Alastair I. Johnston, "Chinese Nuclear Force Modernization: Implications for Arms Control," *Journal of Northeast Asian Studies,* vol. 2, no. 2 (June 1983), pp. 13–28, and his earlier paper written with William G. Saywell, *Chinese Defense Doctrine and Foreign Policy: Options for the Future* (Working Paper No. 11, University of Toronto-York University, 1982); and Robert G. Sutter, *Chinese Nuclear Weapons and American Interests—Conflicting Policy Choices* (Report No. 83–187F, Congressional Research Service, September 27, 1983).

Excellent background studies of the evolution of Chinese defense policy are Harlan Jencks, *From Muskets to Missiles* (Boulder: Westview Press, 1983), and John Wilson Lewis and Thomas Fingar, eds., *China's Quest for Independence: Policy Evolution in the 1970s* (Boulder: Westview Press, 1980). For the Taiwan issue, see "The China-Taiwan Unification Question," two perspectives by Hungdah Chiu and John Quansheng Zhao, *Asian Survey* (October 1983), pp. 1081–1114.

10. See Johnston, "Chinese Nuclear Force Modernization," p. 14, drawing upon an article by Drew Middleton, "Pentagon Studies Prospects of Military Links with China," *New York Times,* January 4, 1980, which in turn cites a secret Pentagon study.

11. For one Soviet evaluation, see the analysis of TASS correspondent Boris Chekhonin, carried in FBIS, *Daily Report—Soviet Union,* 29 December 1983, C 1–2. See also TASS analyst Vasiliy Demidov's report, *ibid.,* 22 December 1983, p. C1.

12. For a more detailed evaluation of prospects with respect to Japanese defense policies, see this author's "The Foreign Policy of Modern Japan," in Roy Macridis, ed., *Foreign Policy in World Politics,* 6th ed. (Englewood Cliffs, N.J.: Prentice-Hall, 1984).

13. Evidence for this was provided by Premier Zhao Ziyang during his visit to the United States and Canada. For his White House speech, see *Beijing Review,* January 16, 1984, pp. 15–16. For the speech to the Canadian Parliament, see *ibid.,* January 30, 1984, pp. 16–18.

14. A survey of Soviet policies in Asia comprehensive in nature is Donald S. Zagoria, ed., *Soviet Policy in East Asia* (New Haven: Yale University Press, 1982). See also, Herbert R. Ellison, ed., *The Sino-Soviet Conflict: A Global Perspective* (Seattle: University of Washington Press, 1982).

15. This is the view of Hisaya Shirai (staff writer of the *Asahi Shimbun*). See his article, "Japan and Siberia: The Big Chill," translated by The Asia Foundation's Translation Service Center, November 9, 1983.

16. An authoritative Soviet view of U.S. policies and the U.S. position in Asia is that of Admiral S. Gorshkov, "Bases for Aggression," *Izvestiya* (December 10, 1983, in FBIS, *Daily Report—Soviet Union,* 13 December 1983, pp. A5–8). For various analyses by Americans, see Richard H. Solomon, ed., *Asian Security in the 1980s* (Cambridge, Mass.: Oelgeschlager, Gunn and Hain, 1980).

17. Dieter Heinzig has provided an accurate evaluation of the Soviet position in Southeast Asia: *Die Sowjetunion in sudostasiatischer Sicht* (Berichte des Bundesinstituts fur ostwissenschaftliche und internationale Studien, Koln, 1983).

18. A Soviet review of USSR involvement was presented on Moscow radio by foreign policy commentator Yuriy Soltan, and is presented in FBIS, *Daily Report—Soviet Union,* 27 December 1983, pp. D1–4.

19. A comprehensive review of Soviet policy toward China is that of Harry Gelman, *The Soviet Far East Buildup and Soviet Risk-Taking Against China* R-2943-AF (Santa Monica: The Rand Corporation, August 1982). For additional writings, see Richard H. Solomon, ed., *The China Factor* (Englewood Cliffs, N.J.: Prentice Hall, 1981) and Harry Gelman, "Andropov's Policy Toward Asia," *Journal of Northeast Asian Studies* (June 1983), pp. 3–12.

20. Two informative articles relating to the military uses of space are Colin S. Gray, "Space Is Not a Sanctuary," and Stephen M. Meyer, "Soviet Military Programmes and the 'New High Ground,' " both in *Survival,* vol. 25, no. 5 (London: International Institute for Strategic Studies, September-October 1983), pp. 194–215.

*Chapter 3*

# THE SOVIET FAR EAST MILITARY BUILDUP: MOTIVES AND PROSPECTS

*by Harry Gelman*

Since the early 1980s, there has been a remarkable contrast between the rapidly shifting political scene in Moscow and the long-term perseverance visible in Soviet policies toward the outside world. Since November 1982, four General Secretaries have led the Soviet Union, but the most striking characteristic of the USSR's external behavior remains its continuity with the past. Nowhere is this more true than in the Far East, where the momentum behind Soviet pursuit of long-established strategic aims shows little sign of slowing down.

The broad outline of these Soviet intentions in Asia remains fairly clear. They may be summarized as follows:

- The vigorous buildup of Soviet military power in Asia, piling on strength where military advantages already exist, and amply compensating in advance for any anticipated increases in strength by the Soviet Union's adversaries.
- The attempt to use these military advantages to protect the security of the Soviet Union by overawing its neighbors.
- The effort, through such intimidation—supplemented by selective conciliatory gestures on minor matters—to separate weaker opponents from stronger ones.
- The effort to defend certain Soviet geopolitical gains staked

out in the 1970s—notably in Afghanistan and Indochina—but not yet consolidated.

- The attempt to get opponents to legitimize those gains, through negotiated understandings, while making no concessions that would jeopardize the advances of the past.
- The biding of time, behind the steady accretion of military power, for such new opportunities to advance the Soviet presence in Asia at acceptable risk as fortune may decree.

This broad pattern of Soviet conduct is hardly unique to the Far East. Indeed, one striking development of the last few years has been a clarification of the extent to which Soviet strategic policies in the East and West interact and tend to link the vital interests of states on both sides of the Eurasian landmass.

In the discussion that follows, the following issues will be reviewed under four major headings. First, trends in Soviet nuclear deployments in Asia will be reviewed in some detail, with consideration of both the implications for the Soviet Union's Asian neighbors and the links that have come to exist between Soviet deployment policies in Europe and Asia. Second, we will assess the status of the Soviet conventional force buildup in the Far East, and its consequences for China, Japan, the United States, and Southeast Asia. Third, Soviet behavior in Afghanistan and Indochina—the two new geopolitical bridgeheads in Asia for the USSR established in the last decade—will be reviewed, together with the implications of some recent trends. Finally, the prospects for the future will be weighed in the light of recent developments.

## Trends in Soviet Nuclear Deployments

Since the late 1970s, Soviet nuclear delivery systems directed against potential Asian targets have undergone a qualitative change, with the deployment to the Far East of the *Backfire* bomber and the SS-20 IRBM. The former has provided the Soviet Union with a long-range bomber of vastly improved speed and survivability, capable of either conventional or nuclear attack, and with a reach stretching out over nearly all of Asia from its bases in Siberia and the Soviet Far East.[1] About 80 are said to be deployed at Asian bases, representing about a third of the total *Backfire* bomber inventory;[2] some are assigned to the Aviation Armies of the Soviet Union and evidently are intended for attack on land targets in Asia, while others have been assigned to Soviet Naval

Aviation (SNA) and apparently are intended for attack on naval targets, above all those of the United States in the Pacific.[3] The strike capabilities of the *Backfire* are further augmented by its capability to carry the AS-4 air-to-surface missile.[4]

The SS-20, meanwhile, has provided the USSR with a missile possessing roughly the same range as the *Backfire,* thus covering almost all of Asia from its Siberian bases.[5] This missile is prized as a theater weapon because of its superior accuracy and reaction time, its mobility—which enhances its survivability—and the fact that it carries three multiple, independently targetable reentry vehicles (MIRVs), which multiply the number of warheads directed at Asian targets by three as new launchers are deployed.[6]

These two primary Soviet "theater" nuclear weapon systems are supplemented by two older, medium-range aircraft with smaller payloads, the Tu-16 *Badger* and the TU-22 *Blinder.* Finally, it is not impossible that at least a segment of the Soviet land-based ICBM force has been designated for use against Asian targets in a depressed-trajectory mode.

## New Weapon Systems in the Soviet Nuclear Inventory

Imposing as it now is, the weight of the Soviet nuclear threat in Asia will almost certainly increase significantly in the remainder of the 1980s. In part, this will be a consequence of the gradual advent of new strategic systems now under development. Although probably intended for intercontinental missions against the United States, many of these new weapon systems will also add to Soviet capabilities against Asian targets. The following factors must also be considered:

1. Several new ICBMs are under development, including one apparently intended for deployment in mobile launchers like those used for the SS-20.[7]

2. The first new *Typhoon* class SSBN, the largest in the world, is already operational, armed with 20 MIRVed SS-NX-20 SLBMs, a missile whose range—over 5,000 miles—"places all of NATO Europe, North America and Asia within *Typhoon's* reach."[8]

3. The Soviet Union is also developing a new strategic bomber—the *Blackjack A,* "the first true Soviet intercontinental bomber in over two decades."[9] This aircraft, somewhat similar to but considerably larger and faster than the American B-1, is expected to become operational in 1987.[10]

4. The capabilities of this bomber will be augmented by its use

with a new air-launched cruise missile(ALCM), the AS-X-15, also being developed. This same ALCM may be deployed on the new *Bear 4* strategic bomber this year[11] and later on aircraft already deployed for theater missions, notably the *Backfire*.[12]

5. In addition, a new sea-launched cruise missile (SLCM)—the SS-NX-21, with an estimated range of some 3,000 kilometers—is nearing completion of development. One striking feature of this weapon is that it can be fired from standard Soviet torpedo tubes.[13] While some of these missiles may be deployed on submarines that are directed against the United States, many of them—perhaps most—are likely to be used for missions in the European theater and in the Far East. It seems plausible that boats of the Soviet Pacific fleet will receive a considerable number of these intermediate-range SLCMs during the 1980s, adding a significant but hard-to-measure increment to the Soviet nuclear threat in Asia.

## The SS-20 Deployments, Asian Security, and Arms Control Negotiations

All these rather ominous impending developments in the Soviet nuclear posture in Asia are superimposed on the one existing element in this posture that is of overwhelming concern to Asians today: the pace of the SS-20 buildup in the Soviet Far East.

Over the last few years, three mutually dependent issues have emerged regarding the SS-20 deployments east of the Urals. One is the question of whether any U.S.-Soviet arms control agreement on INF (intermediate-range nuclear forces) would allow Moscow to transfer to Siberia European theater-based SS-20s, or whether there will be a "global ceiling" on the number of such weapons in any agreement. The second issue is whether those SS-20s already deployed in western Siberia—from which area they can reach targets in both Europe and Asia—are to be included in any such INF agreement. The third issue is the matter of whether anything can be done to halt construction of new SS-20 deployment sites in the Soviet Far East, let alone roll them back.

The first and third questions are of particular concern to Asians; and they became more and more pressing as the INF negotiations moved toward the climax imposed by the December 1983 deployment deadline for the start of the scheduled NATO missile deployments in Europe. Throughout the process, the Soviet leadership repeatedly sought to play off the security interests of the Europeans against those of the Asians, and to confront the United States with conflicting pressures from its friends on both sides of the Soviet Union.

Through most of 1983, the question of SS-20 transferability seemed to dominate the concerns of Asian leaders, no doubt because this had become an increasingly prominent issue in the INF negotiations as the deployment deadline grew closer. In April, Soviet Foreign Minister Andrei A. Gromyko defiantly insisted that:[14]

*We may withdraw part of the missiles from Europe, from the European zone, to Asia if an agreement is reached. This is our business and our right.*

The Soviet Union discovered, however, that adherence to this obstinate position left it exposed to political difficulties in both Europe and Asia: China joined with Japan in voicing public criticism of the Soviet claim to a right to increase the threat to Asia at the expense of Europe, while the NATO consensus continued to reject a formula which left the Soviets free, in effect, to use Asia as a repository for the surplus "European" SS-20s against a time when they might want to move these mobile weapons back again to the European theater. As a consequence, some four months later, the Soviet Union decided to yield on the transfer question. In August 1983, General Secretary Andropov in effect reversed Gromyko's position, now offering to destroy all Europe-based SS-20s over whatever ceiling might be negotiated in an INF settlement acceptable to the Soviet Union.[15]

This position was much better suited to dividing the Soviet Union's opponents. While the Europeans had won their point on the transfer issue (to the benefit of the Asians as well), if Moscow had been willing to make decisive concessions on other INF issues, a major split might have become visible between the interests of the NATO states and those of China and Japan. While Tokyo and Beijing accepted the Soviet concession on SS-20 transfers as a useful initial step, they then redirected their concern to the need to halt and roll back the SS-20 buildup in Asia. A Soviet INF agreement with the United States and the Europeans that did not impose "global" limits on the SS-20s, that halted the buildup in the West but not in the East, could hardly commend itself to Asian leaders.[16]

In fact, the Soviet Union appears to have used the period of the diplomatic struggle over INF in 1982 and 1983 to accelerate the deployment of SS-20 units in Asia. In March 1982, to facilitate the extraction of Western concessions in the INF negotiations, President Brezhnev proclaimed a moratorium on further SS-20 deployments in European Russia. It later became apparent that the Soviets meant by this "moratorium" that they would deploy additional missiles "only" where work on ground installations, even in the most rudimentary form, had already been started. While considerable SS-20 construction thus did go on in the Soviet Union's military districts east of the Urals, a halt was apparently imposed for the time being on new starts in European Russia. Indeed, it seems likely that some extra resources were thereby made available for a quickening of the pace of construction in the East. By May 1983, the Western press reported evidence that the Soviet Union was building at least ten new regimental bases in Siberia to accommodate more than 100 new SS-20 missiles. These bases, said to be in various stages of completion, would—when completed—approximately double the existing number of SS-20s deployed in East Asia (a figure generally listed as 108 until 1983).[17] By early 1984, this building program started to produce results as some of the new missile units were deployed to the field.[18] As of late 1985, even if no further base construction is begun, when current facilities are completed, the Soviets will be able to deploy a total of at least 216 SS-20 launchers in the Far East with a minimum of 648 warheads aimed at Asian targets.[19] These are minimum estimates and could well prove to be somewhat conservative.

This central fact sheds considerable light on the final Soviet INF negotiating concession, announced in October 1983. Andropov now offered to place a freeze on new Soviet Asian deployments of the SS-20 *if* a satisfactory INF agreement were reached with the Europeans *and also if* the United States refrained from deploying any new intermediate-range nuclear weapons targeted on Soviet Asia.[20] The Soviets thus implied that they were willing to trade an ambiguous limit on *the extent of the further increase* in their existing nuclear advantage in Asia in exchange for an agreement in Europe perpetuating and legitimizing their strategic nuclear superiority there. As well, they also sought to place the onus for their failure to halt SS-20 deployments in Asia on U.S. obduracy in Europe.

In any case, it was clear—judging by Soviet behavior during the "moratorium" on SS-20 construction in Europe—that Moscow would have reserved the right to complete all construction already begun in Asia. The program to deploy in the Far East at least 216 SS-20s with 648 warheads was thus sacrosanct for the Soviets, and would almost certainly be completed whether or not the USSR had its way in preventing all American deployments in Europe.[21]

In their INF negotiating position, however, the Soviets sought to make their SS-20 building program in Asia and the future size of their theater nuclear threat against China and Japan hostage to a possible INF agreement in Europe. This linkage faded after the November 1983 Soviet walkout from the INF talks in Geneva; and in the absence of a negotiated agreement, there seems little likelihood that the Soviet Union will agree to a unilateral INF deployment moratorium in Asia (however limited its meaning for the Soviet military buildup in the Far East) merely to conciliate Japan and China. Moscow is even less likely to agree to *reduce* existing Asian deployments for this purpose. Although in the past Brezhnev had vaguely offered to negotiate separately with Asian states about nuclear deployments, it seems highly unlikely, in view of the vast disparity between Soviet and Chinese nuclear strengths and the absence of any Japanese nuclear capability, that the Soviet Union envisions the possibility of reaching formal agreements on the subject with Asians.

What conclusions can be drawn from this panorama of Soviet nuclear development, deployment, and negotiating behavior? First, Soviet leaders seem determined to maintain a continuously updated margin of "theater" nuclear superiority in both Europe and Asia. To prevent American counterdeployments, they evidently are willing to negotiate regarding the size of their margin, but not regarding the fact. In the absence of a willingness by their opponents to sign agreements tacitly legitimizing Soviet superiority, they will do without such agreements, proceeding with their planned deployments and describing them as responses to the behavior of their antagonists. All attempts by the states confronting the Soviet Union to bolster their own defenses in the face of this superiority will meanwhile be strenuously denounced as increasing the danger of war. Their negotiating position, in Asia as in Europe, will be designed to generate maximum tensions between the United States and its allies, and to build public pressures on the governments of the region against either their own defense programs or cooperation with the United States.

Second, it would appear that Soviet leaders genuinely believe that the security interests of the USSR are incompatible with those of their neighbors and can only be adequately protected at the expense of their opponents by maintaining a permanent military advantage of intimidating proportions. This advantage must always be adequate to more than compensate for any worst-case responses by the other side. In Europe, the Soviet margin has therefore been continuously defined since the late 1970s as "equilibrium," despite the fact that this margin has also been continuously growing.[22] In Asia, the Soviet Union probably regards the SS-20 deployment program as covering all contingencies created by the modest Chinese nuclear effort, the similarly modest American nuclear deployments in the vicinity of Asia, and anything further which the United States might conceivably deploy in the future. Nevertheless, Soviet leaders are undoubtedly aware that their margin of theater nuclear superiority in Asia is already much greater than the margin in Europe, and that it will grow even greater as the SS-20 building program and the planned bomber deployments proceed. They evidently also regard this situation as "equilibrium," and will doubtless eventually defend it as such.

Third, the Soviet Union evidently sees this margin of "theater" nuclear superiority on each side of its territory as providing an indispensable instrument of political intimidation, which it does not intend to forego. In Europe, this element in Soviet thinking has long been obvious in Moscow's behavior and was particularly evident during the long Soviet political campaign designed to break Western morale and disrupt NATO over the INF deployment issue. Similarly, in Asia, it is equally obvious that the primary long-term objects of Soviet intimidation through the SS-20 deployment program are China and Japan and their defense dealings with the United States. On both sides of the USSR, a major purpose of this intimidation is to prevent the Soviet Union's neighbors from cooperating in response, and particularly to prevent them from effectively cooperating with the United States— the only power that confronts the Soviet Union on all sides and has the potential to help redress the nuclear balance.

Finally, the Soviet Union also sees its nuclear advantage in Asia as furnishing the essential backdrop and complement to the growth of its conventional forces, and thereby, over the long term, to the incremental expansion of the Soviet geopolitical presence in Asia— an issue to which we now turn.

## The Soviet Conventional Force Buildup in Asia

The Soviet ground, naval, and tactical air buildup in the Far East has been going on now for more than two decades. Initiated in the first year of the Brezhnev regime, it was methodically, although not uniformly, sustained throughout that regime and then continued through the brief reign of Andropov. Since 1965, Soviet ground force strength in the Far East, Siberia, and Central Asia has risen from some 17-20 divisions to 53 divisions, and from some 170,000 ground force troops to nearly half a million men.[23] There is no reason whatsoever to believe that this process has come to an end. The ground forces manpower total, however, will probably continue to rise only slowly in the Far East, as has been the case since the early 1970s when the initial post-Khrushchev spurt in the buildup was completed.

This long-term expansion in Soviet military resources east of the Urals has been only part of the Soviet response to the more general growth in ground force requirements under Brezhnev and Andropov. It is well known that the buildup in the Far East since 1965 has not been at the expense of Soviet capabilities in Europe, but instead has been made possible by a steady enlargement of all the Soviet armed forces, and particularly the ground forces. Similarly, the Soviet deployment of some 115,000 men to Afghanistan since 1979 has not caused any long-term net subtraction from the forces deployed against Western Europe and China, or even from Soviet central reserves. Divisions initially displaced for the Afghan mission have apparently since been either returned to the reserves or compensated for through a further enlargement of the armed forces.[24] Whereas Soviet leaders had a total of 180 divisions at their disposal as recently as 1981, they have over 190 divisions today.[25] This steady expansion of the ground forces has received less public attention in the outside world than the Soviet strategic buildup, or even the growth of the Soviet Navy, but it has had consequences that are at least as important.

The multiplication of the geopolitical tasks imposed on the Soviet ground forces is thus a process that has gone on from the earliest days of the Brezhnev era to the present moment, in parallel with efforts to increase the presence of the Soviet Union on the world scene and to expand the circle of influence and intimidation around the USSR's periphery. As each new task has materialized, there has been a long-term ratcheting upward of the military resources demanded by the expanded interpretation of the requirements of Soviet national interests. Although the capabilities of the Soviet economy—and especially of Soviet manpower—to support these incrementally growing military requirements are certainly not infinite, there has been little indication thus far of a Soviet inclination to scale down political appetites in order to conserve resources.[26]

As noted elsewhere,[27] in the Far East the buildup has gone through discrete stages, and over time Soviet motives for the buildup have changed and broadened. Initially intended to coerce China and enforce the Soviet version of the Sino-Soviet border, the force expansion has by degrees acquired additional purposes: (1) to prevent China from responding to the use of force by the USSR or its clients (i.e., Vietnam) near China's *southern* boundaries; (2) to counteract the growth of American security cooperation with Japan; (3) to maintain the Soviet force advantage against the worst-case possibility of Chinese security cooperation with Japan and the United States; and finally, (4) to assist in the expansion of the Soviet military presence to the south.

Since 1978, the measures devoted to these multiple purposes have clearly entered a new stage. In that year a new high command was set up for all Soviet units in the Far East, formalizing the determination to maintain very large forces in the region indefinitely and to ensure the independent viability of the Far East theater of military operations (TVD) in any circumstances. Modernization of equipment has been accelerated, bringing to the Far East such new Soviet technology as the T-72 tank, the MiG-23 and MiG-27 *Flogger* fighters, and the SU-24 *Fencer* fighter-bomber. Still newer Soviet tactical systems have begun to arrive or are likely to arrive in the Far East over the next few years,[28] including such items as the SU-25 *Frogfoot* fighter-bomber now in use in Afghanistan, the MiG-29 *Fulcrum* dual-capacity interceptor and fighter-bomber, and the SS-21, 22, and 23 short- and medium-range surface-to-surface missiles (SSMs).[29] One consequence of some of these changes will be to significantly augment Soviet short-range tactical nuclear weapons capabilities in the Far East, necessarily directed at China.

In parallel with the reorganization of Soviet Far East forces since 1978, as well as their growth and steady modernization, the Soviet Union has over the same period deployed forces forward in three key Far East areas: Mongolia, the "Northern Territories" adjacent to Japan, and Vietnam. Leaving the last of these for later discussion, it may be noted that the deployments in Mongolia and the "Northern Territories" are clearly intended to put pressure on China and Japan, respectively. In Mongolia, Soviet forces subordinated to the Far East High Command have now been built up to five divisions.[30] These forces are evidently intended as a sword held over China's head, perpetually threatening with Soviet armor the vulnerable invasion route to the North China plain and Beijing. It is not surprising that in the bilateral talks China has conducted with the USSR since 1982, one of the key demands the PRC has presented as prerequisites for a fundamental improvement of Sino-Soviet relations has been a Soviet military withdrawal from Mongolia. Thus far, there has been no response from Moscow.

In the Northern Territories—the Japanese-claimed islands between Hokkaido and the southern Kuriles held by the Soviet Union—the Soviet buildup since 1978 has thus far amounted to the equivalent of a full division, with some additional equipment.[31] It is by now widely agreed that this deployment is intended partly to prevent wartime access by hostile forces to Soviet *Delta*-class missile submarines operating in the Sea of Okhotsk, and partly to convey to Japan the message that under no circumstances will the USSR relinquish control of the islands. In addition, it seems likely that these forces, deployed only a few miles from the Japanese home islands, are intended to complement other efforts to intimidate Japan and to weaken the domestic political consensus which supports Japanese security cooperation with the United States.[32] In this respect, they reinforce such measures as the SS-20 deployment, explicit threats in *Pravda*, and the repeated exercises and deployments all around Japanese airspace and territorial waters of Soviet air and naval units.

An aspect of the Far East buildup of particular concern to Japan, of course, has been the growth of the Soviet Pacific fleet. Now the largest of the four Soviet fleets, it includes some 825 vessels, among them about 135 submarines.[33] Over the years, as the ground force buildup in the Far East proceeded, the number of major surface combatants assigned to the Pacific fleet has also increased from about 50 in 1965 to some 90 today. Once again, the changes since 1978 have been particularly striking, including the addition in 1979 of the *Kiev*-class carrier *Minsk*, three *Kara*-class guided missile antisubmarine warfare (ASW) cruisers, and the growth of an amphibious capability, highlighted by the arrival in 1979 of a very large amphibious transport of the *Ivan Rogov* class. "The Pacific Fleet," notes the Japanese government, "has a naval infantry division that is the sole one in the [four] Soviet fleets and promotes modernization of its equipment."[34] Although Soviet amphibious tonnage is still far too small to constitute a credible sealift capacity for an invasion of Japan, a potential is gradually being created for smaller-scale operations in Northeast or Southeast Asia. The increasing effort that the Soviet Union is devoting to this capability bears watching.

As with other aspects of the Far East buildup, the growth of the Pacific fleet will be paced by the progress of Soviet military development and building programs. The possible advent of Soviet intermediate-range SLCMs directed at Asian land targets has already been mentioned. A new 37,000 ton *Kiev*-class aircraft carrier joined the Pacific fleet in February 1984, making this fleet the first to possess two such carriers.[35] Construction of a much larger aircraft carrier has been completed, the first one intended to carry conventional take-off and landing high-performance jet fighters.[36] When and if such specialized naval fighters are developed, this ship will for the first time begin to redress the serious Soviet deficiency in tactical air cover for naval operations. Although deployment decisions for this carrier are probably still to be made, it is not implausible that it will be sent to the Pacific.

Like the SS-20 deployments and the ground force buildup, the growth of the Pacific fleet is linked by circumstance to Soviet strategic aims in other arenas, far beyond the fleet's home base at Vladivostok. In part, this stems from the fleet's operational jurisdiction, which apparently extends south and westward through the Indian Ocean to the coast of Africa. And in part, it results from Soviet success over the last five years in obtaining and gradually expanding an operational base for naval and air activities in Vietnam. The implications of this development will now be examined.

## Soviet Objectives in Indochina and Afghanistan

Since the time of the Sino-Vietnamese conflict in February-March 1979, the Soviet Union has obtained the use of military facilities in Vietnam that have steadily increased in importance. Beginning with acquisition of the right to make naval port calls and to stage naval reconnaissance flights from Soviet air bases far to the north in the Maritime Provinces, the military benefits obtained from Vietnam have gradually expanded. At Cam Ranh Bay, the Soviet Union has developed, and continues to develop, a facility for intelligence collection and naval support to assist operations in the South China Sea and the Indian Ocean. With the support of this installation, a permanent naval presence of some 20 to 25 warships and auxiliaries has been maintained in the South China Sea, augmented from time to time by visits by major ships such as the *Minsk*.[37] Cam Ranh Bay is reported to be used, in particular, by Soviet submarines.[38]

An important new offensive capability was added in November 1983, when Soviet bombers for the first time were deployed to Cam Ranh Bay. The advent of these ten medium-range Tu-16 *Badgers*[39] appears to mark a new stage in Soviet policy, since this seems to be the first time since 1971 that Soviet-manned bombers with strike capabilities have been deployed to bases outside areas contiguous to the Soviet bloc. This precedent may be more important than the intrinsic capabilities—attack, tanking, and electronic warfare—of the particular aircraft involved. In addition to whatever modest new threat may be presented to American naval operations and facilities in the Southwest Pacific, or to Southeast Asian sea lanes, the deployment raises the prospect of further growth in the Soviet military presence in Vietnam, perhaps some day to include the *Backfire* bomber.

Meanwhile, from Hanoi's point of view, the decision to allow these aircraft basing rights at Cam Ranh Bay may have been influenced by a desire to secure a new element of Soviet protection against any Chinese naval and air deployments in the South China Sea. The *Badgers* thus serve as additional evidence of the Soviet shield behind which Hanoi intends to continue striving to consolidate its conquest of Cambodia against Chinese opposition. For China this event is ominous indeed, for it is powerful evidence that the Soviet Union has no intention of endangering its military position in Southeast Asia by putting pressure on Vietnam to reach a compromise with China over Cambodia. Indeed, it is conceivable that Vietnamese consent to the deployment was obtained, at least in part, as a *quid pro quo* for Soviet rejection of a Chinese demand that the USSR exert such pressure on Hanoi.

From a broader perspective, the arrival of the *Badgers* in Cam Ranh Bay now provides a hint of some of the ultimate consequences that may be anticipated if and when the Soviet Union completes the conquest of Afghanistan. The struggle to suppress the Afghan resistance is now in its sixth year; and although there is as yet no end in sight, there is also no sign of Soviet willingness to settle for less than total control of the country.[40] There is thus every prospect that the military effort in the country will be maintained for as many years as prove necessary to destroy the will and capabilities of the resistance forces. The Soviet Union probably believes that until this occurs and the country is made secure, the strategic fruits of the advance into Afghanistan cannot begin to be gathered. Recent Soviet conduct in Indochina, however, tends to support the interpretation that Moscow hopes eventually to use Afghanistan as a platform for the forward deployment of bombers (among other things) for use in Southwest Asia, and that this is one of the advantages of the occupation of this country that must be deferred until it is pacified.

## Some General Conclusions

In the broadest terms, this survey of trends in Soviet policy in Asia suggests four general conclusions. First, the military buildup will surely go on, although its pace may vary. It is highly unlikely that China will obtain from the Soviet Union the significant concessions it is seeking regarding a reduction in Soviet forces in the Far East, Soviet support for Vietnam, and the Soviet presence in Afghanistan.[41] China and other East Asian states that are now confronted by Soviet military power and efforts at intimidation must expect both trends to grow in the late 1980s, not to contract. They are unlikely to be able to persuade Moscow to give up its efforts to strengthen its influence in the region through a military presence.

Second, although a portion of Soviet military forces in the Far East—particularly some of the SS–20s, strategic bombers, and naval vessels—may be regarded as transferable to other theaters in a dire crisis, this is probably not true of the great bulk of these assets. The long-existing momentum of the strategic and conventional force buildup implies an assumption that large and growing forces will be needed in the Far East for the indefinite future to guard against worst-case eventualities in wartime, as well as to expand Soviet influence in peacetime. With the partial exceptions just noted, the Soviet Union probably does not believe a "swing strategy" to be either feasible or appropriate to its global concerns.

Third, the Soviet Union probably believes its naval and air buildup in the Far East to be particularly cost-effective because it aggravates American resource constraints and accentuates a U.S. dilemma: either to accept the consequences of a less-favorable force balance in the Western Pacific, or to limit the naval forces that can be deployed to the Indian Ocean as a partial offset to the Soviet land and air superiority in Southwest Asia.

Finally, with the movement of the Tu-16 *Badger* bombers to Cam Ranh Bay, Moscow has initiated a forward deployment of offensive forces that may well be a harbinger for the future. It is likely, over time, that there will be more forward deployments of different kinds.[42] During the late 1980s, as circumstances permit, the Soviet Union will probably seek gradually to extract further concrete political and military advantages from its adversaries based on the strategic bridgeheads established in Indochina and Afghanistan in the 1970s. The Soviet Union is, therefore, less likely than ever to yield to China's demand that it give up these bridgeheads which—among other things—encircle the PRC.

### Endnotes

1. *Soviet Military Power, 1984* (Washington, D.C.: U.S. Government Printing Office, 1984), pp. 28–29.
2. *Ibid.*, p. 12. See also, *Defense of Japan, 1984* (Tokyo: Japan Times, Ltd., 1984), p. 31.
3. *The Military Balance, 1984–1985* (London: International Institute for Strategic Studies, 1984), pp. 17, 20.
4. *Ibid.*
5. *Soviet Military Power, 1984*, p. 52.
6. In addition, "the SS-20 launcher has the capability of being reloaded and

refired; the Soviets stockpile refire missiles." (*Soviet Military Power, 1984,* p. 51.)

7. *Ibid.*, p. 24.

8. *Soviet Military Power, 1983* (Washington, D.C.: U.S. Government Printing Office, 1983), p. 21.

9. Joel Wit, "Soviet Cruise Missiles," *Survival,* vol. 25, no. 6 (London: International Institute for Strategic Studies, November-December 1983), p. 257.

10. *Soviet Military Power, 1984,* p. 29.

11. *Ibid.*, p. 31.

12. *Soviet Military Power, 1983,* p. 26.

13. Wit calculates that there may be over 4,000 such tubes in the Soviet Navy. (Wit, "Soviet Cruise Missiles," p. 256.)

14. *New York Times,* April 3, 1983.

15. *Pravda,* August 27, 1983.

16. It can be argued that such an agreement would not really serve NATO's interests either. New mobile SS-20s deployed in central Siberia, even if out of range of Europe, still constitute a reserve that could in principle be drawn on some day for transfer to the West.

17. *Los Angeles Times,* May 8, 1983; *New York Times,* May 8, 1983.

18. By late 1985 the total of deployed SS-20s capable of reaching targets in Asia had grown to more than 170.

19. *Los Angeles Times,* May 8, 1983. This figure does not take into account the fact that each launcher has one "reload" missile, thus potentially doubling the number of warheads (of which there are three on each missile) to a total of 1,296.

20. *Pravda,* October 27, 1983.

21. It is not inconceivable that the Soviet Union, foreseeing that it might eventually make such a conditional Asian moratorium proposal, had accelerated the start of the additional SS-20 bases in Asia partly to make sure that their entire program of planned deployments was "locked in," and would be exempted from any moratorium.

22. See *Progress Report on INF,* 8 December 1983 (a report to NATO Ministers by the Special Consultative Group), p. 33.

23. *Defense of Japan, 1984,* p. 31.

24. See *The Military Balance,* issues 1980-81 through 1984–85.

25. *Soviet Military Power, 1984,* p. 13.

26. Insofar as any such constraint exists, it is clearly in military manpower. It can be argued that a perceived need to ration the allocation of additional troops to the various geopolitical tasks because of the competing needs of the economy has been partly responsible for the reduced rate of growth of Soviet forces along the Sino-Soviet border since the early 1970s, and also for Soviet failure to commit larger forces (which would obviously be useful) to the pacification of Afghanistan. Throughout 1981 the temporary need to reserve large Soviet forces for the possible invasion of Poland was another factor; this particular constraint, however, has now been eased.

27. See Harry Gelman, *Soviet Expansionism in Asia and the Sino-Soviet-U.S. Triangle,* Security Conference on Asia and the Pacific (SeCAP) 58221282, March 1983; also Gelman, *The Soviet Far East Buildup and Soviet Risk-*

*Taking Against China*, R-2943-AF (Santa Monica: The Rand Corporation, August 1982).

28. The Japanese government has said that "there used to be a considerable time lag in delivering the latest weapons systems to the Far Eastern units following their deployment to the European front. But recently there are cases in which the deployment of some newest weapons is almost simultaneous in Europe and the Far East." (*Defense of Japan, 1984*, p. 31)
29. *Soviet Military Power, 1984*, pp. 57–58; *The Military Balance*, p. 19.
30. *Defense of Japan, 1984*, p. 42.
31. *Ibid.*, p. 35.
32. See comments by Hiroshi Kimura in Chapter 6 of this volume.
33. *Defense of Japan, 1984*, p. 33.
34. *Ibid.*
35. *Ibid.*
36. *Soviet Military Power, 1984*, p. 64.
37. *Ibid.*, p. 66.
38. *New York Times*, January 30, 1984.
39. *Soviet Military Power, 1984*, p. 66.
40. Since 1982, the USSR has engaged Pakistan in desultory indirect talks about Afghanistan through the intercession of the U.N. secretary general. It seems quite clear that the Soviet purpose in these talks was to attempt to extract from Pakistan a commitment to close the border in order to halt the assistance flowing to the Afghan resistance in return for cosmetic changes by Moscow that would not alter the fact of Soviet domination of Afghanistan. The Soviets have also conducted talks with Washington for the same purpose, while increasing pressure on Pakistan through diplomatic threats and border violations.
41. See *Asian Security 1984* (Tokyo: Research Institute for Peace and Security, 1984), p. 42. See also, Chapter 5 of this volume.
42. During 1984, the Soviet squadron at Cam Ranh Bay was built up to "24 reconnaissance or combat aircraft, with 8 *Bears* and 16 *Badgers*, including 10 with strike capabilities." (*Soviet Military Power, 1985*, p. 131.) A relevant question is whether the Soviets will eventually also deploy *Backfire* bombers to Cam Ranh Bay, particularly after the *Blackjack A* bomber becomes available for deployment in the Soviet Union.

# Chapter 4

# THINKING ABOUT THE
# NUCLEAR BALANCE IN ASIA

*By J. J. Martin*

### Assessing the Soviet Military Buildup in the
### Asia-Pacific Region

Since 1965, the Soviet Union has been engaged in a major buildup
of armed forces in the Asia-Pacific region, dramatically increasing
the number of its ground, air, and naval forces and improving
substantially their military capabilities. Beginning in 1977, the
Soviets initiated a significant increase in the capabilities of their
nuclear forces located for employment in the Far East theater.
While most of the increases in force size were completed by the
early 1980s, the Soviets continue to replace older conventional and
nuclear weapon systems with modern, more capable versions.

The general purpose force buildup has been analyzed in both its
political and military dimensions by a number of authors, largely as
it affects Sino-Soviet relations and to a lesser extent in the context
of the security interests of the United States and its East Asia
allies.[1] Little analysis has been devoted, however, to the implications of the changes in Soviet nuclear forces. The following analysis
addresses this topic, in an effort to develop interpretive perspectives on the nuclear balance in Asia. The second section of this
chapter describes trends in Soviet nuclear forces in the Asia-Pacific
region and the direct military improvements the Soviets are
achieving with their nuclear force modernization. The third section makes a more comprehensive assessment of trends in the
nuclear balance in Asia by considering U.S.-Soviet-Chinese asymmetries, describing conflicts in which nuclear weapons might be

used, identifying important missions and targets for nuclear forces, deriving key nuclear force characteristics based on these missions and targets, and assessing the impact of trends in the nuclear balance on U.S., Soviet, and Chinese military capabilities to carry out wartime missions.

The implications of this assessment for deterrence and other security interests of the United States, its allies, and its friends in Asia are discussed in the fourth section. The final section recommends approaches to dealing with the continuing Soviet nuclear buildup in Asia.

Much of this chapter concentrates on the warfighting aspects of the nuclear balance in Asia. This focus should not be read as implying that the United States or its allies and friends would benefit from fighting a nuclear war, or that first use of nuclear weapons is a substitute for adequate nonnuclear (conventional) forces. Nevertheless, analysis of Soviet writings and observation of Soviet behavior suggest strongly that deterrence of Soviet attacks is enhanced if the U.S. nuclear force posture causes substantial uncertainty in the minds of Moscow's military planners about the ability of their forces to achieve wartime military objectives. Moreover, the security interests of the United States and various nations in Asia are affected by the likely military outcomes of a prospective nuclear war. Even though the probability of nuclear war is very low, the possibility of a war between nuclear powers leading to use of nuclear weapons affects the security interests of many states in peacetime, in crises, and in nonnuclear wars. For this reason, the Soviet Union seeks to exploit its nuclear buildup for political purposes. The United States and its allies and friends must therefore consider political as well as military responses to this buildup.

While the number of medium-range/intermediate-range ballistic missile (MR/IRBM) launchers in the Soviet Far East has been relatively constant, there has been a major increase in the number of MR/IRBM nuclear warheads and in launcher survivability with deployment of the mobile SS-20 missile system. Deployment of the nuclear-capable *Backfire* medium bomber has significantly increased the combat radius and target coverage of Soviet Strategic Air Armies and Soviet Naval Aviation (SNA) in the Far East. The number of medium bombers in the Asian component of the Strategic Air Armies has remained roughly the same since the mid-1960s, but the number of SNA medium bombers has doubled.[2] The Soviet Union has also been building up the number of nuclear-capable tactical aircraft in the Far East, and has probably been increasing its stockpile of ground force and maritime nuclear weapons in the region.

Analysis of the security implications of this nuclear buildup indicates that it would be politically and militarily unwise for the United States, its allies, and its friends in Asia to depend on first use of nuclear weapons to deter or defend against Soviet nonnuclear attacks in the Asia-Pacific region. While the threat of first use should not be abandoned, conventional forces must be the primary means of deterring or defending against nonnuclear attacks. The primary roles for nuclear weapons should be to deter Soviet nuclear attacks by providing effective responses to such attacks and, through the deterrent effect of these forces, to counter Soviet efforts at nuclear coercion or intimidation of U.S. allies and friends in Asia.

It is important that the United States counter the political impact of the Soviet nuclear buildup in Asia. One way to do this is to keep the Asian nuclear buildup in perspective and not exaggerate its importance. Another way is to emphasize the role that American strategic forces play in countering Soviet Far East nuclear forces.

It is also important to improve the deterrent capabilities of U.S. theater nuclear forces in the Asia-Pacific region. Priority should be given to improving the survivability of U.S. theater nuclear forces and supporting command, control, communications and intelligence ($C^3I$) capabilities, and increasing the military capabilities of long-range theater nuclear strike forces based at sea or in rear areas of the Pacific on U.S. territory.

And finally, it is important that the United States and its allies and friends not depend entirely on American nuclear forces to deter aggressive moves by the Soviet Union or its allies in the region. Conventional forces must be maintained at a level sufficient to deter nonnuclear threats to their interests; otherwise, the choice they will face will be between use of nuclear forces to resist Soviet expansionism or no effective resistance at all.

## Trends in Soviet Far East Nuclear Forces (SS-20s and *Backfires*)

### Background: The Soviet General Purpose Force Buildup

Interpretation of the nuclear balance in Asia must be carried out in the context of an understanding of the balance of general purpose conventional military forces. This is so for two reasons: First, trends in general purpose forces are one guide to determining

Soviet nuclear force trends, since many Soviet nuclear delivery systems in Asia are dual-capable (e.g., surface-to-surface tactical missiles, tactical aircraft, antiship cruise missiles). Second, while the Soviet Union is seeking the capability to prevail in combat without using nuclear weapons, if a war crosses the nuclear threshold, Soviet doctrine calls for employment of nuclear weapons to seize or maintain the general purpose combat initiative and for conventional force operations to exploit the effects of nuclear strikes.[3]

As a result of the Soviet military expansion program over the last 20 years, Moscow's forces in the Far East ". . . are now capable of large-scale offensive as well as defensive operations."[4] Although the Soviets have a growing military presence in the Kurile Islands, the predominant deployment of Soviet ground and tactical air forces in Asia is along the border with China. Soviet forces have a clear capability to defend against a Chinese invasion of the USSR. Moreover, as a result of their general purpose force buildup, the Soviet Union has a substantial combined arms capability for offensive operations into China. However, the size of the People's Liberation Army and the strategic depth of China give it the ability to force a long, debilitating war of attrition on the Soviet Union, should the Soviets invade China for more than brief operations to accomplish limited punitive objectives. Current Soviet difficulties in pacifying Afghanistan only heighten the deterrent effect of China's capacity to conduct an effective "people's war" against a Soviet occupation force inside the PRC.

Soviet naval forces and long-range bombers, while of value for military operations against China, are most relevant to the balance of forces with the United States and Japan in East Asia. This balance is not characterized by the extremes of numbers and qualitative capabilities of the Sino-Soviet military balance and is, therefore, more difficult to assess in a few words. Outcomes of nonnuclear wars between the United States and the Soviet Union and their allies in Asia would depend strongly on factors other than the numerical balance of forces. These include, for example, the amount of time each side has for prewar positioning of forces (many forces of the U.S. Pacific Command are deployed in the eastern and middle Pacific and in the Indian Ocean during peacetime); how each side allocates its forces to various missions and geographic regions over time during the conflict; the bases available to each side (the United States has few bases in the Western Pacific; most are in allied countries, which makes U.S. use of these bases vulnerable to shifts in political attitudes and alignments); and the capabilities of specific weapon systems, operational employment plans, command and control, and training, as they would affect force-on-force engagements.

Soviet air and naval forces do not pose the immediate threat to U.S. and allied security in East Asia that they do in Europe. This is due to the balance of forces in East Asia, the relative economic and political stability of regions in Asia where U.S. and Soviet interests are opposed, and the low likelihood of superpower conflict growing directly from crises in East Asia. Nevertheless, a major war in Europe or Southwest Asia would very likely expand to a global conflict; and in such a war, it is not at all clear that the United States and its allies could dominate the air and naval campaigns in Northeast Asia, particularly early in the war. Soviet air and naval forces in Asia constitute a growing nonnuclear threat to Japan and other U.S. allies, to U.S. and allied forces in the Western Pacific, and to the sea lines of communication (SLOCs) to Northeast Asia.

One commentator sums up the general purpose force balance in Asia as follows:[5]

> *The current balance of U.S. and Soviet [conventional] forces sharply favors the USSR on the land and in forward deployed, land-based air strength. At the same time, it still favors the U.S. in terms of overall naval power in the Pacific and the ability to deploy tactical aviation on carriers or bases throughout the region. The U.S. also retains far superior Command, Control, Communications and Intelligence ($C^3I$) and ASW assets both at the strategic and tactical level. While details are classified, the U.S. has an "electronic shield" based on satellites, ships, airborne sensors, and on ground sites in South Korea and Japan.*

Continuing military challenges in Europe and new ones in the Middle East and Southwest Asia have been diluting over time the number of U.S. general purpose forces available for deployment in East Asia. Ongoing Soviet improvements in its Far East forces threaten to erode further the U.S. advantages cited above, unless there are offsetting increases in the military capabilities of the United States and its allies and friends in Asia. Changes in the nuclear balance in the region—changes that favor the Soviet Union—pose further threats to the security of the United States and its allies and friends.

## Trends in Soviet Nuclear Forces

For purposes of assessing the Soviet nuclear buildup in Asia, it is most useful to think in terms of force categories relevant to two distinct military campaigns: (1) Soviet intermediate-range air, naval, and missile operations throughout East Asia and the Pacific, including China; and (2) a Soviet ground force invasion of China. Considering the range and other combat characteristics of Soviet nuclear forces, their command subordination, and their geographic deployment, the following are the relevant Soviet nuclear weapon systems for each of these campaigns:[6]

- East Asia air and missile operations: longer-range "theater" nuclear force missiles (LRTNF, now generally termed inter-mediate-range nuclear forces, or INF), medium bombers, submarine-launched ballistic missiles (SLBMs), and sea-launched cruise missiles (SLCMs). Soviet intercontinental nu-clear forces, tactical naval nuclear weapons for antisurface ship warfare (ASuW), antisubmarine warfare (ASW), and anti-air warfare (AAW), and land-based surface-to-air missiles (SAMs) also have some relevance to this type of campaign, as do longer-range deep strike tactical aircraft (e.g., *Fencer A*, with a combat radius of 1,800 km).
- Soviet ground force invasion of China: shorter-range INF missiles, tactical aircraft, short-range (battlefield) nuclear forces, and land-based SAMs.

Considering first the Soviet nuclear forces that are relevant to theaterwide strike operations in East Asia, key trend data are shown in the appendix to this volume (see pp. 271-275). This appendix summarizes trends in Soviet intermediate-range nuclear strike forces that have capabilities for theaterwide attacks against U.S. forces in East Asia and against the territories of America's allies and friends, including targets deep in China. These forces include MR/IRBM launchers, medium bombers of the Strategic Air Armies, and medium bombers of Soviet Naval Aviation (SNA). It is these forces that would be of greatest importance for achieving Soviet nuclear missions in air and missile operations in East Asia. SNA bombers would also be a key element in efforts to deny control of the Western Pacific to U.S. and Japanese surface naval forces.

Generally, the number of Soviet MR/IRBM launchers has been roughly constant since the mid-1960s. Similarly, the number of Strategic Air Army medium bombers in the Far East was relatively constant through 1980, then declined to about 120 when Soviet Air Forces were reorganized into five Strategic Air Armies. The number of SNA bombers has, however, more than doubled since the mid-1960s, growing from 55 to 120.

The more significant trend is the substantial increase in the military capabilities of Soviet Far East intermediate-range nuclear forces since the late 1970s—the introduction of the SS-20 IRBM into the Strategic Rocket Forces and the *Backfire* bomber into both the Strategic Air Armies and Soviet Naval Aviation. The SS-20 is a major improvement over the SS-4 and SS-5 missiles it has replaced in the Far East. This system is mobile, improving its survivability in wartime. SS-4s and SS-5s were deployed at fixed sites north of Mongolia, where they were beyond range of U.S. theater nuclear forces in the Asia-Pacific region. They could, however, be attacked by U.S. B-52s, SLBMs, or ICBMs. The SS-20 launchers are deployed in the same general area as the SS-4s and SS-5s, but their mobility makes them difficult to locate for targeting and attack purposes once they have deployed from their garrisons.[7]

The range of the SS-20 is about 20 percent greater than that of the SS-5, as indicated in Table 4–1. This allows the SS-20 to reach more targets than the SS-5, while still operating from bases well inside the Soviet Union, beyond the range of the theater nuclear strike systems of the U.S. Pacific Command.

Most dramatic, however, is the large increase in Soviet theater nuclear warheads resulting from deployment of the SS-20. This trend is shown in Figure 4–1, which graphs the number of warheads on Soviet SS-4s, SS-5s, and SS-20s during the period 1965–1985. SS-11 ICBMs, which began deployment in 1966, have a variable range capability and could be used for theater support; these are not shown in Figure 4–1. Each SS-20 missile has three

Table 4–1    Combat Range/Radius of Soviet Intermediate-Range
                    Nuclear Forces

| MR/IRBMs | First Deployed | Maximum Range |
|---|---|---|
| SS-4 | 1959 | 2000 KM |
| SS-5 | 1961 | 4100 KM |
| SS-20 | 1977 | 5000 KM |

| Medium Bombers | First Deployed | Unrefueled Combat Radius (Two-Way Missions) |
|---|---|---|
| *Badger* | 1955 | 3100 KM |
| *Blinder* | 1962 | 2900 KM |
| *Backfire* | 1974 | 5500 KM |
| *Blackjack* | 1988* | 7300 KM |

*Earliest possible deployment.

Source: U.S. Department of Defense, *Soviet Military Power, 1984* (Washington, D.C.: U.S. Government Printing Office, 1984).

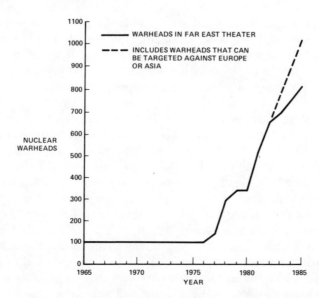

**Figure 4–1** **Soviet MR/IRBM Nuclear Warheads Trend (Far East Theater)**
*Source:* The International Institute for Strategic Studies, *The Military Balance.*

multiple, independently targetable reentry vehicles (MIRVs), and each SS-20 launcher is assessed to have one refire or reload missile. Consequently, the number of Soviet MR/IRBM warheads in the Far East, which was constant at about 100 since the mid-1960s, began to increase sharply when the SS-20 deployment began in 1977, surpassing 1,000 warheads by late 1985. SS-20 MIRVs significantly increase the number of fixed targets in East Asia the Soviets can attack. The large number of SS-20 warheads, the mobility of the launchers, and the SS-20 reload and refire capability provide the Soviets with a survivable theater nuclear reserve in the Far East for restrike after an initial exchange. Being land-based, this force is capable of quick responses under the centralized control of the Soviet General Staff or Far East High Command.

Deployment of the *Backfire* bomber with both the Strategic Air Armies and Soviet Naval Aviation in the Far East is a second major improvement in Soviet capabilities for theaterwide air and missile operations. *Backfire* bombers appear to be replacing the older *Badger* and *Blinder* medium bombers in the Strategic Air Armies in Asia; in Soviet Naval Aviation, however, *Badgers* and *Blinders* are being retained as *Backfires* are deployed.

The *Backfire* is a long-range aircraft capable of performing

nuclear strike, conventional strike, anti-shipping, and reconnaissance missions. Its low-level penetration capabilities make it a
more survivable system than its predecessors.[8] The naval version
of the *Backfire*, equipped with AS-4/*Kitchen* air-to-surface missiles
(ASMs), is a major nuclear or conventional threat to U.S. carrier
battle groups (CVBGs) and other surface shipping.

Of greatest significance is the unrefueled combat radius of the
*Backfire* on two-way missions. The combat radius of the *Backfire* is
almost twice that of the *Blinder* and substantially larger than that of
the *Badger* (see Table 4–1). The 5500 km combat radius of the
*Backfire* gives it a capability to reach targets in all of China, all of
Northeast Asia, most of Southeast Asia, and parts of North America, as shown in Figure 4–2. The naval version of *Backfire* is able to
hold at risk surface forces and shipping in all of the Western and
Northern Pacific, provided the Soviets can locate these targets
sufficiently well to bring them under attack. If operated or staged
from bases in Vietnam, the *Backfire* could cover significant areas of
the Southern Pacific as well. Figure 4–2 also shows the projected
combat radius of the Soviet *Blackjack* bomber, which is now

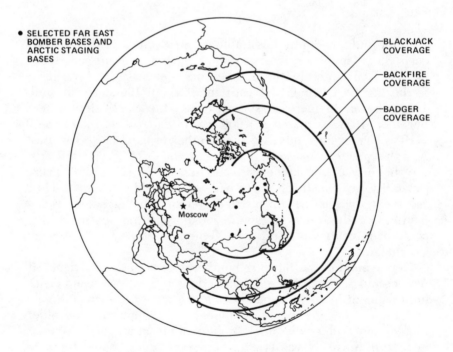

Figure 4–2   Medium Bomber Coverage from Soviet Bases (Unrefueled, Two-
Way Missions) *Source: Soviet Military Power*.

undergoing flight testing. The *Blackjack* could be deployed as early as 1988.

Soviet strategic forces also can contribute to air and missile operations in the Far East, although their primary mission is to attack targets in the United States. Over 30 ballistic missile submarines are deployed with the Soviet Pacific Fleet, including 9 *Yankee*-class SSBNs and 15 *Delta*-class SSBNs. Approximately 30 *Bear* and a dozen *Bison* intercontinental bombers are deployed in the Far East. SS-11 and SS-18 ICBMs are based in the Siberian, Transbaykal, and Far East military districts.[9]

Turning briefly to Soviet nuclear forces that could support ground force operations against China, one finds far less data available publicly than is the case for intermediate-range nuclear forces. Soviet intermediate-range nuclear forces would have an important role in a campaign against China by holding at risk or attacking missile launchers, airfields, nuclear storage and production facilities, and political or military command and control centers. Since the primary difficulty faced by the Soviet Union in an invasion of China is the large number of Chinese ground forces, nuclear-capable weapon systems of the Soviet ground forces and nuclear-capable tactical aircraft also are important.

Soviet shorter-range INF missiles and short-range battlefield nuclear weapon systems are organic to Soviet ground force units. Hence, the number of such systems and their nuclear warheads presumably increased by at least a factor of 2.5 as the number of Soviet divisions in the Far East grew from less than 20 in the mid-1960s to the current level of more than 50. There are some 200 *Frog* launchers, over 100 *Scud* launchers, and 40 *Scaleboard* launchers in the Far East. These are mobile, nuclear-capable surface-to-surface rocket and missile systems. The *Frog* and *Scud* missiles are expected to be replaced by nuclear-capable SS-21 and SS-23 surface-to-surface missile (SSM) systems. These modernized SSMs have greater range than the systems they will replace, and they are more accurate. Soviet ground forces in the Far East are also receiving nuclear-capable 152 mm artillery pieces.[10]

The number of Soviet tactical aircraft in the Far East has grown by a factor of six since the mid-1960s, and presumably there has been accompanying growth in the number of nuclear-capable tactical aircraft. Whether there has been corresponding growth in the size of the tactical nuclear bomb stockpile in the Soviet Far East cannot be determined from public sources. Modern strike aircraft such as the *Flogger* and *Fencer* are being deployed in the Far East; the *Flogger* and *Fencer* are assessed to have a nuclear delivery capability.[11]

The Soviet Union has an antiballistic missile (ABM) defense around Moscow that could be effective against the small attacks China could launch against the Soviet capital. In addition, the Soviets are developing ABM components that could be used in a widespread defense beyond the 100 launcher limit of the ABM Treaty, and are developing the SA-X-12 SAM, which has some antitactical ballistic missile capability.[12]

Several strategic objectives appear to underlie the Soviet nuclear buildup in Asia. The first is to achieve the capability to fight and prevail in a nuclear war. Second, through this nuclear war-fighting capability as well as its general purpose forces, the Soviet Union seeks to deter attacks on itself. Third, but by no means least, the Soviet Union wants to have a manifestly powerful nuclear force to help achieve peacetime political goals such as disruption of Western alliances.

## The Nuclear Forces of China and the United States

Opposing Soviet nuclear forces in Asia are U.S. and Chinese nuclear weapon systems. The United States maintains nuclear forces to help deter attacks on itself and its allies. These forces are also intended to be of sufficient size and capabilities to help control escalation and to enable the United States to conclude any conflict with the Soviet Union rapidly while protecting the vital interests of the United States and its allies.

China, on the other hand, appears to be following the philosophy of General Gallois, rather than building up its nuclear forces rapidly along more orthodox U.S. or Soviet lines. The Chinese goal seems to be a minimum force for proportional deterrence—a force sufficient in numbers and operational capabilities to inflict damage on an enemy that is disproportionately greater than the prospective benefits the enemy might stand to gain by attacking China.

China currently has deployed 50 DF-2 MRBMs and 60 DF-3 IRBMs that can reach targets in the Soviet Far East. In addition, four DF-4 and two DF-5 ICBMs—missiles that can reach Moscow and other targets in the western military districts of the USSR— are deployed. There are no reports of Chinese tactical nuclear weapons; if such weapons are available, they could be delivered by fighter aircraft or by approximately 120 H-6 medium bombers (variants of the Soviet Tu-16/*Badger*). One SSBN, capable of carrying 12 CSS-NX-4 SLBMs, is reported to be on sea trials. Two *Han*-class SSNs are said to carry cruise missiles with nuclear warheads. China's nuclear weapons stockpile is now believed to number several hundred.[13] Because of the limited number of Chinese nuclear weapons, the relative inaccuracy of their delivery systems, and the probable low penetration capability of Chinese fighters and bombers through Soviet air defenses, China's nuclear force is capable primarily of effective attacks on Soviet urban-industrial targets—largely those in the USSR's Far East provinces.

U.S. strategic and theater nuclear forces also oppose Soviet nuclear forces in the Far East. *Minutemen* ICBMs can reach Soviet targets in the region, as can *Trident I* (C-4) SLBMs. Currently, five *Ohio*-class *Trident* SSBNs are deployed in the Pacific, with more planned. Fourteen B-52s are based on Guam for conventional or nuclear support to operations in the Asia-Pacific region; and more B-52s are available in the continental United States.[14] The *Tomahawk* land-attack cruise missile, equipped with a nuclear warhead (TLAM/N), began to be deployed on U.S. Navy attack submarines and surface ships in 1984. Navy carrier-based tactical aircraft with nuclear bombs also contribute to U.S. theater nuclear capabilities, as do Navy nuclear-capable fleet air defense SAMs, ASW rockets, and air-delivered ASW nuclear depth bombs.[15]

The characteristics of U.S. theater nuclear forces in the Asia-Pacific region seem to reflect requirements developed for the European theater. A notable example is delivery system range or combat radius, which is adequate for systems deployed in Europe, but—for the same systems deployed in the Asia-Pacific region—falls short of reaching many important targets in the USSR. On the other hand, Soviet theater nuclear forces seem to be determined by requirements for multiple theaters, not just Europe.

To recapitulate, the number of Soviet MR/IRBM missile launchers in the Far East has been relatively constant since the mid-1960s, with a small increase beginning in the late 1970s; the number of medium bombers in the Strategic Air Armies in the Far East has remained about the same since the mid-1960s, but the number of SNA medium bombers has doubled. Of greatest significance is the Soviet trend to upgrade the capabilities of INF missiles and aircraft with deployment of SS-20 missiles and *Backfire* bombers, resulting in a major increase in IRBM nuclear warheads and a substantial increase in range and target coverage for both IRBMs and medium bombers. The Soviets have also been building up the number of shorter-range INF missile launchers and short-range battlefield nuclear systems, and improving their range and accuracy. And they have increased the number and combat capabilities of nuclear-capable tactical aircraft and sea-based nuclear weapon systems in the Far East.

## Thinking About the Nuclear Balance in Asia

What do these trends mean for the nuclear balance in the Asia-Pacific region? What are the important characteristics of this balance? What do trends in the nuclear balance mean for deterrence? More than four years of detailed analysis of Far East military issues by the author suggests that assessment of the following sequence of issues is fundamental to understanding trends in the regional nuclear balance:

1. Establish a basic frame of reference by identifying enduring U.S.-Soviet-Chinese asymmetries in the Asia-Pacific region.
2. Determine conflict situations in which nuclear weapons might be used.
3. Within these conflict situations, determine important missions and targets related to nuclear forces.
4. Determine important nuclear force posture characteristics in light of these missions and targets.
5. Assess the impact of trends in the Asia-Pacific nuclear balance on U.S., Soviet, and Chinese capabilities to carry out the foregoing missions.
6. Determine the implications for deterrence and other security interests of the United States, its allies, and friends.

The remainder of this essay sketches out an analysis along these lines. Before proceeding, however, one other point must be discussed to avoid a potential pitfall. Most U.S. defense specialists, and perhaps some Asian specialists who have been trained in American institutions, tend to be influenced (perhaps unconsciously) by analytic constructs derived from European military problems. There are major political-military differences between Europe and the Asia-Pacific region, however, that should be kept explicitly in mind.

In Europe, the area of potential conflict is relatively small and potentially cohesive compared with the large and politically diverse Asia-Pacific region. Both the United States and the Soviet Union operate within established alliances in Europe. In Asia, the United States has multiple, regional alliances; the Soviet Union does not have an extensive alliance structure; and China's alignment in a U.S.-Soviet war is a major uncertainty—one that poses a far greater potential problem for the USSR than for the United States. Except for Mongolia, the Soviet Union does not have the buffer of client states between itself and its adversaries that it has in Europe.

In a European war, the dominant type of military campaign would be ground force operations with air support; naval operations would be important only if the conflict continued for more than a few weeks. In Asia, ground force operations would be important in a Sino-Soviet conflict and on the Korean peninsula; for general war in the Asia-Pacific region, however, naval forces and medium-range bombers and missiles would dominate the conflict. While the Soviets have extensive air defenses in Asia and have the advantage of interior lines of communication in a war against the United States and its allies, neither is as well-developed as in the western USSR. In a Sino-Soviet conflict, China would have the advantage of interior lines of communication.

A further complication in Europe is that deployment of modernized theater nuclear forces by the United States and its allies is heavily conditioned by the politics of arms control. Although there are clear political constraints on U.S. deployment of nuclear weapons in Asia, the Soviets are not able currently to manipulate arms control negotiations to undercut the American or Chinese nuclear weapons posture in Asia, as they have been seeking to do in Europe.

## U.S.-Soviet-Chinese Asymmetries

Focusing now on the Asia-Pacific region, U.S.-Soviet geostrategic and force posture asymmetries would have major effects on wartime operations. Geostrategic asymmetries are long-lasting, in the absence of fundamental political realignments in Asia. For example, most major threats to U.S. forces in Asia are based on Soviet territory, while the U.S. forward-deployed forces in the Pacific depend on some form of basing or base support located on allied territory. This results in asymmetrical escalation risks, with the United States and its allies facing greater risks of nuclear escalation if they attack Soviet threats in the USSR than the Soviets face in attacking U.S. and allied threats in East Asia.

A second geostrategic asymmetry relates to strategic depth: there is considerably more land available in the Soviet Far East for dispersal of forces than is available to the United States and its allies in East Asia. China, of course, also has substantial room for force dispersal. U.S. and allied naval forces can use the vast area of the Pacific Ocean for dispersal, but this is an ocean in which Soviet forces also operate, and therefore does not have the sanctuary quality that the Soviet Far East landmass potentially offers Soviet forces.

U.S. military dependence on base support from its East Asian allies, the growing requirement for cooperative (if not joint) U.S. and allied military operations, and the commitments of the United States to its allies in Asia all make it essential for the United States to be able to counter Soviet use of nonnuclear or nuclear threats to coerce U.S. allies. This constitutes another geostrategic asymmetry, in that American coercion of Soviet allies in Asia would not damage the political-military posture of the USSR to as serious a degree as would successful Soviet coercion of U.S. allies.

U.S.-Soviet military asymmetries are also significant. While these can change over time, they are likely to persist at least through the 1980s. Soviet nuclear strike forces in Asia generally have greater range than American theater nuclear forces in the Pacific (B-52s are an exception), giving the Soviets advantages in threatening U.S. and allied bases and forces and in surviving U.S. theater nuclear attacks. These advantages are partly offset, however, by U.S. strategic forces.

The Soviets have major advantages over the United States and its allies in capabilities for chemical warfare operations.[16] On the other hand, the Soviet Union uses an SSBN operating concept in which it deploys its ballistic missile submarines in waters near the Soviet Union. This concept requires a significant portion of Soviet naval forces to protect SSBN operating areas, keeping them from other missions such as interdiction of U.S. and allied sea lines of communication.[17] The United States has no such requirement for general purpose force protection of its SSBNs.

Sino-Soviet asymmetries are also of interest. One obvious asymmetry is in nuclear forces. China's force is small compared to that of the Soviet Union. China's ballistic missiles do not have the accuracy or hard target destruction capability possessed by Soviet missiles, and China's nuclear forces are more vulnerable to a Soviet nuclear attack than are Soviet nuclear forces to a Chinese attack. However, as discussed subsequently, many of China's missiles are mobile and concealed, making it difficult—if not impossible—for the Soviet Union to have high confidence of executing a disarming strike against Chinese nuclear forces.

Another, more complex asymmetry is in general purpose forces. China has approximately 160 ground force divisions, compared with approximately 50 Soviet divisions in the Far East. Most of China's ground forces are, however, infantry divisions, while Soviet divisions have advantages in armor, mobility, and firepower. Soviet tactical air capability to support ground operations is qualitatively superior to that of China, as are Soviet air defenses. These Soviet advantages are offset, however, by asymmetries in strategic vulnerabilities that would work counter to any incentives the Soviets might have to attack China in a crisis or worldwide conflict—Soviet concerns about fighting on multiple fronts; China's potential for imposing a long war on the Soviets should they invade China for more than a brief period; China's nuclear capability to inflict urban-industrial damage on the Soviet Union that could be disproportionately costly compared with Soviet gains from attacking China; and the dispersed nature of China's population and its military and economic assets, which would reduce the strategic effect of Soviet nuclear attacks on China.

## Nuclear Conflict Situations

Analysts can construct nuclear war scenarios in great political-military detail. For understanding the nuclear balance, however, three characteristics of potential nuclear conflicts in Asia are important: (1) the general nature of wars in which nuclear weapons might be used, (2) the timing of nuclear use, and (3) the reasons why one side or another might initiate nuclear war.

Only three potential conflict situations in Asia appear to threaten the interests of some nuclear power sufficiently that it would consider employing nuclear weapons to defend these interests:

1. A North Korean invasion of South Korea that could not be contained or reversed by ROK and U.S. conventional forces. Any use of nuclear weapons poses escalation risks, but the Soviet Union is not likely to be involved directly in a limited attack on South Korea. Therefore, limited nuclear weapons employment by the United States in Korea is not likely to escalate to U.S.-Soviet nuclear war. U.S. use of nuclear weapons in a Korean war would, however, have profound effects on attitudes in Japan, China, and other regional states. These are important issues, but they are beyond the scope of this chapter. Hence, Korean war scenarios will not be analyzed further here.[18]
2. General war (worldwide conflict) between the Soviet Union and its allies on the one hand and the United States and its allies on the other hand. A worldwide war, perhaps growing out of a war in Europe, would almost surely involve fighting in Asia. However, war between the United States and the Soviet Union and between their respective allies that was confined only to the Asia-Pacific region seems unlikely.
3. Sino-Soviet war.

Considering only the dynamics of conflict in Asia, and assuming that nuclear weapons are used at all, early first use of nuclear weapons seems likely only in a war limited to the Korean Peninsula in which the Soviet Union is not directly involved. In the Asia-Pacific part of a worldwide conflict, the pace of air and sea operations is likely to move more slowly than in Europe, in part because forces are more dispersed in Asia and because the overall balance of general purpose forces is more even than in Europe. In these wars, it is less likely than in Europe that vital interests would be in such immediate jeopardy that the United States or the Soviet Union would resort to early first use of nuclear weapons.

All this is, however, highly speculative; early use of nuclear weapons by one of the nuclear powers cannot be ruled out in Asia. In fact, nuclear weapons might be employed in the Asia-Pacific region at an early stage as a result of "horizontal" escalation from Europe. For example, if NATO followed its doctrine and initiated use of nuclear weapons early in a war in Europe, the Soviet Union—fearing that NATO's first use would be followed by U.S. nuclear attacks on Soviet forces in Asia, as well as by additional NATO nuclear attacks—might well respond with nuclear weapons against targets in both Europe and the Asia-Pacific region. Alternatively, the Soviet Union might initiate use of nuclear weapons in Europe to preempt NATO's use or, possibly, to ensure that the war was concluded quickly, to avoid providing opportunities in a prolonged war for insurrection in the Warsaw Pact countries. Believing the risk to be high that the United States would respond to this nuclear attack with nuclear strikes on Soviet military targets in both Europe and Asia (the latter in order to exacerbate Soviet problems in fighting on multiple fronts), the Soviet Union might undertake nuclear attacks in Asia simultaneously with its initiation of nuclear war in Europe.

Even if there were no horizontal escalation from Europe, nuclear weapons use could not be ruled out as worldwide war or a Sino-Soviet conflict unfolded over time. Reasons for nuclear use could include excessive loss of critical military forces by one or more sides, deterioration of one side's general military situation to the point of near collapse, or perceptions (correct or incorrect) that the adversary was about to initiate use of nuclear weapons.

## Key Missions and Targets

Considering the two conflict situations most pertinent to this chapter (general war and Sino-Soviet conflict), we now explore the military missions that are important in terms of the nuclear balance. In addition to missions that involve nuclear attacks, it is essential to examine missions involving: (1) nonnuclear attacks on nuclear forces, since attrition of nuclear-capable delivery systems in conventional war would affect each side's ability to carry out nuclear attacks; (2) air defense operations, since these can protect nuclear-capable delivery systems and impose attrition on dual-capable aircraft in both conventional and nuclear war; and (3) nonnuclear attacks on nonnuclear forces, since these would affect incentives to use nuclear weapons and the timing and conditions of nuclear use should it occur.

Table 4–2 summarizes forces and targets related to six major U.S. and Soviet missions in general war:

1. Destruction or neutralization of nuclear threats.
2. Protection of SSBN operating areas (a mission only for the Soviet Union).
3. Destruction or neutralization of U.S. carrier battle groups (a mission currently only for the Soviet Union).
4. Destruction or neutralization of general purpose land-based air strike and $C^3I$ capabilities.
5. Control of vital ocean areas, including sea lines of communication (a mission currently important only for the United States and its allies).
6. Maintenance of a survivable nuclear reserve for restrikes or coercion after an initial nuclear exchange.

U.S. allies can contribute to many of these missions by assisting in nonnuclear attacks on Soviet nuclear forces, by providing active and passive defenses of U.S. and allied targets for Soviet attacks, and providing early warning of Soviet air attacks.

The list of critical missions in a Sino-Soviet conflict is not as long. Table 4–3 summarizes forces and targets related to three key missions in a Sino-Soviet conflict:

1. Destruction or neutralization of nuclear threats. While potentially vital for China, its attack and defense capabilities are so meager relative to the Soviet nuclear threat that this mission is not feasible for Chinese forces. China's strategy appears to rely for deterrence on passive defenses (dispersal and hardening of its nuclear forces) and threats of nuclear retaliation against a handful of Soviet cities.
2. Support to ground force operations.
3. Destruction or neutralization of general purpose air strike capabilities.

## Nuclear Force Posture Characteristics

Based on an analysis of the targets shown in Tables 4–2 and 4–3, several nuclear force posture characteristics appear to be important for assessing the balance of U.S., Soviet, and Chinese nuclear

**Table 4–2  Key General War Missions and Targets**

| Mission | Forces Used to Execute Mission | Targets for U.S. and Allied Forces | Targets for Soviet Forces |
|---|---|---|---|
| Destruction or Neutralization of Nuclear Threats | Nuclear attack<br>Nonnuclear attack<br>Air defense<br>ASW | IRBM launchers<br>Intercontinental & medium bombers<br>Frontal aviation deep strike aircraft<br>Ballistic missile submarines<br>Supporting bases<br>Supporting air defenses | Long-range bombers<br>Carrier-based tactical aircraft<br>Ballistic missile submarines<br>TLAM/N ships and submarines<br>Supporting bases<br>Supporting air defenses |
| Protection of Soviet SSBN Operating Areas | Nuclear attack<br>Nonnuclear attack<br>Air defense<br>ASW | Not applicable | ASW forces (SSNs, P-3s)<br>ASW surveillance<br>Supporting bases |
| Destruction or Neutralization of U.S. Carrier Battle Groups | Nuclear attack<br>Nonnuclear attack<br>Air defense | Not applicable | Aircraft carriers<br>Escort ships<br>Tactical aircraft |
| Destruction or Neutralization of General Purpose Land-Based Air Strike Capabilities | Nuclear attack<br>Nonnuclear attack<br>Air defense | Intercontinental & medium bombers<br>Deep strike tactical aircraft<br>Supporting bases<br>Supporting air defenses | B-52s<br>Tactical aircraft<br>Supporting bases<br>Supporting air defenses |

| Control of Vital Ocean Areas (Including SLOCs) | Nuclear attack<br>Nonnuclear attack<br>ASW<br>Fleet air defense | SNA bombers<br>Submarines & surface ships<br>Supporting bases<br>Supporting air defenses | Not applicable |
| --- | --- | --- | --- |
| Maintenance of Survivable Nuclear Reserve (Restrike or Coercion after Initial Nuclear Exchange) | Nuclear attack<br>Nonnuclear attack<br>ASW<br>Air defense<br>Counter-C$^3$I | Surveillance & target acquisition systems<br>Command & control<br>Attack capabilities that threaten U.S. TNF reserves | Surveillance & target acquisition systems<br>Command & control<br>Attack capabilities that threaten Soviet Far East nuclear reserves |

**Table 4-3 Key Sino-Soviet War Missions and Targets**

| Mission | Forces Used to Execute Mission | Targets for | |
|---|---|---|---|
| | | Chinese Forces | Soviet Forces |
| Destruction or Neutralization of Nuclear Threats | Nuclear attack<br>Nonnuclear attack<br>Air defense<br>ABM defense (Moscow only)<br>Special forces<br>ASW | Mission not practical for Chinese forces | ICBMs<br>MR/IRBMs<br>Medium bombers<br>SSBNs and cruise missile submarines<br>Nuclear weapons storage and production facilities<br>Supporting bases<br>Supporting air defenses |
| Support to Ground Force Operations | Nuclear attack<br>Nonnuclear attack | Soviet ground forces threatening key areas of China<br>Soviet logistics support, including land and sea lines of communication | Chinese ground forces opposing rapid advance of Soviet ground forces |
| Destruction or Neutralization of General Purpose Air Strike Capabilities | Nuclear attack<br>Nonnuclear attack<br>Air defenses | Strike aircraft<br>Supporting bases<br>Supporting air defenses | Strike aircraft<br>Supporting bases<br>Supporting air defenses |

forces in the Asia-Pacific region. These characteristics are summarized below and discussed in more detail in the appendix to this chapter (see pp. 271-275)

1. Nuclear forces must be able to survive enemy nonnuclear attacks (for perhaps a considerable period of time) and enemy nuclear attacks. Survivability in turn depends on the targetability of friendly nuclear forces, the physical hardness of these forces, and their defenses.
2. Surviving nuclear forces must be able to penetrate enemy defenses, which depends on the fraction of the friendly nuclear force that consists of ballistic missile systems and the ability of manned aircraft and cruise missiles to exploit weaknesses in enemy air defenses.
3. Penetrating nuclear forces must be able effectively to attack those enemy targets that are, at the time of the attack, of paramount importance for the ongoing military campaign. Effective attack depends on the range or combat radius of friendly nuclear forces, the ability to locate mobile enemy targets, the response time of friendly nuclear forces, and delivery system accuracy and nuclear warhead yield.

## Trends in Mission Capabilities

The analysis to this point has identified potential nuclear conflict situations in Asia and developed key missions and targets related to nuclear forces. This permits determination of important nuclear force posture characteristics for carrying out the key missions. Consideration of trends in these important nuclear force posture characteristics then permits one to determine and assess trends in U.S., Soviet, and Chinese capabilities to execute key nuclear-related missions. This last step requires extensive study and detailed exposition. Only summary observations can be made here. As in foregoing sections, general war missions are addressed first, then those associated with a Sino-Soviet conflict.

*Destruction of Nuclear Threats.* Observed inversely, one side's capability for this mission is the ability of the other side's nuclear forces to survive attacks.

U.S. capabilities to destroy Soviet nuclear forces in Asia can be summarized as follows. American nuclear forces have a substantial capability to destroy fixed nuclear threat targets that are within range (e.g., bomber main operating bases, naval bases). Significant elements of Soviet nuclear forces are, however, difficult for the United States to locate and attack effectively, particularly in a short period of time;[19] these Soviet forces include SS-20 launchers that have dispersed from garrisons, dispersed medium and intercontinental bombers, and missile-launching submarines at sea. As the Soviets continue to deploy SS-20s and *Backfires*, they are acquiring an increased capability to operate nuclear forces beyond the range of U.S. theater-based delivery systems, while still being able to reach most U.S. and allied targets in the Asia-Pacific region. U.S. strategic forces have adequate range to reach these Soviet nuclear forces.

U.S. and allied aircraft can make nonnuclear attacks on Soviet bomber main operating bases and naval bases, but this currently would require large raids to penetrate air defenses. Moreover, insufficient numbers of the modern conventional munitions required for this mission are deployed with U.S. and allied air forces. Technology offers prospects in the near future for substantial improvement in nonnuclear capabilities to attack Soviet bomber and naval bases effectively (e.g., cruise missiles, scatterable mines, runway-cutting munitions, smart area munitions, precision-guided munitions for attacking hard structures), but current budgets will not provide these systems as rapidly or in the quantities that appear warranted by the threat. Moreover, except for B-52s carrying conventional ordnance, current and programmed air and cruise missile delivery systems for nonnuclear munitions do not have adequate range to reach many Soviet nuclear forces deployed in Asia.

The Soviet Union, with its SS-20s (supplemented by ICBMs for use against deeper targets), has a highly effective nuclear strike capability against fixed bases in Asia that support U.S. nuclear-capable forces. It has a modest, but growing, nonnuclear air strike capability against deeper bases such as Guam. U.S. ballistic missile and TLAM/N-capable submarines at sea are, however, likely to be highly survivable under Soviet nuclear or nonnuclear attacks.

For decades the Soviets have devoted substantial resources to acquiring capabilities to destroy U.S. aircraft carriers, which they see as a major nuclear threat. With large, repeated bomber/ASM raids, coordinated with submarine attacks, the Soviets can make nonnuclear attacks on aircraft carriers operating within range of Soviet Naval Aviation. (Soviet nuclear attack capabilities against U.S. carrier battle groups are discussed below.) Specific outcomes depend on the details of the outer and inner air battles around the carrier battle groups, U.S. and allied ASW efforts, and electronic warfare capabilities and tactics; they are difficult to summarize in a brief assessment. Both sides continue to make improvements in nonnuclear attack and defense capabilities, but the balance is now such that the U.S. Navy prefers to have several carrier battle groups operating in mutual support before proceeding into areas where they would be subjected to large Soviet Naval Aviation raids.

The primary difficulty faced by the Soviets in attacking carrier battle groups is to locate battle groups early enough to mass bomber and submarine forces against them. Increasingly, the Soviet ability to locate carrier battle groups for attack purposes depends, on the one hand, on details of Soviet surveillance and $C^3$, and on the other hand, U.S. and allied counter-$C^3$ efforts. As TLAM/N is deployed on U.S. surface combatants, Soviet problems in locating and attacking surface nuclear threats at sea will be compounded, because of the increase in the number of ships they will have to find and destroy.

*Protection of SSBN Operating Areas.*   By operating their ballistic missile submarines in ocean areas protected by air and naval forces, the Soviets can impose high costs on U.S. ASW forces seeking to attack Soviet SLBM assets. Soviet SS-N-8 and SS-N-18 SLBMs deployed on *Delta*-class SSBNs can reach targets in almost all of North America from protected home waters (primarily in the Sea of Okhotsk); intermediate-range SLBMs on *Yankee*-class SSBNs can reach Asian targets from these same operating areas.[20] U.S. SSNs could more readily carry out attack operations against Soviet ballistic missile submarines in protected havens than could U.S. ASW aircraft or surface ships, but prospects for rapidly destroying the majority of Soviet SSBNs do not appear high. Moreover, U.S. SSNs are needed for other missions, such as protection of carrier battle groups and sea lines of communication.

The Soviet Union places high priority on protecting its ballistic missile submarines, but this mission ties up a significant proportion of Soviet naval forces. Thus, by merely posing a threat, U.S. and allied ASW forces can inflict a kind of "virtual attrition" on Soviet naval forces, without actually carrying out attacks on Soviet ballistic missile submarines.

*Nuclear Attacks on U.S. Carrier Battle Groups.*   Provided the Soviets can locate a carrier battle group, a significantly smaller number of air-launched or submarine-launched cruise missiles is required for high probability of sinking the aircraft carrier if these missiles have nuclear warheads, as compared with the nonnuclear attack problem discussed earlier. Trends that counter one another make survivability of U.S. carrier battle groups in a nuclear environment difficult to assess. Soviet deployment of *Backfire* bombers enlarges significantly the threat area within which carrier battle groups must operate if they are to come within striking range of Soviet targets ashore. However, enlarging the threat area makes it more difficult for the Soviets to position submarines for coordinated air-submarine attacks. U.S. deployment of the *Aegis* air defense system is increasing the fleet's ability to defend against nuclear, as well as nonnuclear, attacks. TLAM/N deployment is increasing the number of nuclear-capable strike ships the Soviets must bring under attack and allows both carrier battle groups and independently operating ships to attack Soviet targets ashore from greater stand-off distances. Chances for carrier battle group survival in a nuclear war depend considerably on the effectiveness of U.S. and allied nonnuclear and nuclear attacks on Soviet Naval Aviation bomber bases, air defense effectiveness in attriting SNA bombers in nonnuclear war, and ASW effectiveness against Soviet attack and cruise missile submarines in nonnuclear war.

*Nuclear Attacks on Air Bases and $C^3I$.* The Soviet Union has a highly capable ballistic missile nuclear threat against U.S. and allied general purpose air bases in the Asia-Pacific region (SS-20s, SLBMs, ICBMs). There is a small number of these bases and they have no ballistic missile defenses. Moreover, the flight times of the Soviet missiles are so short (on the order of 8 to 15 minutes) that it appears impractical to launch aircraft on tactical warning of the attack. This Soviet capability makes it unlikely that the United States or its allies could sustain land-based tactical air or maritime patrol air operations after a Soviet nuclear attack on air bases.

U.S. nuclear capabilities for destroying Soviet air bases, while not as swift or decisive as the Soviet capability, would seriously impair Soviet air operations for a considerable period of time. The Soviet Union can disperse its aircraft in depth, requiring the United States either to attack many tens of dispersal bases or to execute a complicated coordination of surveillance systems and nuclear strike plans to attack the bases to which the Soviets have actually dispersed their aircraft. Attack of deep Soviet dispersal bases would require use of B-52s or SLBMs. Use of subsonic delivery systems (e.g., tactical or strategic aircraft, or cruise missiles) to attack deeper Soviet bases would allow the Soviets time to launch aircraft on warning of the attack, unless counter-$C^3$ measures were effective in denying the Soviets a launch-on-warning option. In any event, U.S. nuclear attacks would have a high probability of destroying Soviet general purpose main operating bases, which are necessary for sustained air operations.

The Soviet theater ballistic missile capability would be as effective against fixed U.S. and allied $C^3I$ installations in the Asia-Pacific region as against U.S. and allied air bases. Space-based $C^3I$ would survive a Soviet theater nuclear attack, but fixed ground stations in

Asia would probably be destroyed, as would some airborne or sea-based C³I capabilities; and some U.S. C³I satellites would probably be destroyed by Soviet antisatellite (ASAT) systems if such attacks were launched. Surviving aircraft carriers and large surface combatants would be particularly important for reconstituting U.S. and allied command and control capabilities after a Soviet theater nuclear attack.

Soviet C³I installations are deployed in large numbers for redundancy, and they are hardened. Some are mobile, and some are space-based.[21] Therefore, more U.S. nuclear warheads are needed to attack Soviet Asia-Pacific C³I installations, as compared with the number required by the Soviets to attack U.S. and allied C³I installations. Nevertheless, U.S. nuclear attacks could cause widespread destruction in the Soviet C³I network. Some rudimentary Soviet C³I capability would, however, probably remain.

*Control of SLOCs.* American use of nuclear weapons would significantly reduce the Soviet threat to shipping in vital Asia-Pacific sea lines of communications, especially if nuclear weapons were used against Soviet Naval Aviation bases and naval C³I facilities. But the submarine threat probably would not be entirely eliminated, even if the United States used nuclear ASW weapons. Of more serious import, in a nuclear war the Soviets could and probably would use nuclear weapons to destroy the Asia-Pacific ports at which the sea lines terminated.

*Survivable Theater Nuclear Reserves.* Both the Soviet Union and the United States would be likely to have surviving reserves of theater nuclear forces after an exchange of nuclear strikes in the Asia-Pacific region. The extent to which these forces could be utilized in an extended conflict would depend on how well each side's command and control and logistics support could be reconstituted after a theater nuclear exchange.

Surviving Soviet nuclear forces would consist primarily of ICBMs, SS-20s, and SLBMs. Some dispersed medium or intercontinental bombers might also survive, but the Soviets would be hard-pressed to mount a sustained air campaign in the aftermath of a theater nuclear exchange. A rudimentary land-based C³I capability probably would remain, but air defenses and logistics support would be decimated.

Most surviving U.S. theater nuclear forces would be at sea— SLBMs, TLAM/N, perhaps some carrier battle groups. Surviving theater C³I would be primarily that which remained at sea. B-52s and ICBMs from CONUS could provide theater support. There would be little remaining land-based ASW capability and logistics support in the forward area.

Turning briefly to nuclear-related missions in a Sino-Soviet conflict, the major trends can be summarized as follows.

*Destruction of Nuclear Threats.* As noted above, China has little capability to destroy or neutralize Soviet nuclear threats and is not likely to be able to change this situation materially in the next decade, even should it choose to try.

The Soviet Union has nuclear strike capabilities against Chinese MR/IRBMs, ICBMs, and air bases supporting nuclear-capable aircraft. Considering China's ability to disperse, conceal, and otherwise protect its nuclear forces, however, the USSR cannot have high confidence of denying Chinese nuclear retaliation against Soviet cities, especially in the Far East. Moreover, the Soviets are not likely to be able to destroy Chinese cruise missile or ballistic missile submarines at sea on the precise time schedule required for a coordinated disarming first strike against Chinese nuclear threats. Over time, as China's nuclear force grows larger and more diverse, this situation will worsen for the Soviets.

*Nuclear Support for Ground Force Operations.* As a consequence of the limited size of China's nuclear stockpile, the vulnerability of its air bases to Soviet nuclear and nonnuclear attacks, and the extensive air defenses organic to Soviet ground forces, China has only a modest capability to undertake effective nuclear attacks against Soviet ground force concentrations. Such attacks would make an invasion of China costly to the Soviet Union, but are not likely to be decisive in halting or rolling back a Soviet invasion.

The USSR, on the other hand, has ample battlefield nuclear forces to attack Chinese ground force concentrations and help prevent or overcome the massing of Chinese forces at major defense lines. Nuclear weapons would, however, be far less useful in sustaining deep penetrations into China against dispersed Chinese hit-and-run operations in a long war. Any Soviet use of nuclear weapons against China risks Chinese retaliatory nuclear attacks against Soviet cities.

*Nuclear Attacks on Air Bases.* Through dispersal of nuclear forces, China probably can maintain a capability to destroy some Soviet main operating bases, but not enough to influence decisively the outcome of a Sino-Soviet war. As China's nuclear force grows, however, its nuclear strike capability against the Soviet Far East air base system will increase correspondingly.

The Soviets, with a much larger nuclear force than China, can effectively attack China's main operating bases, destroying many aircraft, much of the associated command and control, and much of the logistics infrastructure of China's air force.

## The Impact of the Soviet Nuclear Buildup on U.S. and Allied Security Interests

The foregoing analysis highlights some Soviet military strengths and weaknesses. By sustaining programs since the mid-1960s that have expanded and improved general purpose ground, air, and naval forces in the Far East, the Soviets have constructed a substantial capability for nonnuclear war in Asia. Soviet general purpose forces provide the ability to conduct combined arms, ground and air campaigns against China, and air, missile, and naval campaigns against the United States and its allies in East Asia and the Pacific Ocean. These forces can defend the USSR against a Chinese invasion. They also have a strong and growing capability for short, punitive invasions of China. China's strength lies in its ability to impose a long, costly war of attrition on the USSR should it seek to invade and hold Chinese territory. However, continued Soviet improvements in Far East forces, if permitted to go unchecked or unmatched, could result in a Soviet capability to seize and hold key Chinese border provinces, especially in the Northwest (Xinjiang) and the Northeast (Manchuria).

Soviet nonnuclear air, missile, and naval forces for use against the United States and its allies in Asia are limited by their inadequate numbers when measured against a large and diverse set of nonnuclear missions ranging from protection of SSBN havens, to strikes on air and naval threats to the Soviet homeland, to securing Soviet interests in Southwest Asia and the Indian Ocean. Unless offset by U.S. and allied nonnuclear force improvements, the growth in numbers and capabilities of Soviet nonnuclear forces in the Far East eventually will overcome these limitations.

Considering the Soviet buildup of nuclear forces in the Far East, the increase in both numbers and military capability (e.g., range or combat radius) of theaterwide strike forces is of major significance. Of equal significance for China is the buildup of Soviet battlefield nuclear forces and tactical air nuclear capability to support ground force operations. Soviet nuclear forces could destroy many Chinese nuclear forces, air bases, command and control facilities, and other fixed military or civil installations, and could effectively support Soviet breakthrough operations against massed Chinese ground forces. The Soviets could not, however, have high confidence of disarming China's nuclear strike forces and preventing Chinese nuclear attacks on key Soviet cities; nor does it appear likely that Soviet nuclear forces can deal decisively with China's capability for a long war of attrition.

In a general war with the United States and its allies, Soviet Far East nuclear forces could destroy major bases, command and control sites, and other fixed installations in either a first strike or a response to American nuclear strikes. Moreover, the Soviet Union would have a substantial theater nuclear reserve both ashore and at sea after a theater nuclear exchange in Asia. U.S. theater nuclear forces have limitations in reaching deep dispersal areas in the Soviet Far East, but they could destroy air and naval main operating bases and SS-20 operating bases, many dispersal bases and land-based nuclear forces, many command and control facilities, and other fixed installations. U.S. strategic forces could reach targets deeper in the Soviet Union. After a nuclear exchange in Asia, most surviving U.S. theater nuclear forces would be at sea.

While ongoing or programmed improvements in U.S., Soviet, and Chinese nuclear forces will change the military balance in detailed, marginal ways, they are not likely to make fundamental changes in this assessment for the next decade. What, then, are the implications of this nuclear balance for the security interests of the United States, its allies, and its friends in peacetime, crises, and wartime?

## Peacetime Diplomacy and Deterrence

To date, the ongoing Soviet nuclear buildup in Asia has not had significant effects on peacetime diplomacy. Certainly, Soviet general purpose force actions have had far greater public visibility— the border clashes with Chinese forces in the late 1960s, for example; Soviet military occupation of disputed islands in the Southern Kuriles in 1978 and 1979; and the attack on Korea Air Lines Flight 007 in 1983. Moreover, unlike their practice in Europe, Soviet leaders have not sought recently to exploit their nuclear forces in diplomacy with Asian nations.

In one sense, recent changes in the Soviet nuclear force posture in Asia may seem irrelevant to peacetime relations. Asian countries have already been in the shadow of Soviet nuclear forces for over three decades, and changes since 1965 do not alter the general impression in Asia that the overall U.S.-Soviet strategic balance makes nuclear war a remote possibility. Since the risk of nuclear war is so low, what difference can improved Soviet nuclear war-fighting capabilities make?

This question can be answered not so much in military terms as in a growing Soviet potential to use its Far East nuclear forces to influence Asia-Pacific affairs in peacetime. Soviet achievement of strategic parity with the United States has raised questions about the ability of U.S. strategic forces to deter attacks on U.S. allies (particularly nonnuclear attacks), making regional nuclear and nonnuclear balances potentially more important in deterring regional attacks. The Soviet Union clearly is seeking to achieve theater nuclear superiority in Asia and to improve the military utility of its theater nuclear forces. Moreover, Soviet leaders are actively trying to exploit popular fears of nuclear war in efforts to achieve peacetime foreign policy gains in Europe and the United States. They combine generalized public threats of catastrophic violence in the event of war with military capabilities for rapid and decisive nuclear or nonnuclear combat in attempts to influence the domestic politics of Western nations through appeals to antinuclear groups. Such Soviet efforts have been directed toward dividing the United States and its allies, preventing deployment of new or improved theater nuclear forces in Europe (enhanced radiation/ reduced blast weapons, *Pershing II*, ground-launched cruise missiles), and at achieving arms control agreements on terms favorable to the USSR.

Unless countered, the Soviet Far East theater nuclear buildup has the potential to cause similar political problems in Asia. One way to counter the political impact of the Soviet nuclear buildup is to make sure that Asian nations maintain a proper perspective regarding the Soviet nuclear threat. For example, the United States should not exaggerate the importance of the SS-20 and *Backfire*. Moreover, the role of U.S. strategic forces in countering Soviet Far East nuclear forces should be emphasized.

One reason the Soviets have not tried to mount a major propaganda campaign in Asia to exploit their Far East nuclear strength has been that political situations in Asian nations have not provided them with suitable opportunities. To the extent possible, the United States and its allies should avoid nuclear strategy or force posture actions that could prove controversial in Asia, to limit future Soviet propaganda opportunities.

Nevertheless, the ongoing modernization of Soviet Far East nuclear forces has important implications for Asian security, both militarily and for what these modernization programs indicate about Soviet attitudes. One consequence of the Soviet nuclear buildup may be to increase Soviet confidence in forestalling U.S. or Chinese nuclear responses to Soviet nonnuclear—or even limited nuclear—attacks in Asia. Soviet political and military leaders appear to desire high confidence of rapidly and successfully concluding military actions before setting such actions in motion. The erosion of deterrence that could result if the Soviet nuclear buildup were to continue unchecked should be halted by actions intended to undermine the confidence of Soviet leaders that they can achieve quick successes in military operations. Deterrence in Asia has rested to a considerable extent on the threat of escalation to high levels of nuclear destruction. Far more effective for deterring hostile Soviet military actions are military response capabilities specifically directed at reducing Soviet confidence in the success of the military missions their nuclear forces are intended to support. Improving deterrence does not, therefore, require deployment of nuclear forces to match SS-20s and *Backfires;* indeed, such deployments could be politically divisive in Asia. Preferred directions for enhancing deterrence are to improve:

- Survivability of nonnuclear and nuclear forces and associated $C^3I$ systems in Asia.
- Nonnuclear long-range strike capabilities in Asia.
- Nuclear long-range strike capabilities based at sea or in rear areas of the Pacific on U.S. territory.

U.S. threats to use nuclear weapons contribute to deterrence of Soviet nonnuclear attacks. The threat of nuclear weapons employment against general purpose forces also imposes military risks on the Soviets should they mass these general purpose forces; by compelling dispersal of general purpose forces, nuclear weapons enhance the effectiveness of conventional defenses.

However, the United States, its allies, and its friends should not depend on nuclear threats to deter Soviet nonnuclear attacks in Asia. The Soviet Union would surely make nuclear responses to U.S. or Chinese nuclear attacks. The foregoing analysis indicates that nuclear exchanges would not result in net strategic advantages for the United States, China, or their allies; in fact, given current trends in the Soviet nuclear buildup, nuclear exchanges in Asia might result in net strategic advantages for the USSR.

Moreover, a doctrine of first use of nuclear weapons to deter or defend against Soviet nonnuclear attacks is not likely to instill confidence among the publics in Asian countries. People recognize that their interests would not be served by nuclear war. While they might tolerate a doctrine of first use of nuclear weapons so long as the potentially catastrophic problems with this doctrine remain obscure, Soviet propaganda in crises or wartime would exploit latent (or not so latent) public fears to cause possibly grave political problems in various Asian nations. Such problems are already evident in Europe in a period of relatively good relations between the superpowers; think how difficult they could become in a deep crisis.

There is no need to forego the threat of first use of nuclear weapons. As just noted, this threat contributes to deterrence and enhances the effectiveness of conventional forces. But the primary role for nuclear weapons in Asia should be to deter Soviet first use of nuclear weapons. This should be achieved by threatening responses that undermine the confidence of Soviet leaders in their ability to achieve their military objectives in a war in Asia.

## Crises

In a deep crisis between the Soviet Union and one or more countries with major interests in Asia, the Soviet Union would surely seek to use its nuclear strength to incite internal strife within key countries in Asia, to divide allies, and to exact concessions. The recent and continuing military improvements in Far East nuclear forces would contribute to the overall impression of Soviet nuclear strength, but it would be the size of Soviet nuclear forces and the general threat of catastrophic destruction that would operate most effectively to achieve Soviet political aims in a crisis.

Specific military improvements in U.S. nuclear forces would likewise contribute to the impression of countervailing U.S. strength and would probably influence—perhaps to a considerable degree—the decisions of Soviet leaders in a crisis. Specifics of the U.S. nuclear posture would, however, have marginal influence on the behavior of U.S. allies and friends in a crisis, unless future basing of American nuclear forces were to lead some countries to believe they were unnecessarily exposed to Soviet nuclear attacks. In general, however, the actions of Asian countries in a crisis would be affected mostly by their assessment of where their own interests lay, the manner in which the United States was conducting itself in the crisis, the capabilities of nonnuclear forces, and the overall impressions in these countries of the extent to which U.S. nuclear forces neutralized Soviet nuclear threats.

## Wartime

Having adequate military counters to Soviet nuclear forces is most important in wartime—particularly nonnuclear war—to deter Soviet use of nuclear weapons and to offset the "virtual" effects of Soviet nuclear forces on U.S. and allied nonnuclear military operations.[22] It is in wartime situations that the specifics of the Soviet nuclear buildup in Asia would have the greatest effect on U.S. and allied security interests, in the ways discussed in foregoing sections of this chapter.

Consideration of wartime situations yields the most compelling

arguments for improved U.S. and allied nonnuclear forces to deter
or defend against Soviet nonnuclear attacks. At best, American
nuclear forces can neutralize Soviet nuclear threats. Responsible
Asian leaders are unlikely to be interested in U.S. first use of
nuclear weapons to defend against Soviet nonnuclear attacks,
given the large nuclear responses the Soviet Union can make
against U.S. allies in Asia, as well as against the United States
itself. Asian publics are unlikely to support American first use,
even if their leaders were to urge them to do so.

## Dealing with the Soviet Nuclear Buildup in Asia: Offshore Nuclear Forces and Improved Conventional Defenses

The United States, its allies, and its friends should not depend on
threats of the first use of nuclear weapons to deter or defend
against Soviet nonnuclear attacks in Asia. U.S. nuclear forces have
a vital, continuing role to play in deterring or responding to Soviet
nuclear attacks in Asia; through this capability they also have a vital
role to play in countering Soviet attempts to coerce Asian nations
with veiled or explicit nuclear threats. The following paragraphs
briefly suggest future directions for U.S. and allied force modernization, and comment on the potential of arms control negotiations
for dealing with the Soviet nuclear buildup in Asia.

Survivability is of paramount importance for a viable U.S.
nuclear force posture in the Asia-Pacific region. Actions must be
continued or increased to improve the survivability of U.S. nuclear
forces and U.S. and allied $C^3I$ and logistics support for U.S.
nuclear-capable delivery systems. These forces and support elements must be survivable under Soviet nonnuclear or nuclear
attacks. Allied countries can contribute, for example, through
improved active and passive defenses of $C^3I$ and logistics which,
while not dedicated to support of nuclear forces, contribute a key
military infrastructure that would sustain both nuclear-capable and
strictly conventional forces in wartime. Japan and other allies can
also provide surveillance for early warning of Soviet air raids on
U.S. carrier battle groups or bases on Pacific islands such as Guam.

U.S. nuclear force improvements in the Asia-Pacific region
should be directed particularly at a better capability for long-range
strikes against Soviet military targets ashore. Improvements are
needed in the survivability of long-range nuclear strike assets
deployed in the Asia-Pacific region, in their range, in the number

of these assets available early in a war with the Soviet Union, and in the survivability of their C³I. To avoid divisive controversy within Asian nations and to limit Soviet opportunities to divide the United States and its Asian allies, U.S. efforts to improve its long-range nuclear strike capabilities in the Asia-Pacific region should focus on SLBMs, carrier-based tactical aircraft, sea-based cruise missiles, and B-52s based on American territory in rear areas.

To reduce dependence on first use of nuclear weapons while countering a growing Soviet nonnuclear threat, the United States and its allies in Asia need to continue to make a variety of improvements in conventional air, naval, and ground forces. Of particular importance for the issues discussed in this chapter are improvements in long-range conventional bomber and cruise missile capabilities for attacks on air bases, naval bases, C³I, and other key military targets in the Soviet Union. Improved early warning and air defenses, hardening of vital C³I and other military facilities ashore, dispersal of forces, and other measures to improve the survivability of U.S. and allied conventional forces against Soviet nuclear and nonnuclear attacks (including Soviet chemical attacks) should also be given priority.

Finally, it should be stated that arms control is not a panacea for U.S. and Asian military planning problems, and may not even be a viable approach to mitigating the Soviet nuclear threat in Asia. If arms control negotiations with the Soviet Union are entered into with inadequate political and technical preparations, they can easily become nothing more than an additional means for the Soviets to try to manipulate the domestic politics of Asian nations.[23] The United States and its Asian allies and friends should examine together what political and military conditions need to exist in order to have reasonable prospects that arms control talks with the USSR would enhance Asian security.

Future U.S. arms negotiations with the Soviet Union, even though focused on strategic and European forces, can affect Asian security. The most obvious example relates to negotiations on SS-20 limits. The United States, China, and other Asian nations should consult on what SS-20 levels in Asia might be acceptable from both political and military perspectives and how, if at all, these might be influenced through INF talks with the Soviet Union. A range of SS-20 levels in Asia may be acceptable from a military viewpoint, since many important military capabilities in the Asia-Pacific region are difficult or impossible to target with SS-20s (e.g., ships or submarines at sea). Moreover, eliminating or reducing SS-20 launchers to a low level would not in itself eliminate the Soviet nuclear threat to Asia, since Soviet ICBMs,

SLBMs, bombers, tactical aircraft, battlefield nuclear weapons, and maritime nuclear weapons would remain. SS-20s in Asia should not become an obsession with the United States and Asian nations. Neither should the Soviet nuclear buildup in Asia go uncountered.

# Appendix: Nuclear Force Posture Characteristics

Targets related to the U.S., Soviet, and Chinese nuclear force postures include forces and facilities on land, sea-based forces, and air-breathing systems (aircraft and cruise missiles) attempting to penetrate air defenses. Some of these targets are nuclear delivery systems and their support, subject to attack by both nuclear and nonnuclear means; others are general purpose forces, bases, and command and control, subject to attack by nuclear and nonnuclear forces. Land-based targets include mobile missile launchers; hardened point targets (e.g., missile silos, command and control bunkers); air, naval and support bases; ground force concentrations; and air defenses. Sea-based targets include carrier battle groups, surface combatants operating independently (e.g., ships carrying TLAM/N), and submarines. Aircraft and cruise missiles in flight are targets for air defenses.

Based on analysis of this set of targets for major Asia-Pacific conflicts, several nuclear force posture characteristics appear to be of major importance. In general, nuclear forces must be able to survive enemy nonnuclear attacks (for perhaps a considerable period of time) and enemy nuclear attacks; surviving nuclear forces must be able to penetrate enemy defenses and effectively attack those enemy targets that are, at the time of attack, of paramount importance for the ongoing military campaign.

Nuclear force survival under enemy nonnuclear or nuclear attacks depends on:

1. Targetability of friendly nuclear forces (mobility, depth of the basing system, operational capability for dispersal of nuclear forces, the ability to deny the enemy information on the location of friendly nuclear forces).

2. Physical hardness of nuclear forces to the effects of nonnuclear and nuclear munitions.
3. Defenses of friendly nuclear forces.

Nuclear force penetration of enemy air defenses depends on:

1. The fraction of the friendly nuclear force that consists of ballistic missile systems, which are essentially invulnerable to currently deployed defenses in Asia. In the future, if antitactical missile defenses are deployed or as modernized air defenses with phased-array radars and high-acceleration SAMs are deployed, ballistic missiles will be increasingly subject to interception by defenses in Asia.
2. The ability of manned aircraft to exploit weaknesses in air defenses through use of stand-off missiles, electronic warfare techniques, low altitude penetration, defense suppression attacks, and saturation of air defenses.
3. The ability of cruise missiles to exploit weaknesses in air defenses through low radar cross sections, low altitude penetration, and saturation of defenses.

Effective nuclear attack on enemy targets depends on:

1. Adequate range or combat radius to reach enemy targets.
2. The ability to locate moveable land-based or sea-based targets sufficiently well for effective targeting and attack.
3. Response time, to carry out required attacks before moveable targets can relocate or launch out from under the attack. Response time is a combination of delivery system speed (ballistic missiles have a major speed advantage over aircraft or cruise missiles) and the rapidity with which the friendly command and control system can assimilate and transmit targeting information.
4. Delivery system accuracy and nuclear warhead yield.

## Endnotes

1. See, for example, Harry Gelman, *The Soviet Far East Buildup and Soviet Risk-Taking Against China,* R–2943–AF (Santa Monica, The Rand Corporation, August 1982), and the chapters in this volume by Gelman, Yao, Ha, and Kimura.
2. Soviet Air Forces were reorganized beginning in the late 1970s. Formerly, the Soviet Air Forces consisted of Long-Range Aviation, Frontal Aviation, Air Defense Forces, and Military Transport Aviation. The current structure

includes Strategic Air Armies (consisting of long-range bombers, medium-range bombers, reconnaissance aircraft, and some tactical aircraft); Air Forces of the Military Districts and Groups of Forces (including tactical aircraft, fighter-interceptors, reconnaissance aircraft, and helicopters); and Military Transport Aviation. Soviet Naval Aviation units are subordinate to fleet commanders and consist of land-based and carrier-based bombers, anti-submarine warfare aircraft, and reconnaissance aircraft. See Department of Defense, *Soviet Military Power, 1985,* 4th ed. (April 1985), pp. 33, 79–84, 101–102. For simplicity, the terminology of the current Soviet Air Forces organization is used when discussing trends from earlier periods.

3. For discussion of Soviet nuclear doctrine, see Fritz W. Ermarth, "Contrasts in American and Soviet Strategic Thought," *International Security,* vol. 3, no. 2 (Fall 1978), pp. 138–55. See also *Soviet Military Power, 1984,* 3rd ed. (April 1984), pp. 50–51.

4. *Soviet Military Power, 1983,* 2nd ed. (March 1983), p. 51. Forces for employment in the Far East include those deployed in the Central Asia, Siberian, Transbaykal, and Far East military districts. For details of the Soviet general purpose force buildup, see Harry Gelman, "The Soviet Far East Military Buildup: Motives and Prospects," Chapter 3 in this volume.

5. Anthony H. Cordesman, "The Military Balance in Northeast Asia: The Challenge to Japan and Korea," *Armed Forces Journal International* (November 1983), p. 96.

6. For definition of U.S. categories for Soviet theater nuclear forces, see the appendix to this chapter.

7. *Soviet Military Power, 1981,* 1st ed. (September 1981), p. 27, has a map showing general basing areas for Soviet MR/IRBMs. See also, *Soviet Military Power, 1984,* 3rd ed., p. 52.

8. *Soviet Military Power, 1985,* 4th ed., p. 34.

9. *Ibid.,* pp. 26, 33; *Soviet Military Power, 1983,* 2nd ed. (1983), pp. 24, 53.

10. *Soviet Military Power, 1985,* 4th ed., p. 38.

11. *Soviet Military Power, 1983,* 2nd ed., pp. 52–53; *Soviet Military Power, 1984,* 3rd ed., p. 57.

12. *Soviet Military Power, 1985,* 4th ed., pp. 46–48.

13. The International Institute for Strategic Studies, *The Military Balance, 1984–1985,* London: IISS, 1984, pp. 90–91. The missile nomenclature "DF" (Dong Feng, which means "East Wind") is that used by the IISS.

14. G. Jacobs, "Soviet Forces and the Pacific Basin," *Jane's Defense Review,* vol. 4, no. 2 (1983), p. 133; *Soviet Military Power, 1985,* 4th ed., p. 33.

15. Secretary of Defense Caspar W. Weinberger, *Annual Report to the Congress, Fiscal Year 1984,* Washington, D.C. (February 1, 1983), pp. 222, 235; *Annual Report to the Congress, Fiscal Year 1983,* Washington, D.C. (February 8, 1982), p. III-59.

16. *Soviet Military Power, 1985,* 4th ed., pp. 71–72.

17. *Ibid.,* pp. 31–32, 92. See also, Cordesman, "The Military Balance in Northeast Asia," p. 101, and Jacobs, "Soviet Forces and the Pacific Basin," p. 133.

18. See Fuji Kamiya, "Prospects for a New Korean War: Implications for Security in Northeast Asia," Chapter 10 in this volume.

19. Slow attrition of one side's nuclear forces (e.g., over days) allows that side opportunities to launch its nuclear forces from under the attack.

20. *Soviet Military Power, 1985*, 4th ed., pp. 31–32.

21. *Ibid.*, pp. 27–28.

22. Virtual effects of nuclear forces are those military effects resulting from the presence of nuclear forces, without their actual use. Examples of virtual effects include dispersal of ground, air, or naval forces because of the threat of nuclear attacks (reducing the military effectiveness of these forces), or decisions not to deploy general purpose forces into high nuclear threat areas for fear of their loss should the war become nuclear.

23. For an analysis of the role of arms control in Soviet security, see Helmut Sonnenfeldt and William Hyland, *Soviet Perspectives on Security*, Adelphi Paper 150, The International Institute for Strategic Studies, London (Spring 1979), pp. 21–23.

*Part Two*

# REGIONAL PERSPECTIVES ON THE SOVIET NUCLEAR THREAT

*Chapter 5*

# SOVIET MILITARY DEPLOYMENTS IN THE ASIA-PACIFIC REGION: IMPLICATIONS FOR CHINA'S SECURITY

*By Yao Wenbin*

The Asia-Pacific region has traditionally been of strategic significance for the Soviet Union; but developments in the international situation since the late 1970s have given this region heightened importance for the security of the USSR. Soviet military forces and activities there have been continuously strengthened. This chapter attempts to analyze Soviet defense strategy in Asia and the significance for the security of the People's Republic of China (PRC) of Moscow's still-growing military deployments in the region.

## Soviet Strategy in Asia

Soviet military strategy in Asia is an important component of the USSR's global strategy and reflects Moscow's worldwide ambitions and concerns. Soviet military actions in this region are thus subject to continuous adjustment as Moscow's global strategy develops and changes. Since the late 1970s, the Soviet Union has been confronted with important changes in its security environment, among which the following three aspects are directly related to its strategy in Asia:

1. A new period in the U.S.-Soviet rivalry has taken shape, one that is quite different from that of the 1970s. Each of the two superpowers has readjusted its global strategy, making their rivalry more intense. The United States gradually shook off the inhibiting effects of the war in Vietnam and adopted a more assertive policy toward the Soviet Union of "overall deterrence" and a strategic concept of "flexible counterattack" in an attempt to reverse its previously passive and unfavorable position. Constrained by many factors, Soviet expansion has been more cautious than in the latter 1970s, but Moscow's basic policies and strategic objectives remain unchanged. Facing a more assertive U.S. policy of direct confrontation, the Soviet Union has not given way in the slightest. It has intensified its rivalry with the United States in various military and strategic fields in an effort to maintain and increase its past gains. The pattern of the U.S.-Soviet rivalry has thus changed from that of the 1970s, when the Soviet Union was on the offensive and the United States on the defensive, into an intricate and complex mix of actions in which each power is at once on the offensive and the defensive, making some gains and enduring some losses.

2. Changes have taken place in the Asia-Pacific region. By completely ending the turmoil of the "Cultural Revolution" and eliminating the effects of Leftist ideology, China has entered a new period of rapid social development and is making every effort to implement the "Four Modernizations" economic construction program. In its foreign policy, China adheres to the principles of independence, opposition to hegemonism, and the upholding of world peace, and has improved relations with the United States, Japan, and several other Asian countries. The United States has reversed its "strategic retreat" from the Asia-Pacific region, enhanced its military strength in the Western Pacific, and is vigorously pursuing a multinational alliance strategy, with U.S.-Japan military cooperation as its cornerstone. Japan has further strengthened its military ties with the United States, developed friendly relations with China, and adopted a firmer attitude toward the Soviet Union. All this, coupled with the thorough exposure of the true nature of Soviet "hegemony" and expansionism in Afghanistan and Indochina, has put the Soviet Union in a more isolated position in the region.

3. The Asian region has assumed increasing global importance,

and its economic power has been growing in relation to the rest of the world. The U.S. trade turnover and investment growth rate in the region now exceed those in Europe. Japan's economic strength continues to grow, and its gross national product, now third highest in the world, approaches that of the Soviet Union. The Soviet Union has paid more and more attention to the development of its Far Eastern provinces and to increasing its economic ties with Asian countries. Economic development in the Asia-Pacific region is expected to have greater vitality and potential than that in Europe.

Strategically, the Asia-Pacific region has become increasingly important in both Soviet and U.S. global strategies. It is becoming evident that the Soviet Union considers the Asian region an important "front" for containing U.S. military forces and strengthening its two-front operational deployment. The United States has also laid increasing stress on the Asia-Pacific region. It has abandoned its "swing strategy" and sees Northeast Asia as a key to deterring and containing the Soviet Union. All of this suggests that there has been a significant change in the traditional American attitude of regarding Europe as of central importance to its interests, with Asia occupying a much lesser position, thus leading the Soviet Union to pay greater attention to Asian questions as well. Against this background, the Soviet Union has seen an urgent strategic need to make adjustments in its Asian strategy.

Politically, the main trend in Moscow's approach to the region is the launching of a peace offensive, with a view to dividing various antihegemonic forces in the Asian region and sowing discord in U.S. relations with China, Japan, and other Asian countries. The Soviet leadership thus hopes to extricate itself from the predicament of isolation and to expand its influence. For this purpose, the Soviet Union in recent years has repeatedly expressed its willingness to normalize relations with China, to expand economic cooperation with Japan, and to increase bilateral exchanges in various fields with the ASEAN countries. On many occasions it has advanced the idea of adopting confidence-building measures in the Far East. It has proposed through Mongolia the signing of a nonaggression treaty by all Asian countries. And it has supported Vietnam's proposals for such transparent devices as regional talks in an attempt to peddle its Asian Collective Security System again in disguised fashion.

Militarily, the Soviet Union concentrates its efforts on strengthening operational capabilities and offensive deployments throughout the entire Far East theater, attempting to rely on its military strength to seek new advances and to enhance preparations for war. To this end, it has, over the past few years, attached special importance to improving its theater nuclear attack capability in the Asia-Pacific region, increasing the strength and activities of its naval and air forces, and augmenting the capability for theaterwide coordinated operations. Moreover, the Soviet Union has steadily stepped up its penetration into and expansion to South and Southeast Asia and has tried to extend its military presence outside the USSR and overseas to the maximum extent possible, in order to gain a favorable strategic position in relation to the United States.

To sum up, the primary objective of current Soviet strategy in Asia is to consolidate and expand its positions in the region, weaken and edge out American influence, and pursue its global strategy in coordination with its rivalry with the United States on the European and Middle East/South Asia fronts. This strategy does have its defensive aspects, but its primary character is offensive. It employs political, economic, military, and other means, but its mainstay is military strength. It is directed at all Asian countries, with the United States as the primary target. It is not only oriented to the rivalry with the United States, but also takes into consideration the operational needs of future warfare. It can be said that Moscow's present Asian strategy is essentially one of pursuing hegemonism in the region and rivaling the United States there. Improving military strength and operational deployments persists as the focal effort of Soviet strategy in Asia.

## Soviet Military Activity

Guided by its strategy, the Soviet Union has made new efforts since the late 1970s to improve its military strength and operational deployments in the Asian region, as was given prominence by President Brezhnev's trip to the Soviet Far East in 1978. Improvements have been made to the Soviet regional military posture in a number of important respects.

### Command Structure

In early 1978, a Far East theater command was set up in Ulan Ude, to direct and coordinate the military operations of the forces of the Far East, Transbaykal (including Soviet forces in Mongolia), and Siberian military districts and of the Soviet Pacific fleet. This was the first permanent Soviet theater command established in peacetime, and is an important step for strengthening military deployments on the eastern front. In the light of the increasing Soviet attention in recent years to the study of and preparation for a two-front war, and to the Soviet operational concept of emphasizing the conduct of "theater strategic operations," it is evident that the Asia-Pacific region is seen as operationally very important to Moscow's military planning.

## Theater Nuclear Forces

Theater nuclear forces have been strengthened significantly. Since 1977, more than 170 SS-20 intermediate-range missiles have been deployed in the Asian region and new sites continue to be constructed. Some 80 *Backfire* bombers of the Soviet Air Force and Naval Aviation are stationed in the region. They represent one of the most significant additions to Soviet military power in Asia. These deployments are coordinated with and closely related to the Soviet concern with maintaining theater nuclear superiority in Europe. They have further enhanced Soviet military backing for its strategy in Asia, posing an increased nuclear threat to Asian countries. Moreover, given the fact that the SS-20 missile is mobile, its simultaneous deployment in Europe and Asia gives the Soviet Union more bargaining chips in the nuclear arms race and arms control negotiations with the United States.

## Naval Forces

The strength and activities of the Soviet Pacific fleet have been substantially increased. Currently, it has more than 800 ships of various types—more than any other Soviet fleet—with a gross tonnage second only to the North Sea Fleet. With the introduction over the past few years of *Delta-III*-class nuclear ballistic missile submarines (SSBNs), nuclear-powered attack submarines (SSNs), and such major surface combatants as the *Novorossisk* aircraft carrier and *Kara*-class cruisers, together with some logistic support ships, the strategic attack and oceangoing capabilities of the Pacific fleet have increased considerably.

Soviet forces have made increasing use of Cam Ranh Bay basing facilities, not only stationing a naval task force detachment and some long-range reconnaissance aircraft and ASW patrol aircraft there, but deploying Tu-16 *Badger* medium-range bombers for the first time on a Soviet base in Southeast Asia.[1] This significantly strengthens Moscow's naval position in the Western Pacific and its capabilities for controlling such important sea lines of communication as the Strait of Malacca and the Bashi Channel. It can also give support to Soviet military operations in the Middle East, the Persian Gulf, and the Indian Ocean area, and poses a certain threat to China's coastal areas in the south and to the U.S. air and naval bases at Subic Bay and Clark Field in the Philippines.

## Gound Forces

Some improvements and adjustments in the deployment of ground forces in the Asian region have also been made. There has been little change in their strength, which remains at about 53 divisions. The operational deployments in the Transbaykal Military District and in Mongolia have been augmented, and a garrison unit (equivalent to one division) was formed on Japan's Northern Territories. The main emphasis has been on the replacement of weapons and equipment and improving combined-arms and combat capabilities. T-72 tanks, various types of armored combat vehicles, new artillery pieces, and other weapons and equipment have been deployed, and a large number of combat and service support units have been newly formed and integrated.

Some changes have taken place in the organizational structure and weapons of the Soviet Air and Air Defense Forces. The changes in structure, basically completed in 1982, primarily resulted in the change of command systems of the Air Force Long Range Aviation, the formation of new army aviation, and the redivision of air defense districts. The rate of replacement of weapons and equipment was accelerated, and new types of combat aircraft such as MiG-23, -25, -27, Su-24 fighters and Mi-24 helicopters were introduced. These measures have further increased the capabilities of the Air Force to conduct theater operations and to coordinate operations with the ground forces; they also have improved the unity and flexibility of the air defense operational command.

## Future Directions

Soviet military strength in the Asia-Pacific region is expected to continue to grow for some time to come. While the current level of personnel strength will probably be maintained, there will be a trend toward more rapid replacement and upgrading of weapons. Growth in theater nuclear forces and in the strength of the navy and air forces will continue. We can also anticipate further improvements in force structure and organization so as to enhance theaterwide combined-arms operations. This increasing military strength will continue to be the primary element behind the Soviet Union's Asian strategy.

## China's Security

The Soviet military buildup and operational deployments in the Asian region have direct implications for China's security in that they endanger regional peace and stability. They cannot but cause concern to the Chinese people and to the peoples of other Asian countries.

The unrelenting Soviet military buildup in the Far East since the mid-1960s constitutes a significant threat to China's security. This basic posture is clear and has not changed: Soviet ground forces and frontal and army aviation in the Asian region are directed mainly at China. SS-20 missiles and *Backfire* bombers deployed in the region are capable of attacking areas deep inside China. The Soviet Pacific fleet poses a threat to China's coastal areas. In addition to deploying military forces with China as their primary target, the Soviet Union has constantly staged military exercises of different scales in areas adjacent to China's northern border and with China as the presumed enemy. In recent years, the Soviet military presence in South and Southeast Asia has increased, effectively encircling China from the north, west, and south. All this clearly indicates that the threat to China's security comes mainly from the Soviet Union, from its continuous military buildup in the Asia-Pacific region, and from its hegemonist policy.

It is precisely for the reasons just outlined that China has explicitly indicated in direct Sino-Soviet consultations that the Soviet Union should remove the "three major obstacles" as a basis for normalizing relations. If the Soviet Union sincerely wants to improve bilateral Sino-Soviet relations, it should take practical steps to eliminate its military threat to China by (1) withdrawing its troops from the Sino-Soviet border area and Mongolia, (2) withdrawing its forces from Afghanistan, and (3) ceasing to support Vietnam in its aggression against Kampuchea. In the meantime, China has unswervingly given its support to the Kampuchean people in their struggle against Vietnam's hegemonism and to the people of Afghanistan in their struggle against Soviet aggression. China holds that only by doing so can the Soviet Union and Vietnam be eventually forced to withdraw their occupation forces. This is the only basis on which a just settlement of the issues of Kampuchea and Afghanistan can be achieved, thereby thwarting

Moscow's strategy of southward expansion and defending peace and justice in the regions of Southeast and South Asia.

Soviet military deployments in the Asian region also pose a threat to the security of other Asian countries and to American strategic interests. It has become evident that all Soviet measures to enhance its military deployments in the region are diametrically opposed to those of the United States. Over the past few years, both the Soviet Union and the United States have sought to achieve a favorable strategic position in the region, regarding this as an important means of containing its adversary and preparing for a two-front or multi-front war. The growing Soviet theater nuclear forces and Soviet naval and air power are directed primarily at the United States, while the new U.S. *Tomahawk* cruise missiles and growing naval and air power are directed at the Soviet Union. Soviet Pacific fleet forces have been deployed forward to the South China Sea in an attempt to threaten the U.S. naval transit route from the Pacific to the Indian Ocean; at the same time, the U.S. Seventh Fleet has staged exercises farther forward into the Sea of Japan with a view to being able to encircle and contain Soviet naval power close to the Soviet coast. It is this sharp strategic contention that has made the U.S.-Soviet confrontation in the Asia-Pacific region increasingly intense. As a result, the rivalry between the two superpowers in the region is becoming more turbulent.

China is a developing socialist country that follows a foreign policy of independence. China is always opposed to hegemonism and to the superpowers' practice of exerting pressure on other countries, perpetrating aggression, or pursuing expansionist policies by relying on their military power. China never attaches itself to or yields to any power or group of powers. Its position of opposing the strengthening of Soviet military deployments in the Asia-Pacific region is consistent and clear-cut. China wants to establish and develop friendly relations with all countries, including the Soviet Union, on the basis of the Five Principles of Peaceful Coexistence.

China is facing the arduous task of domestic economic construction, which requires a peaceful environment and lasting international stability. China does not want war; but confronted with the realities of the day, it must take necessary measures to bolster its defenses to preserve its own security. To modernize its defenses, China will adhere to the principle of mainly relying on its own national efforts while, at the same time, being willing to import advanced technology and equipment to the extent possible. Strengthening its military forces, including the development of a nuclear force of limited size, is entirely for self-defense and for the prevention of aggression. The Chinese government has repeatedly and explicitly declared that China will not be the first to use nuclear weapons at any time or under any circumstances; it has also stated unconditionally that China will not use nuclear weapons against nonnuclear countries. A modernized, powerful China will be an important factor for stability in Asia and will make an active contribution to the containment of Soviet expansion and the safeguarding of peace and security in the region.

## Endnote

1. See Harry Gelman, "The Soviet Far East Military Buildup: Motives and Prospects," Chapter 3 in this volume.

*Chapter 6*

# THE SOVIET MILITARY BUILDUP: ITS IMPACT ON JAPAN AND ITS AIMS

*by Hiroshi Kimura*

It is an undeniable fact, amply described in other chapters, that the Soviet Union has steadily built up its military forces in East Asia and in the vicinity of Japan. The primary questions raised by this buildup are: Why, and with what objectives, are Soviet forces being expanded in the region? And if one accepts the interpretation, as do many observers, that the buildup is counterproductive for Soviet interests in the region, what motivates the Kremlin to pursue a policy that many foreign observers see as self-defeating? The main aim of this chapter is to answer these questions from a Japanese perspective by assessing the impact of the Soviet military buildup on Japan and by examining the major factors that motivate and determine Soviet foreign and military policy toward Japan.

### Evolving Japanese Approaches to Defense: Gradual or Dramatic Change?

There is debate abroad about whether Japanese attitudes and policies toward national security matters have recently undergone significant changes. One school of thought, which includes American defense officials, concludes that basic changes have not yet taken place. It is pointed out, for example, that Japan continues to keep defense spending extremely low relative to the United States and its other allies (at just about 1 percent of GNP) and persistently adheres to such self-imposed constraints as the Three Non-Nuclear Principles and the policy of not sending the Self-Defense Forces (SDF) overseas. In contrast, another school of thought, which includes Soviet observers, deliberately overdramatizes the "remilitarization" of Japan and argues that fundamental changes in Japan's security policies have in fact taken place. Proponents of this group draw attention to the fact that Japan has steadily increased its military budget (now the eighth largest in the world) over the past few years, that it seems to recognize only two and a half of its Three Non-Nuclear Principles, and that it is increasingly involved in Washington's global efforts to counter the Soviet Union.

The disparities between these two viewpoints are based largely on *how* one examines certain facts—that is, by what dimensions and with what standards one chooses to measure and interpret recent occurrences in Japan. From the perspective of those who would like to see a heavily armed Japan, the changes that have occurred in recent years appear to be very moderate, insufficient, and unsatisfactory. From the point of view of those who prefer Japan to remain unarmed or at the most lightly armed, the changes look quite formidable.

The correct assessment of what has occurred in Japan's approach to national security and defense lies somewhere between these two extremes. While some significant changes have taken place in terms of the Japanese public's perceptions of defense issues, these attitude changes have yet to be fully converted into changes in policy. And although there have been some changes in policy, they are not large enough to constitute a dramatic departure from Japan's postwar defense policy. If the direction has been set for major changes, the pace of change has been gradual rather than drastic.

Keeping in mind the limited scope of this "change," let us now examine in greater detail the most noticeable areas of recent development in public attitudes and defense activities.

## Japanese Perceptions of the Soviet Threat

Regardless of what the government in Tokyo may call it—whether a "potential threat" or simply a "threat"—an increasing number of Japanese have begun to identify the Soviet military buildup in the Far East as the primary challenge to the security of Japan. Because of the incremental nature of this perceptual change, it is difficult to pinpoint exactly when it began to take place. It is clear, however, that the period from 1978 to 1980 marked an important turning point. During 1978-1979, after the Sino-Japanese peace treaty was signed and the 1950 Sino-Soviet treaty of friendship and alliance (which identified Japan as a common enemy) was abrogated, China ceased to be seen as a potential threat. In a complete reversal of policy, Beijing not only avidly endorsed the U.S.-Japan Security Treaty, but began to defend vigorously the need for a rapid Japanese military buildup in response to Soviet "hegemonism."

During this same period, the Japanese learned that the Soviet Union had embarked on the deployment of its military forces to the islands of Kunashiri, Etorofu, and Shikotan off Hokkaido. Regardless of Soviet motives, the psychological impact of these actions on the Japanese, who continue to regard these Northern Islands as an integral part of Japan, has been great indeed. Moreover, Moscow's invasion of Afghanistan in late 1979 reinforced the Japanese sense of a security threat from the Soviet Union—a concern that has superseded most other Japanese international priorities, including the territorial question of the Northern Territories, which has dominated Japanese-Soviet relations during the entire postwar period. The impact of the Soviet intervention in Afghanistan led to official statements in the Japanese Diet in February 1980 by Prime Minister Masayoshi Ohira and Director General of the Defense Agency Kichizo Hosoda in which the Soviet Union was characterized as a "potential" and "serious" threat to Japan.

Soviet behavior since 1980 has only served to strengthen the perception of the Soviet Union as the main threat to Japan's security. In January 1983, Yurii V. Andropov, then the CPSU's General Secretary, and Andrei A. Gromyko, Foreign Minister, were reported as having said that the Soviet Union would "redeploy to the Soviet Far East some of the SS-20 missiles which might exceed the agreed upon quota for the European zone in the INF negotiation at Geneva, in order to counter the American military buildup around Japan."[1] The SS-20 mobile intermediate-range ballistic missile is believed to have enough range to cover the distance from almost any point in the Soviet Far East to every corner of Japan. Approximately one-third of all the SS-20s in the Soviet arsenal, 108 at that time and now more than 170, has been deployed in the Soviet Far East and targeted on Japan and other countries in Asia. The words expressed by Soviet leaders demonstrate their intention and strategy to exploit the Japanese concern about this extremely powerful and sophisticated missile as an instrument for manipulating the Japanese attitude toward the confrontation between two military superpowers. The Korean Air Lines incident of September 1, 1983 reinforced this view. The shooting down of the civilian aircraft, among other things, reminded the Japanese that the Soviet armed forces have not grown merely for appearance sake, nor only to pursue politico-diplomatic functions; rather, they have been expanded for use when needed as a coercive means to fulfilling operational military purposes.

## The Development of U.S.-Japan Defense Cooperation

How has the shift in public perceptions of the threat to Japan's security affected defense policy? Recent Japanese governments have begun to stress more and more the necessity for Japan to strengthen cooperative ties with the United States and the NATO countries in order to counter the Soviet threat. Based on his conviction that the security of Japan is inseparably linked with that of the rest of the world, former Prime Minister Ohira declared that Japan would undertake sacrifices for the "Western Community." Mr. Ohira's successor, Zenko Suzuki, went one step further toward what can be called the "globalization" of Japanese security interests. In a communiqué issued jointly with President Reagan in May 1981, the Japanese Prime Minister recognized that "the alliance between Japan and the United States is built upon their shared values of democracy and liberty." Acknowledging the "desirability of an appropriate division of roles" between the two countries, Suzuki further promised that Japan would take steps to bolster its military capabilities and extend its defense perimeter several hundred miles off its shores and out to 1,000 miles of its sea lanes.

Yasuhiro Nakasone, perhaps the most articulate and outspoken political leader of postwar Japan, has been trying harder than any of his predecessors to accelerate the process of the globalization of Japan's defense and foreign policies. In order to clarify this position, the Japanese Prime Minister has repeatedly stated that "the fundamental principle of Japanese diplomacy" lies in making efforts "to promote solidarity with the Western countries, particularly with the United States," and "to fulfill her [Japan's] obligations as a member of the Western Community." When former Prime Minister Suzuki referred to Japan-U.S. relations as an "alliance," quite a sensation resulted in Japan due to the term's strong connotation of a *military* alliance. The resulting furor,

however, did not prevent the much bolder Prime Minister Nakasone from going one step further. He not only confirmed that
relations between Japan and the United States are indeed a
military alliance, but during his January 1983 visit to Washington,
he further described those relations as *unmei kyodotai* (a community bound together by a common destiny).

Regarding Japan's position on American nuclear arms control
negotiations with the Soviet Union, Nakasone clearly associated
Japan with the United States and the NATO nations at the Williamsburg Summit in May 1983. The final joint statement of that
meeting contained a sentence which declared: "The security of our
countries is indivisible and must be approached on a global basis."
This sentence was fully endorsed by the Japanese Prime Minister,
and according to some sources, was placed in the statement
specifically at Nakasone's request. In any case, Nakasone's actions
can be interpreted as a shift in policy orientation from the postwar
Japanese orientation of an "exclusively defensive defense" to a
more active commitment and a larger Japanese role in security
affairs on a global scale.

Concerning the question of Japan's role in countering the Soviet
threat in East Asia and the Pacific, Prime Minister Nakasone made
several sensational statements during his visit to Washington in
January 1983. First, he expressed his government's determination
that "the whole Japanese archipelago should be like an unsinkable
aircraft carrier putting up a tremendous bulwark of defense against
infiltration of [Soviet] bombers." Second, responding more specifically than did Prime Minister Suzuki to American requests for
Japan to blockade the three key straits of Tsushima, Tsugaru, and
Soya in an effort to restrict the movements of the Soviet Pacific
fleet, he went so far as to say: "[One of Japan's] largest objectives is
to have complete and full control of the three straits that go
through the Japanese islands so that there can be no passage of
Soviet submarines or other naval activities." Third, Nakasone
demonstrated a serious commitment to the concept of a 1,000-mile
sea lane defense, which had been mentioned first but never
elaborated on by his predecessor, Suzuki. Nakasone put the concept in more concrete terms, by explaining to an American audi-
ence: "Our desire would be to defend the sea lanes between Guam
and Tokyo and between the Straits of Taiwan and Osaka." The
Nakasone government also agreed to a U.S.-Japan study on joint
sea lane operations. Giving this planning effort an official endorsement, the 1983 edition of Japan's Defense White Paper elaborated
on the concept and used the term "sea lane defense" for the first
time in an official government document.

# The Practical Evolution of U.S.-Japan
# Defense Ties

Since the end of World War II, Japan has developed a unique concept of self-defense, that is, an "exclusively defensive defense." This concept, which limits the use, level, and geographical scope of the Self Defense Forces (SDF), has resulted in the adherence to several self-imposed principles, including the prohibition of sending troops overseas; prohibition of the possession of weapons used exclusively for the destruction of foreign territory such as ICBMs and long-range bombers; prohibition of the exercise of the right of collective self-defense; restrictions on the exportation of weapons and military technology; and the three principles regarding nuclear weapons of "not possessing, not manufacturing and not introducing them into Japan." Although these principles are sustained as formal policy, in recent years the Japanese government has begun to interpret them in an increasingly flexible way. The following are some of the measures that have been implemented by the Nakasone administration and its two predecessors (Ohira and Suzuki) or will be adopted as a result of this more flexible attitude toward Japan's defense activities.

1. *1,000-Mile Sea Lane Defense*. The geographical area in which Japan can utilize the SDF is not necessarily limited to Japan's land, sea, and airspace as such, but will be decided on according to specific circumstances. Whereas the mission assigned to the Maritime Self Defense Forces by the National Defense Program Outline of 1976 was to conduct warning and surveillance within Japan's territory and neighboring sea and airspace, both the Suzuki and (in particular) Nakasone cabinets have redefined the constitutionally defensive geographical area of Japan to include an expanded perimeter "several hundred nautical miles off its shores and 1,000 miles of sea lanes."

2. *Participation in Naval Exercises*. Since 1980, when Prime Minister Ohira for the first time allowed the SDF to participate in the Pacific Rim naval exercise RimPac 80, Japanese administrations have made it almost a rule to participate in joint naval exercises in the Pacific Ocean together with the navies of the ANZUS member countries (the United States, Australia, and New Zealand). The rationale for permitting the Maritime SDF to take part in such exercises is that this type of training is different from sending troops overseas "for the purpose of using force," which is regarded as constitutionally impermissible.

3. *Sharing the Cost of U.S. Forces in Japan*. While Japanese

governments have judged unconstitutional Japan's participation in any international arrangement for collective self-defense, they have regarded the right of self-defense as permissible as long as it is intended to defend Japan's own land and people. The Japan-U.S. Security Treaty arrangement is therefore considered constitutional, precisely because while it does obligate the United States to defend Japan, it does not require Japan to reciprocate. In an effort to make this arrangement more equitable, Japan has assumed some of the labor and other costs for bases and facilities required for the stationing of American forces on Japanese territory. In recent years, Japan has been spending more than one billion U.S. dollars annually for the upkeep of these facilities, where the United States deploys some 47,000 troops—a cost of $21,000 per American soldier, the highest share of the cost of U.S. overseas deployments anywhere in the world.

4. *Transfers of Military Technology.* Acting on a suggestion initially made by his predecessor Zenko Suzuki, Prime Minister Nakasone agreed to provide advanced Japanese defense-related technology to the United States. This decision, long-awaited by the United States, signaled a major reversal of Japan's policy of restricting the flow of weapons and military expertise to any foreign country. The rationale for the decision was that such transfers to the United States, a nation with which Japan has a security arrangement, does not run counter to Japan's self-imposed principles on the export of weapons.

5. *Deployment of F-16s.* Japan has agreed to an American proposal for the deployment of some 48 F-16 fighter-bombers at Misawa air base in northern Japan, beginning in 1985.

6. *Interpretation of the Non-Introduction of Nuclear Weapons.* Regardless of the accuracy or inaccuracy of the so-called "Reischauer testimony,"[2] the Japanese government has never attempted to raise questions as to whether U.S. warships making transit visits to bases in Japan are armed with nuclear weapons. The government is expected to continue this policy on port calls by U.S. naval ships, even those equipped with *Tomahawk* long-range cruise missiles (which can be armed with either conventional or nuclear warheads).

7. *Increase in Defense Spending.* Despite domestic political and fiscal constraints, Japan's defense budget has gradually increased in recent years. The percentage of GNP spent for defense has grown as follows over the last several fiscal years: 1977, 0.88 percent; 1978 to 1980, 0.90 percent; 1981, 0.91 percent; 1982. 0.93 percent; 1983, 0.97 percent; 1984, 0.99 percent; and 1985, 0.997 percent. It seems only a matter of time before the 1976 cabinet

policy of imposing a ceiling of 1 percent of GNP on defense spending will be dropped. (In fact, using NATO's definition of defense costs, the Japanese figure is already 1.6 percent of GNP.) If salaries for SDF personnel are increased by 3 percent, defense expenditures could exceed the 1 percent limit in fiscal year 1986.

What has made these changes acceptable to the Japanese people and government? There are, of course, many reasons which have to do with the perception of threat, policy orientations, and practical measures concerning defense and security affairs. The following factors, however, seem to have played a predominant role: the Japanese feeling that there has been a relative decline in American supremacy in the political, military, and economic spheres; an increasing recognition of the indivisibility of the security of Japan and that of the rest of the world and, hence, the need to share the defense burden with the Western nations; a heightened Japanese self-confidence and even a growing sense of nationalism brought about, and buttressed by, economic achievements and other successes. Yet, without a doubt, the outstanding factor has been the impact on Japanese thinking of the Soviet military buildup throughout the world and, in particular, in the vicinity of Japan.

Given the complicated and dynamic nature of these changes in attitude and policy, it is very difficult, perhaps impossible, to assess how much of Japan's rapid and substantial defense buildup has been driven by the Soviet military buildup in the Far East, but it would not be an exaggeration to say that without it, most of these changes would not have occurred in the first place. In other words, an awakening to the "Soviet threat," a change in the defense consciousness of the Japanese public (something the Soviet Union calls the "resurgence of militarist tendencies"), heightened military cooperation with the United States, and the "NATO-ization" process have all been directly stimulated by or have been accelerated by the Soviet military buildup.

If the cause-and-effect relationship between this military buildup and the transformation in Japanese security perceptions and policies is accepted as correct, then a further question must be asked: Why does the Soviet Union continue to pursue such a self-defeating policy, provoking precisely the development that it says it does not want to take place? This question has relevance if the following are regarded as the general objectives of Soviet foreign policy toward Japan: (1) to prevent closer ties between Tokyo and Washington; (2) to thwart the "globalization," or "NATO-ization," of Japan; (3) to prevent Japan from cooperating with China; (4) to arrest the growth of "militarism" in Japan; (5) to promote more active economic cooperation with the Soviet Union; and (6) to diminish or contain the Japanese demand for the return of the Northern Islands. The continuing Soviet military buildup seems to run counter to the achievement of these objectives.

## Soviet Foreign Policy Toward Japan

The answer to the question of why the Soviet Union pursues a self-defeating policy toward Japan seems to lie, first of all, in the fact that the Soviet leadership at present has no effective instrument of influence at their disposal apart from the threat of military superiority. For quite some time now, Marxist-Leninist ideology and the Soviet socioeconomic system have ceased to hold any appeal for the majority of Japanese. Neither geographic proximity nor economic complementarity provide a convincing basis for an improvement in Soviet-Japanese bilateral relations. Moreover, few of the Kremlin's tactics in dealing with Japan (such as its attempt to drive a wedge between Japan and the United States and other Western nations, the maneuver to improve relations with China, and the separation of politics from economics) have produced any positive results. Consequently, the only means of influence left to exploit is that of military pressure. It is, of course, one thing for the Soviet Union to put forward the excuse that it has no other means of influence, but quite a different one for others to accept such a rationale. Moscow must also come to see that this approach is not just ineffective; it is counterproductive.

The second reason, related to the first, seems to lie in the firm Soviet belief that military strength carries extraordinary weight in any assessment of the "correlation of forces" in international affairs. Soviet leaders seem to feel that military power is the most effective instrument for achieving almost any national goal. In other words, they believe that military power can be converted into political influence. To make things worse, some Soviet Communist Party *apparatchiki* and high government officials in charge of Japanese affairs still appear to adhere to the notion that the Japanese people can be easily intimidated and, if pressed hard and often enough, will ultimately capitulate to Soviet terms.

The Japanese, however, are not easily impressed nor influenced by demonstrations of naked military might. They have concluded from their own defeat in World War II that military means do not lead to the achievement of national goals. Accordingly, whether for good or ill, they are extraordinarily insensitive to any Soviet bluff with military might. Thus, because Soviet leaders do not seem to comprehend that a deliberately tough policy eventually works against their interests, as was made evident by the KAL incident, they have not yet demonstrated any intention whatsoever to alter their policy of further increasing Soviet military strength in the Far East. The recent deployment of another aircraft carrier, the *Novorossiysk*, to the region further illustrates this point.

A third reason seems to lie in the institutional structure within which Soviet foreign policy is made. On the basis of private conversations with Soviet specialists on Japan, many Japanese and Americans have concluded that some of these analysts know that Soviet actions toward Japan have been neither intelligent nor effective. They know, for example, that there *is* a territorial problem between Japan and the Soviet Union, despite official Soviet assertions to the contrary. The problem, however, is that these specialists do not have much influence on the Kremlin's decisionmaking with regard to Japan. They are simply *institutniki* (area specialists in institutes attached to the USSR's Academy of Sciences) or *mezhdunarodniki* (internationalists), who are used as researchers rather than advisers or policymakers. The bureaucratic distinction between them and the actual decisionmakers in the Kremlin is—according to defectors from these institutes—much more marked than that between American area specialists and elected officials in the White House.

Ivan Kovalenko, deputy chief of the party's International Department, currently occupies the highest position in the Communist Party of the Soviet Union (CPSU) held by a Japanologist. He has been identified as the "commander-in-chief" of Soviet policymaking toward Japan. However, his influence on Soviet policy decisions affecting Japan seems to be smaller than the influence of Mikhail Kapitsa, a Sinologist and one of the Soviet Deputy Foreign Ministers, on Soviet-China policy. To make things worse, Kovalenko, who was in charge of public relations and the Communist education of Japanese war prisoners in Siberia, appears to Japanese who have met him to believe that Japanese are easily intimidated. Such a notion is out-of-date: Japanese have been increasingly regaining self-confidence; they have fully recovered from World War II through their achievement of an economic miracle. Many Japanese believe that as long as Kovalenko or someone else with similarly outdated views occupies an important position in Soviet policymaking toward Japan, the possibility for an improvement in bilateral relations is slim.

The last but perhaps the most convincing answer to the question of why the Soviet Union continues its military buildup seems to lie in its global strategy. The Soviet Union looks on Japan as a small country with no natural resources with which to conduct an independent foreign policy. In the words of one Soviet spokesman, Dmitrii Petrov, the head of the Japanese Section, Institute of Far Eastern Studies, Soviet Academy of Sciences:[3]

> *extraordinary poverty in natural resources makes the Japanese economy exclusively dependent upon foreign trade . . . Here lies one of the problems of Japan.*

He also pointed out the military weakness of Japan:[4]

> *Japan, in size of armed forces, quality of military technique, size of military budget and all other indexes, cannot be compared to the USA and countries of the Common Market. Japan does not have her own atomic weapons nor does she independently decide strategic problems.*

These observations and remarks were made ten years ago. During the decade since that time, Japan has, of course, undergone a tremendous transformation, thereby making some of the above assessments rather dated. Japan managed to overcome the 1973–74 oil shock, is bound to overtake the Soviet economy in terms of gross national product and technological sophistication, and is considered to have the capability to surpass—and in some areas of economic performance, in fact, has surpassed—even the United States. These economic accomplishments seem recently to have brought a realization to the Soviets, albeit belatedly and still insufficiently, that a lack of natural resources is not necessarily a handicap for the Japanese. The Soviet Union is now eager to learn from the Japanese economy and Japanese management how to put right its own sluggish, inefficient economy. Particular interest is shown in the fields of electronics, computers, semiconductors, and other Japanese high technologies.

When it comes to the military field, however, the Soviet assessment of Japan remains essentially unchanged. True, Moscow has lately embarked on a campaign against the "remilitarization" of Japan, but, if one looks at this closely, certain characteristics at once emerge. The first salient feature is its *preventive* character. What Moscow is concerned about is clearly not the present level of Japan's military capabilities—which are almost insignificant when compared with Soviet military forces in terms of budget, size, or weapons—but about its *potential*, its capacity to grow into an effective military force in the future. I. I. Ivkov, presumably the pen name of I. Kovalenko, candidly admitted that "the process of the militarization of Japan has not yet become all-embracing."[5] Having said this, however, Ivkov hastened to call attention to the fact that Japan commands "advanced, up-to-date technology," which, in the Soviet judgment, could be "quickly and easily switched, converted or re-equipped to serve military purposes."

In short, Japan has, in the Soviet view, "a powerful military-industrial potential, which makes it possible for Japanese ruling circles, when necessary, to build up a multimillion-man army and equip it with advanced military technology."[6] Put another way, what worries the Soviet Union is the *direction* in which Tokyo is moving and the historical experience of a *rapid* transformation in Japan once set on course. Lest they have to confront such a transformation of Japan too late, the Soviet leaders seem determined to nip in the bud what they refer to as the "resurgence of Japanese militarism." Aside from this concern, however, the Soviet Union believes, in general, that without nuclear weapons, Japan is not yet a full-fledged and independent military power. In 1981, one Soviet spokesman concluded: "Today and *in the near future* Japan will be unable independently to resolve strategic questions and conduct offensive large-scale operations."[7] (Emphasis added.)

In the Soviet perception and in its list of foreign policy priorities, the United States still occupies the dominant position—so much so that Moscow does not seem to realize the need to develop a policy specifically oriented toward Japan alone. Suggesting that the Soviet Union's policy toward Japan is nothing other than a function, or almost an automatic extension, of Soviet global strategy, Basil Dmytryshyn, professor at Portland State University, holds that the Soviet Union simply does not have a clear, distinct, positive policy toward Japan. Offers that have been made to improve Soviet-Japanese relations have been merely "spinoffs of Soviet policy toward the United States and/or toward China." Such an interpretation seems a valid one and has received confirmation even from Soviet spokesmen. For example, Yuri Badura, a former Tokyo correspondent and currently deputy director of the international department of *Izvestia,* writes in his article contributed to the Japanese periodical *Jiyu* (Freedom) as follows:[8]

> *The title prepared for my article by the Japanese editor, i.e., "What Does the Soviet Union Want from Japan," is misleading and somewhat perplexes me because there is nothing that can be specifically called a Soviet policy toward Japan among Soviet foreign policy goals. . . . Even when concrete questions regarding Japan are being considered, they are based on the general line of foreign policy adapted for the party and government.*

The basic strategy of Soviet foreign policy seems to be "let us do business with the United States first, leaving the others for a later stage." In Soviet foreign policy priorities, the global confrontation with the United States occupies first place. Relations with Japan are only secondary, subordinated to the primary objective of struggle with the United States. The Soviet Union seems to believe that whether or not it does a good job vis-à-vis the United States more or less determines its interactions with other countries in other regions. More concretely, to lose the battle with its major adversary, the United States, might mean that it would no longer be very useful to pursue efforts elsewhere. Conversely, if the Soviet Union were to win this major battle, it would make victory or success in other areas a lot easier, if not automatic.

Only on the basis of such a Soviet perception of the world situation and with such a foreign policy strategy can the continuance by the Soviet Union of a counterproductive policy toward Japan be explained. In short, the Soviet Union firmly believes in or expects final victory over its arch opponent, the United States, and so does not care very much in the interim about temporary losses or failures in its diplomacy toward Japan.

It should be said again, however, that Soviet strategy toward Japan is based on premises that are increasingly out of date, including the belief that military strength carries extraordinary weight in the "correlation of forces" and that the United States is the major and almost exclusive threat to Soviet interests. If the Soviet Union is to conduct a successful foreign policy toward Japan, it must undergo *inter alia* a kind of mental "re-programming," from the obsession with military strength to a more nonmilitary-oriented mentality (including economic, scientific-technological, and psychological factors). After such "mental surgery," the Soviet leaders may see the urgent need for a distinct foreign policy toward Japan—one that is not simply an extension of that toward the United States but is independent enough to be distinguished from it, and which takes full account of the specific conditions of Japanese perceptions, values, and views. This will, of course, be difficult to put into effect, and certainly cannot be done overnight.

## Recommendations

Finally, what should be done to counter the continuing accumulation of Soviet military power in the Asia-Pacific region? It is essential that efforts be made to ensure that Soviet gains in the region and elsewhere in the world achieved by military means do not materialize. To this end there is an overriding need to formulate a comprehensive regional security strategy and to coordinate this with a global one. The strategy must be implemented coherently and consistently, although with flexibility. Its major components, with which the United States, Japan, their allies and friendly states in the region will be concerned, are as follows:

1. It is essential to make an accurate assessment of Soviet military strength—neither an under- nor an overestimation. The inclination to overestimate Soviet military power must in particular be guarded against. Evidence suggests that Soviet military forces, in reality, are not as impressive as outsiders may imagine them to be. This is evident, for instance, in testimony by the pilot V. Belenko, who defected to the United States via Japan in 1976 with his MiG-25; in the two-and-a-half-hour chase by the Soviet air defense forces of the KAL passenger aircraft in the fall of 1983; and in the writings of V. Suvorov and other former Soviet officers who have defected.[9] Presumably, due to their deep-rooted inferiority complex and their belief that a tough posture with military muscle is the most effective way to generate political benefits, the Soviet Union has deliberately not made any special efforts to fill in the gap between the outside world's perception and the reality of Soviet military might—as was evident in the "missile gap" argument of the late 1950s. So long as what is actually needed to ensure our security is provided, it is unnecessary and even unwise to be intimidated by the excessive accumulation of Soviet military power. To be so is to end up playing into the hands of the Soviet Union, which is particularly interested in political benefits gained through the deliberate demonstration of military might.

2. It is essential that the Soviet Union be continually reminded that the accumulation of military power is not necessarily accompanied by an increase in political influence. Georgi A. Arbatov, director of the Institute of the United States and Canadian Studies in Moscow, recognized this axiom when he said (while clearly having in mind the growth of U.S. military forces): "It is increasingly difficult to translate military power into political influence."[10] Influential Soviet foreign policymakers must be encouraged to realize this, as it seems that only a very small minority of the *mezhdunarodniki* do so at the moment. It would be useful and effective to bring the Kremlin to understand that its coercive diplomacy, which relies heavily on the political use of military forces, is often self-defeating, particularly in the case of Japan.

3. Many foreign policy specialists assert that the most appropriate global policy to be pursued by the United States toward the Soviet Union is that of inducements for restraint and counterpressures in response to expansionist actions. This author subscribes to such a view, with the only reservation that there should not be

excessive resort to counterpressures or the stick. If the Reagan administration relies too heavily on a tough stance based on strength, it may turn out to be counterproductive. The Soviet Union, under its new leader Mikhail Gorbachev, is currently facing serious problems, difficulties, and dilemmas in almost all fields, domestic and foreign. In such circumstances, it would not be wise for the United States to drive the Soviet Union too hard or too far into a corner, since this would only help the regime appeal to Russian patriotism and to justify further sacrifices in the already low living standard of the Soviet people. Such an American policy would only enable Soviet leaders to further strengthen their military forces.

4. It is important for the United States to provide reassurance about the reliability of its commitment to the defense of the Asia-Pacific region. The Soviet SS-20 nuclear missiles stationed east of the Urals could, if launched, hit and destroy in 8 minutes or so not only Japan but most of the regional countries without posing a direct threat to the United States. Faced with such a threat, it is only natural that people in the area have become increasingly apprehensive regarding actions the United States would take in case of a Soviet nuclear attack. With the aim of at least psychologically alleviating such concerns, it is necessary to deploy *Tomahawk* or other types of cruise missiles aboard American naval ships in the area.

5. On the Japanese side, it is essential that an effort be made to increase her military strength. While a carrot-and-stick strategy toward the Soviet Union is suitable for Japan as well as for the United States in dealing with Moscow, great care should be taken lest Japan end up employing primarily or solely the easier means of accommodation with the Soviet Union (such as economic cooperation in the development of Siberia), leaving the harder means of military confrontation solely to the United States. This is especially important because many Americans still entertain suspicions that, through low spending on defense, Japan has been materially better off and more successful in competing with the U.S. economy while the United States pays for the defense of the alliance. The facts that Japan spends on defense less than 1 percent of GNP while the United States spends 6.4 percent, that Japanese pay $96 per capita for defense while Americans pay $798, appear as symbols of a refusal to bear a fair share of the security burden of the Western community.

In this light, it is extremely important for the Nakasone government to go beyond the 1 percent limit on defense spending. More concretely, Japan should make substantial improvements in such areas as air defense, antisubmarine warfare and surface naval capabilities, and in combat sustainability through increases in logistics, particularly in stocks of ammunition, spares, and fuel. In these and other fields, there is a large gap between what the Japanese government plans to do and what the Reagan administration wants it to do. Given the domestic political problems facing the Nakasone government, it would be more realistic and more productive for the United States to press the Japanese government first to reach on schedule the targets set by the Mid-term Defense Program Estimate for 1983 to 1987. There seems little point in trying to revise this program, inadequate though it is, until it has been achieved.

6. Japan faces a dilemma between U.S. expectations of a rapid increase in defense capabilities and the fears of other Asian nations of a major Japanese military buildup. In the light of their memories of Japanese militarism in the 1930s to 1940s and the "economic imperialism" of the postwar period, apprehensions among Asian nations are understandable if not justified. These nations want the United States rather than Japan to be the primary military power in the region. Though it is hard to assuage or eliminate such concerns for all time, in part because of the psychological legacy of the past, this kind of dilemma is not insurmountable, provided that U.S.-Japan defense cooperation is explained and discussed regularly and sufficiently with the concerned Asian governments. These governments regard it as natural and justifiable for Japan to be able to defend her home islands and the surrounding waters, but they strongly oppose the resurgence of a strong and militaristic Japan. Most of them have endorsed the need for Japan to assume some share of the burden with the United States of defending the sea lanes of communication, which are essential to Japan's survival as an economic power. However, they would not like to see a Japanese military presence in their own immediate waters. In other words, if these nations are assured that there is a definite and reasonable limit to the increase in Japan's military capabilities, they are unlikely to oppose heightened U.S.-Japan defense cooperation.

## Endnotes

1. *Die Welt*, January 17, 1983.
2. See *Asian Security 1981* (Tokyo: Research Institute for Peace and Security, 1981), p. 15, and *Asian Security, 1984*, pp. 203–06.
3. D. V. Petrov, *Iaponiia v mirovoi politike* (Moscow: Izdatel'stvo "Mezhdunarodye otnosheniia," 1973), pp. 39–40.

4. *Ibid*, p. 41.
5. I. I. Ivkov, "Iaponskii militarizm podnimaet golovu" [Japanese militarism rears its head], *Problemy dal'nego vostoka [Far Eastern Affairs]*, no. 3 (1978), p. 46.
6. Ivkov, p. 46.
7. D. V. Petrov, "Militarizatsiia Iaponii—ugroza miru v Aszii" [Militarization of Japan is a threat to peace in Asia]. *Problemy dal'nego vostoka*, no. 1 (1981), p. 51.
8. Yuri Bandura, "Soren wa Nihon ni nani o nozomuka?" [What does the Soviet Union want from Japan?], *Jiyu* (January 1982), p. 158.
9. See, for example, John Barron, *MiG Pilot: The Final Escape of Lieutenant Belenko* (New York: McGraw-Hill, 1980), p. 224; Viktor Suvorov, *Inside the Soviet Army* (New York: Macmillan, 1982), p. 296.
10. G. A. Arbatov, "O Sobetsko-amerikanskikh otnosheniikh" [On Soviet-American Relations], *Kommunist*, no. 3 (February 1973), p. 105.

## Chapter 7

# THEATER NUCLEAR WEAPONS AND JAPAN'S DEFENSE POLICY

*by Masataka Kosaka*

The emergence of the intermediate-range nuclear forces (INF) issue and the unremitting Soviet military buildup in the Asia-Pacific region over the past 20 years have, for perhaps the first time, posed a severe problem for the military policy of the U.S.-Japan alliance. Nuclear matters have often caused difficulties among the Atlantic allies, not the least because nuclear weapons have a strong psychological and political impact, the effects of which cannot easily be forecast. But until the mid-1980s, the Japanese public regarded such concerns as irrelevant to their security and largely ignored the unchecked Soviet military buildup, especially the new deployments of SS-20 missiles and the nuclear-capable *Backfire* bombers. The reasons were plain. Soviet nuclear weapons were largely limited to strategic purposes, and their use was regarded as a negligible possibility. The United States was the dominant power in East Asia, especially on the seas and in the air, and provided a sufficiently strong shield for its allies in the region. Friendly relations with the United States and domestic stability were thus both a necessary and sufficient condition for security. There was no need for any serious calculation of the conventional military balance, let alone the nuclear one.

Neither of these two assumptions holds true today. As technology has developed, medium- and short-range nuclear missiles have been deployed in the theater in substantial numbers. They are more readily usable than the bulky and cumbersome older "strategic" weapons, and so must be taken into account as part of the operational Soviet military presence in the region. At the same time, Soviet conventional forces have now been built up and are in a position to challenge U.S. dominance in the Asia-Pacific region. The pattern and pace of the expansion of Soviet conventional and nuclear forces has been described in earlier chapters, but it is worth summarizing here its general dimensions. Soviet ground forces have grown from less than 20 divisions in 1965 to 53 in 1985; there are now about 2,200 combat aircraft in place of 300 or so; and the Soviet Pacific fleet, once negligible in size, is now the largest of the four Soviet fleets. Since 1977, SS-20 intermediate-range nuclear missiles and *Backfire* nuclear-capable bombers have been deployed in the Far East, together with other aircraft and ships with dual capability, nuclear or conventional.

Nuclear policy presents a very delicate problem for the United States and its allies. If rash, it can destabilize the military balance and divide allies, as has been witnessed in Europe. Merely to deploy nuclear missiles to counter Soviet theater nuclear forces does not necessarily seem an effective course. This chapter, therefore, discusses the general problems that nuclear weapons bring to the alliance, and then examines the security policy of Japan to see what changes are needed and what actions are best avoided.

## The Nature of Nuclear Weapons

The present situation is paradoxical: on the one hand, there is a growing recognition that nuclear weapons are difficult, almost impossible to use; on the other hand, countries now devote massive resources to acquiring whole varieties of them, as if they mean to use them. Why is this, and what should be our attitude toward it?

The paradox is rooted in the basic characteristics of nuclear weapons. First, to wage unlimited nuclear war cannot be a rational act and, therefore, will not take place except as an act of desperation. Since atomic weapons were first detonated in 1945, specialists and laymen have never stopped discussing them, giving rise to a wide diversity of views about their effects on national security and the conduct of warfare. But the unusability of the weapons seems clear enough because their destructive power is now too great and too indiscriminate. It is meaningful in this regard that they have never been used since the end of World War II. Even when nuclear arsenals were limited and nuclear war did not threaten the end of the planet, they were not used. Now that the large numbers of nuclear weapons deployed by the United States and Soviet Union, if used, would cause serious environmental destruction, the probability of their use has further decreased. The kind of environmental destruction that would result from a large-scale nuclear war is not exactly known. Some have predicted "nuclear winter," and others "scorched earth." Either of these developments would mean destruction on a scale that would render the tens of millions of deaths that might result directly from nuclear war almost negligible.

Second, while there is a theoretical possibility of limiting nuclear war, in practice it seems quite unlikely. There has been continuous discussion of such a concept since the middle of the 1950s. Most analysts have warned that the use of tactical and theater nuclear weapons cannot be strictly limited, and that once tactical nuclear weapons are used there is no guarantee that war will not escalate beyond that level. And even a limited nuclear war could be devastating. As Alain Enthoven wrote in 1971 regarding a "limited" nuclear war in Europe:[1]

*Even under the most favorable assumptions, it appears that between 2 and 20 million Europeans would be killed, with widespread damage to the economy of the affected area and a high risk of 100 million dead if the war escalated to attacks on cities.*

Thus, the possibility of nuclear war remains. Such a war, if limited, might not lead to widespread environmental destruction; but casualties at the level of 20 million dead are not unimaginable. Limited nuclear war is not probable; but it is possible.

Third, nuclear weapons give, or are thought to give, decisive advantage if one country has a monopoly of them or has a very clear superiority. A nuclear power will not submit passively to losing in conventional war and to the sacrifice of its vital interests against a nonnuclear power. At the very least, nuclear weapons can give a veto power on vital issues.

Fourth, nuclear superiority can give the appearance that one power is stronger than the others. The question of who is ultimately the strongest, however, will not vanish. Nuclear arms may be seen as the *ultima ratio*, the ultimate weapons, but such a judgment is absurd if their use can only lead to a self-destructive doomsday. However, human beings can and do make intellectual errors; otherwise, the argument as to whether there is "parity" between the United States and the Soviet Union or whether one has "superiority" over the other would not take place. In fact, former U.S. Secretary of Defense James Schlesinger argued for the concept of "essential equivalence" as being important for symbolic purposes (despite the meaninglessness of precise numerical comparisons of nuclear weapons), in large part because strategic offensive forces have come to be seen by many—however regrettably—as important to the status and stature of a major power. Lack of perceived "equality" could become a source of serious diplomatic and military miscalculation.[2]

The psychological impact of nuclear weapons, coupled with continuous technological innovation, has stimulated the nuclear arms race. New technologies may seem to hold the promise of giving the possessing power a decisive advantage, or making limited nuclear war more practical. Simply phrased, there is a view that "the newer the weapons, the better." A balance hardly emerges or is negotiated between the nuclear powers before some new technology creates the expectation or fear of one power getting ahead of the others, at least in a certain sector of the nuclear arsenal. The new intermediate-, medium-, and short-range nuclear missiles are the latest manifestation of the arms race. With the remarkable improvement in missile accuracy, collateral damage can be minimal, making the new missiles different in effect from the tactical nuclear weapons deployed in the late 1950s and the early 1960s. Many of them have a counterforce capability and may be regarded as not having so horrendous or provocative an effect in actual use as strategic nuclear weapons.

As a result, a theoretical interest in limited nuclear war has been recently revived, with all its political implications. Many conflict scenarios involving the use of tactical or short-range "theater" nuclear weapons have been produced which appear "realistic." Nevertheless, the fundamental difficulty of limiting nuclear war has not disappeared. Once the very clear line of demarcation between nuclear and nonnuclear conflict is crossed, there is no guarantee that war will not escalate to the strategic level.

In this connection, it is worth noting that the same technologies that have produced the new intermediate-range nuclear forces— that is, precise guidance and target acquisition—have diminished and will further diminish the significance of medium- and short-range nuclear weapons. This is so because precision guidance enables conventional explosives to destroy many military targets that formerly could be dealt with only by theater nuclear weapons. This is not the case for all targets, however; some missions will still require nuclear warheads. There is a role for INF, and they will remain in the armory. Unfortunately, these new missiles are mobile and hence pose serious problems for arms control. Verification of their numbers may only be possible through the use of such heretofore unacceptable measures as on-site inspection.

The superpowers are thus doomed to the thankless tasks of dissipating considerable resources on the development and deployment of nuclear weapons and preparing for nuclear conflicts that are unlikely to come. The task of sustaining a credible nuclear deterrent force is essential, but fruitless in that the weapons (hopefully) will never be used.

## Nuclear Deterrence and Alliance Relationships

If nuclear weapons are unlikely to be used in warfare, it is also the case that their mere possession has demoralizing effects on publics at large and causes divisions among allies. Nuclear weapons have such disproportionate destructive power that their use can only be justified in the most extreme cases. There is no easy rationale for their employment, even in a just war of defense; their use would almost always be seen as immoral. If, therefore, too much weight is placed on nuclear weapons in security policy, people will become skeptical of the policy itself. Unjust means can mar the most righteous of aims. Signs of such public rejection of the legitimacy of nuclear weapons are already evident in the antinuclear movements. To justify the possible use of such weapons on the grounds that national defense is of supreme importance is to commit the intellectual error of regarding any means as justified by the end of national security.

While public demoralization may be a long-term problem, the divisive effects on an alliance relationship of nuclear policy is a more urgent one. Indeed, it has already arisen more than once, not only in America's relations with Japan, the nation with a "nuclear allergy," but with other allies of the U.S. in Europe and the Asia-Pacific region.

The role of nuclear weapons is to deter war. Their effectiveness as instruments of deterrence cannot be clearly demonstrated, however, as no one can be sure that an adversary desisted from attacking because the deterrent—nuclear or conventional— functioned, or because of other factors, or because the adversary had no intention of attacking at all. As a mirror image of this problem in logic, the Japanese people clearly appreciate their friendly relations with the United States, which instinctively make them feel secure. But they are not very enthusiastic about military cooperation with the United States. There are many reasons for this, but an important one is that it is impossible to prove that the security of Japan would have been at greater risk without it; indeed, there are those who feel that Japan is more vulnerable to military pressures from America's adversaries because of its defense cooperation with the United States.

It is also difficult to be confident about "extended deterrence," not least because it is very difficult to prove its effectiveness. Deterrence is a matter of intricate psychology. When A wants to deter action by B, it is vital how B predicts A will act under various circumstances. In a situation of mutual deterrence, this process also occurs for B; and there is no clear theoretical solution to this problem of the mutual assessment of actions by two adversaries. The question, "Will the United States act to protect Paris at the risk of sacrificing New York?" is a simple one, but the sense of doubt underlying it is a powerful political force that cannot be refuted easily.

It can safely be assumed that extraordinary determination would be required for a decision to actually use nuclear weapons, especially on behalf of allied states. Many factors contribute to making an adversary refrain from nuclear use: (1) such extreme action is very difficult to justify; (2) public opinion would be overwhelmingly against it; (3) the destructive power is too huge and too indiscriminate to have military rationality; and (4) the uncertainties about the outcome of nuclear war are too great even if one tries to limit it. These factors also make the deterrent effect of nuclear weapons against nonnuclear attacks questionable, especially if a nuclear power's vital interests are not directly affected. Obvious doubt arises once consideration is given to the circumstances and the scale of military attacks that are required for a nation to decide to resort to nuclear weapons and for the nuclear weapons to act as a deterrent.

This is the basic reason why a limited nuclear war strategy unnerves rather than assures allies. Although it is not designed as a warfighting scenario, but rather has the aim of enhancing deterrence, it generates among allies more apprehension than reassurance. Dependence on nuclear weapons gave America's allies a sense of security only when the United States had obvious nuclear superiority over the Soviet Union.[3]

In a seeming contradiction, the deterrence through nuclear weapons that is stressed by the United States tends to make its allies irresponsible security partners, for if nuclear weapons are seen as the basis for deterring conventional as well as nuclear attacks, the allies tend to lose a feeling of responsibility for their own conventional defense and become apathetic: if the United

States alone has sufficient nuclear capability for the Western alliance and nuclear weapons are the main means of defense, what other nations do does not matter very much. If the United States has the will to use nuclear weapons to defend its allies, they are safe. If not, they are vulnerable. Security policy thus degenerates into a matter of confidence among allies and a constant testing of wills between rival camps. The role of allies is reduced to that of a "trip wire."

Many have pointed to this effect of apathy and irresponsibility among allies resulting from American dependence on nuclear weapons for deterrence. As early as the beginning of the 1960s, Henry Kissinger argued that "the destructiveness and range of modern weapons have a tendency to produce both extreme nationalism and neutralism."[4] At the same time, it must be admitted that the lack of allied responsibility has caused increased dependence on U.S. nuclear weapons. Japan resisted successfully the American demand that it rearm. European NATO countries agreed at Lisbon in 1952 to build up conventional strength to the level of some 50 divisions by the end of the year, with more later, to provide a credible conventional defense, but they did not carry out this pledge.

There were good reasons for allied recalcitrance in both cases. In the early 1950s, Japan could argue that its economy had not yet recovered from World War II and that it had no resources to spend on armaments without sacrificing the standard of living of the people; rearmament might lead to a destabilization of society, a greater threat than the military forces of the Soviet Union, which at that time had little capability to project forces abroad. To the Europeans as well, social stability and the rebuilding of their economies could be considered as more fundamental to security than an increase in defense forces. By depending on American nuclear weapons and not increasing their own conventional forces, the European allies could obtain security at a lower cost and achieve greater economic growth and prosperity.

With the advent of strategic nuclear parity, however, it is no longer possible to attain the same level of security by the same method. The need to respond to this new situation is beyond doubt. But inertia persists. The greatest danger resulting from the dependence on nuclear weapons is that it weakens the determination of the Western nations. If political will is weakened enough, there is a possibility that the Soviet Union may one day think it can gamble on the United States not using nuclear weapons even if it is losing against a Soviet conventional attack. Andrei Sakharov has pointed to the possibility that the Soviet Union might resort to a conventional attack on the West on the assumption that the United States and its allies, aware of the horrible consequences of the use of nuclear weapons, would rather lose than use them.[5]

A loss of Western determination could also give the Soviet military capability a degree of political influence that might eventually result in "Finlandization" or political self-neutralization. In this connection, it is important to note that nuclear weapons have both military and political-psychological effects (indeed, probably more political and psychological than military). An important function of the deployment of the Soviet SS-20 IRBM has turned out to be one of engendering a mood of defeatism among both Europeans and Japanese. Put crudely, these weapons tend to spread the psychology of "better red than dead," and they may already have done so to some extent. It is doubtful whether the Soviet Union calculated on this before building the SS-20; but the antinuclear movements in Europe seem to have taught Soviet leaders to use the missiles primarily for their political effect. European leaders, thanks to political determination and some good fortune, have managed to withstand the pressures of their antinuclear movements; but the significant nonmilitary use of the SS-20 has been clearly demonstrated.

Indeed, it can even be argued that the Soviet threat has been primarily political, as did George Kennan in the late 1940s.[6] The Soviet Union clearly has an antipathy for the West, grown out of both historical and ideological circumstances. The Russians have lived in an insecure environment for centuries. They have been invaded by foreign countries time and again. Conversely, Russia has also had the concept of the state "as an ideological entity destined eventually to spread to the utmost limits of global expansionism of the earth,"[7] a belief in becoming the Third Rome, a concept now justified by the doctrine of Marxism-Leninism. Their sense of insecurity has made the Soviet leaders very cautious; but their Marxist orientation to history makes them patient and willing to wait until an opportunity presents itself in which to expand without risk. They thus prefer to make gains by political rather than military means, although the latter is seen as part of the former. Kennan accordingly argued that it was not Russian military power that threatened the West but Soviet political influence.

## Managing Alliance Relations

Given the nature of nuclear weapons and their psychological and political effects, it is clear that one of the central tasks of foreign and security policy is to manage alliance relationships to ensure allied unity, cooperation, and a responsible role for all the associated nations. Henry Kissinger's statement of the early 1960s is still valid:[8]

> *The most delicate problem faced by the United States in its Atlantic policy is to promote cohesion without undermining the self-confidence and the political will of its allies.*

Peacetime cooperation among allies is now needed to an extent never seen in the past for the following three reasons: first, the huge destructive power and vastly increased range and speed of modern weapons enables such forces to be used quickly and decisively. The defenses must therefore be on constant alert. Second, there is military bipolarity, in which the military capabilities of the two superpowers far exceed those of other countries. Were it not for American nuclear deterrence, the Soviet Union could threaten the rest of the world with its nuclear forces and destroy key Western military facilities. Even if conventional capability alone is taken into account, only the United States can vie with the Soviet Union. The security of the allied nations of the West thus depends on the military power of the United States.

Third, the aim of the Western alliance is deterrence, for which not only formal commitments but also more tangible guarantees are felt necessary. Deterrence is largely a psychological matter, for which purpose unity is essential. If allied cohesion is strong, the adversary will feel a greater probability that deterrence will be extended, and the allies will feel secure. For this reason, the Western allies have always endeavored to get from the United States an unequivocal commitment to their security. The NATO allies have considered that the stationing of American troops on their soil is essential to deterrence, and Japan requested the United States to maintain its military bases on its territory in the early 1950s. There has been consultation and cooperation and, in the case of Europe, an integrated command has been created.

On the other hand, tight integration of allied military forces makes the allies less independent, and perhaps less responsible. As the disparity of military power between the United States and its allies is great and will remain so, it is only natural that U.S. forces should play the primary role, with the allies assuming subsidiary roles. But such subsidiary roles can make for irresponsibility.

There is no easy way of resolving this contradiction; a combination of measures is needed. Basically, confidence is the product of overall relations within the alliance. If the allies broadly share

common goals, they can act cooperatively without losing independence. Mutually beneficial economic relations certainly contribute
to the formation of a sense of shared interests. Generally speaking,
the Western alliance has done well in its efforts. For example,
frequent summit conferences have helped to create a sense of
community as the heads of state have tried to meet the challenges
of the 1970s.

But military policy must also be planned, keeping in mind the
basic contradiction mentioned above. For example, discussion of
the circumstances in which theater nuclear weapons might be used
tends to strain allied relationships, contrary to the intention of
close defense coordination. Experience with the Multilateral Nuclear Force (MLF) in the early 1960s, and INF deployments in the
1980s, is evidence of the problems that arise due to the nature of
nuclear weapons and to the way they tend to obscure the military
roles played by individual allies.

It is necessary to clearly define allied responsibilities and to
establish a system by which these are carried out. The responsibility of the allies of the United States should be to reinforce
conventional military power. Of course, there is nothing absolute
about the division between nuclear and nonnuclear forces: conventional deterrence is meaningful only when it is buttressed by
nuclear deterrence. If it were not for U.S. theater nuclear forces in
Western Europe, the conventional forces of the NATO alliance,
however skillfully deployed and used, could easily be nullified by
nuclear strikes by SS-21, SS-22, and SS-23 missiles. In the Western Pacific region the military capabilities of America's allies could
be paralyzed by similar attacks.

But stance and stature are very important in contemporary
international relations. There is the fact that nuclear weapons have
psychological and political as well as military effects. And
"Finlandization" may be more probable than military conquest.

It must be pointed out here that the U.S. nuclear weapons give
both assurances and concerns to the allies: The allies know that
America's nuclear arsenal is the basis of their security policy. But
they are also worried about the possibility that the United States
may actually use its nuclear weapons in a way detrimental to their
interests, as was clear from the turmoil created by President
Reagan's remark about the possibility of a limited nuclear war.

The dilemma should not be resolved in a theoretical way but
pragmatically. A case in point is conflicting approaches to a declara-
tory policy of no-first-use of nuclear weapons. Such a policy may be
justified on several grounds: If the role of the allies is defined as
conventional defense and it is made clear that U.S. nuclear weap-

ons are there only to deter Soviet use of nuclear weapons, allies' responsibilities will be clear and may contribute to sounder relations within the alliance. On the other hand, it can be argued that it is in the interest of the alliance to heighten deterrence by maintaining a higher degree of uncertainty with regard to the possible use of nuclear weapons. Conversely, some assert that there are not many uncertainties anyway regarding use of nuclear weapons, and it may be a better policy in the long run to state the truth publicly. And others point out that an unambiguous no-first-use policy would upset the three major European allies, Germany most of all, because of the relative weakness of their conventional defenses. Perhaps it is counterproductive to try to resolve the above dilemma in a clear-cut way.

## Japan's "Underdeveloped" Security Policy

Japan's contemporary security policy can be described as underdeveloped, but its relatively unelaborated form has the potential for growth into a reasonable and sound defense posture within the Western alliance.

The policy is "underdeveloped" in that Japan depends on the United States for security and does not contribute to the common defense of the "Free World," as many critics have pointed out. Japan has, in fact, benefited from the special relationship with the United States in many ways, apart from the economic benefits of belonging to the GATT-IMF system of free trade and enjoying ready access to the large American market—issues that are not explored here. First of all, the United States has provided Japan, through the alliance relationship, with a "nuclear umbrella." Second, a powerful conventional military shield created by the U.S. Seventh Fleet and the Fifth Air Force has kept the seas around Japan and the airspace over the country safe. In addition, the United States is committed to cooperating with Japan in countering any localized aggression against Japan with conventional weapons. The defense policy of Japan is to have the ability to counter localized and limited aggression on its own,[9] but since the required military capability has not yet been attained, it must be said that U.S. military power continues to guarantee Japan's conventional security. As Nagai Yonosuke has put it, Japan is like a youth who has grown up but is not yet a full adult with responsibility and rights.[10]

But there are some roots in Japan's security policy that can produce a defense posture appropriate to the present world situation. These roots are the idea of comprehensive security and nondependence on U.S. nuclear weapons except for deterrence. The concept of so-called comprehensive security may be wise in two senses. The first premise of comprehensive security is that the balance of power in international politics is not constituted by military power alone, but is all-encompassing of a nation's capabilities, including economic power and cultural vitality.[11] Actually, there is a paradox in contemporary international politics in that military force—and nuclear weapons in particular—can be decisive but is seldom used, while nonmilitary means can always be used and their long-term accumulated effects may change international relations.

Such thinking is not unique to Japan. It influenced the United States after World War II as American leaders assessed the destruction of the European economy and the social insecurity caused by it. The Marshall Plan for European economic recovery was designed to correct this dangerous weakness in the East-West balance. Thus, the United States concentrated its efforts on bringing about the economic reconstruction of Europe. American military expenditures in the late 1940s were 4 percent of GNP, but before increasing its military budget the United States increased its economic aid to Europe. Marshall Plan assistance totaled close to 2 percent of GNP. In line with the same basic thinking, the United States, even while pressing for Japan's rearmament, accepted Japan's argument that for the time being Japan's contribution to the Free World lay in the reconstruction of its economy.[12] It can be argued that the United States has changed its thinking and now attaches too great a role to military force, although Soviet military spending at nearly 15 percent of GNP is the root of American concerns about the contemporary East-West military balance.

The second premise of comprehensive security is that an effective response to the Soviet challenge should be asymmetrical rather than symmetrical. The reason lies in the differences in nature between a free society and a totalitarian political system. The Soviet Union, which is basically a militarized social system, can easily increase its armed forces without further damaging its society, whereas the democratic countries can militarize only with pain and serious ill-effects. It is, therefore, unwise and, indeed, useless to try to overwhelm the Soviet Union by superior military force. A combination of adequate defense capability and other means will work better. It has been said that "the biggest deterrent to the Russians is a healthy economy in America." Though this is certainly an overstatement, inasmuch as a military component is essential to deterrence, there is no doubt that a healthy Free World economy and social system is the fundamental basis for countering the Soviet challenge.

Arms control, or avoiding dependence on U.S. nuclear weapons, constitutes an important element in Japan's security policy. Exemplifying this are the "three nonnuclear principles." The first two—not to possess and not to produce nuclear weapons—have actually become part of international law in the form of the Non-Proliferation Treaty (NPT). The third principle—not to introduce nuclear weapons—is less generally accepted and has recently been a subject of some dispute in Japan.[13] But the three are, on the whole, consistent with the principle of arms control that the nuclear balance would be stabilized if a nuclear power did not station nuclear weapons in places other than where they are clearly necessary to its own defense, and that the proliferation of nuclear weapons should be prevented. It was this thinking that led the United States to agree to withdraw nuclear weapons from Okinawa upon Japan's request in the late 1960s, at the time of the negotiation for the return of the islands to Japanese jurisdiction. Arms control has become part of the security policy of most countries, and the deployment of intermediate-range or "theater" nuclear forces has increased the need for such controls, however difficult it might be to institute them.

However, Japan should not be too proud of its position on nuclear weapons, for its policies were not created intentionally: Japan's security policy was born out of necessity and has developed through the interaction of opposing points of view. It is, in a word, an accidental product of circumstances and politics. Accordingly, many problems related to it have not been well considered. Japan's security policy was also made possible, to a large extent, by American wisdom. It was G. F. Kennan who emphasized the importance of Japan having a healthy society and a strong economy but with negligible military forces. It was John Foster Dulles who did not pressure Japan to rearm substantially. It was those who were concerned with the reversion of Okinawa who agreed to withdraw nuclear weapons from the island and paid due respect to Japan's three nonnuclear principles.

Basically, Japan's contemporary approach to its national security was made possible because the country was in the fortunate position of facing little threat from the Soviet Union in the 1950s and 1960s. In addition to Japan's insular position, the military capabilities of the Soviet Union were concentrated in the west, facing Europe, with only a part in the east. From the middle of the 1960s, Japan was further helped by the bitter confrontation between the Soviet Union and China. In such a fortunate position, Japan could take a somewhat detached and semi-utopian view about its security.

Nonetheless, Japan's security policy did acquire sound aspects. The two basic tenets of this policy must be sustained: the response to the Soviet challenge should be asymmetrical rather than symmetrical, so that Japan can utilize the economic and political strength that the Soviet Union does not possess and cannot hope to possess; and Japan should hold to its nonnuclear security policy, not depending on American nuclear weapons except for deterrence against Soviet nuclear weapons.

## The Need for Improved Conventional Defenses

The trouble with Japan's contemporary security policy is that its basically sound guidelines have not been fully implemented. This is especially problematic in view of the growing Soviet military presence in the Asia-Pacific region. An important and well-known reason for this failure to update the country's defense posture is the domestic political situation. Public opinion on foreign and security policy has been split in two from the time of the signing of the San Francisco Peace Treaty in 1951, as the Japan Socialist Party (JSP) and other elements of the opposition have been opposed to the U.S.-Japan Mutual Security Treaty. They have exerted a considerable restraint on government policy. Though clearly in the minority, the opposition is single-minded and, therefore, effective. In addition, several important and influential institutions, notably the press, are sympathetic to the opposition point of view. They have all enjoyed the symbolic power of Article 9 of the Constitution, which renounces war and the possession of a national capability to wage war.

But there is no reason for an excuse. Japan's present-day security efforts are in lamentable condition, to say the least. First, take a brief look at the efforts to achieve a comprehensive security capability. Though excellent in theory, it has actually been an excuse, even a lie, to avoid greater defense efforts. The argument for it smacks strongly of a rebuttal to demands that Japan increase its self-defense capabilities. The unstated thrust of the argument is not for an increase in economic assistance but for the prevention of an increase in military expenditure. Japan's ratio of official aid to GNP is, in fact, on the low side among the industrially advanced nations. True, official aid has been increased in recent years, but it has just passed 0.35 percent of GNP, well below the figure for many of the West European states (for the Dutch the figure in 1984 was 1.02; France, 0.77; and West Germany, 0.45; for the United States the figure was 0.23). It is unlikely that Japan's official aid will go much beyond the OECD average of 0.36 (as of 1984) any time soon, because few responsible Japanese think in such terms.

As for nondependence on U.S. nuclear weapons, Japan has simply depended on the United States for conventional defense as well. It is true that Japan has not depended on American nuclear weapons in the way that West European countries have, but this is possible because the threat from Soviet conventional forces is minimal and the U.S. Seventh Fleet has dominated the Pacific. But this situation is now changing: the Soviet Union has increasingly built up conventional ground forces, air forces, and naval strength on its Pacific Coast and in the Western Pacific. Japan should, therefore, have sufficient conventional strength if it is to avoid dependence on American nuclear weapons other than to deter Soviet nuclear weapons. But Japan has not acquired this conventional military strength.

Since the mid-1970s, there has been awareness in Japan that such defense efforts are necessary. But the will to carry them out has not been strong enough to overcome the obstacles. The first obstacle is represented by the so-called political taboos. Originally, there was a taboo against Japan maintaining any military forces. Recently, the most important taboo has been that military spending should not exceed 1 percent of GNP. The government set the 1 percent ceiling in 1976 in order to get the Defense Program Outline (DPO) approved in the face of strong opposition,[14] but the ceiling has since made the buildup of the Self-Defense Forces (SDF) very slow. The second and more recent obstacle has been the financial crisis. This difficulty emerged at just the time when most Japanese approved of the existence of the U.S.-Japan Mutual Security Treaty and the SDF, and in principle began to admit the need for Japan to assume larger defense responsibilities. The current financial stringency means that the government cannot increase most expenditures and has been forced to reduce some. In such a situation, it is difficult to increase the military budget. There is also inertia among the Japanese elites, many of whom consider that Japan should only increase its defense capability just enough so as not to worsen the U.S.-Japan relationship, since the nation's security depends on a favorable mood in this relationship.[15]

These barriers and restraints exist as political facts and cannot be ignored. Accordingly, there is a need to be realistic and proceed carefully, using resources effectively and wisely. The following points, however, embody the direction in which heightened security efforts should be made:

1. The development and maintenance of an effective surveillance system to monitor the overall behavior of Soviet forces, the movement of Soviet military aircraft, and the passing of Soviet warships through the straits. The Soviet Pacific fleet has more ships than its American counterpart, but the U.S. Navy has a far stronger attack capability. The movement of Soviet forces can be deterred and countered by the functioning of an effective early warning system.

2. Improvement of Japan's air defenses, especially so as to neutralize the threat of Soviet *Backfire* bombers, which are a serious danger to the U.S. Seventh Fleet. The Japanese government has taken a position that it will assume responsibility for the defense of two sea lanes out to a distance of 1,000 nautical miles. This cannot be done in the near future as it involves very considerable cost. Japan must begin with a task of higher priority, developing the capability to control the straits and seas near Japan, including longer-range air defenses.

3. The basic task of the SDF is to defend the homeland. To do this, it must acquire the capability to prevent the landing of enemy military forces on the home islands by using a variety of guided missiles. The focal point of Japan's defense is Hokkaido, which is near Soviet territory and is strategically important as its northern shore faces the Sea of Okhotsk. The SDF must deploy larger forces there and give them sustainability and resilience. If it is difficult to station larger forces there in peacetime, the SDF must have a realistic rapid reinforcement plan, making such preparations now as this plan requires.

4. In order to use the nation's limited defense resources effectively, integration or better coordination of the three services of the SDF is essential. In this regard, it must be noted that the Japanese command, control, and communication system is hardly sufficient to the needs of modern defense.

In addition to greater conventional military contributions by Japan, better coordination and stronger cooperation between the United States and Japan is required to face the new defense situation created by the advent of theater nuclear weapons in the Asia-Pacific region. Even though Japan does not associate itself with U.S. nuclear policy, as mentioned above, Japan does not want to find its security "decoupled" from the American nuclear deterrent. In other words, Japan wants to enjoy the benefits of the

American "nuclear umbrella" without placing its hands directly on it. It is a difficult policy position, and may be selfish to a certain extent. But it will be maintained as it has its *raison d'etre*. It follows, then, that Japan must do much more in the nonnuclear dimensions of defense so that the U.S.-Japan alliance will increase its cohesion and hence the assurance it gives to Japan's security.

In the past few years the United States and Japan have moved in the right direction in the development of defense cooperation. The establishment of "guidelines for bilateral defense cooperation" in 1978 was an important step forward. In accordance with this plan, studies on joint operations and other issues have been undertaken. In 1983 Prime Minister Nakasone pledged Japan to transfer military-related technologies to the United States. One can say that the U.S.-Japan relationship began to become an "alliance" for the first time in the early 1980s as defense cooperation acquired genuine aspects of mutuality and reciprocity. But there is still much more to be done.

## Endnotes

1. Alain C. Enthoven and K. Wayne Smith, *How Much Is Enough?* (New York: Harper & Row, 1971), p. 128.
2. James Schlesinger, *Annual Defense Report FY1976*, p. II–7.
3. Michael Howard, "Reassurance and Deterrence," *Foreign Affairs* (Winter 1982–83), Vol. 61, No. 2, pp. 309–324.
4. Henry Kissinger, "Coalition Diplomacy in a Nuclear Age," *Foreign Affairs* (July 1964), vol. 42, no. 4, pp. 525–545.
5. Andrei Sakharov, "The Danger of Thermonuclear War," *Foreign Affairs* (Summer 1983), vol. 61, no. 5, pp. 1001–1016.
6. NSC-20-2, George F. Kennan, *Memoirs 1925–1950*, p. 361.
7. Johns Lewis Gaddis, *Strategy of Containment* (London: Oxford University Press, 1982), p. 33.
8. Kissinger, "Coalition Diplomacy in a Nuclear Age, *op. cit.*"
9. The Defense Program Outline of 1976 stipulated that the military forces of Japan should be planned so as to raise the cost of aggression by acquiring the capabilities to block military invasion with "limited small-scale conventional military forces" independently.
10. Nagai Yonosuke, "A State in the Moratorium Stage," *Chūō Kōron* (January 1981).
11. The term "Comprehensive Security" became widely and publicly used in the time of the Ohira Cabinet in the late 1970s, but the philosophy itself has existed since the early 1950s. (See *Asian Security 1982*, Tokyo: Research Institute for Peace and Security, 1982.)
12. Kennan contributed to the modification of the U.S. occupation policy in

Japan through his work on the U.S. State Department Policy Planning Staff. His thoughts are reflected in NSC-13.

13. Some people interpret the third principle as prohibiting the visit of U.S. naval ships with nuclear weapons to Japanese ports. But this was not the intention of the makers of the three principles. The third principle was meant to preclude the deployment of missiles with nuclear warheads on Japanese territory without the consent of the Japanese government. Inclusion of port-calls and transits under the third principle is nonsensical from a legal point of view. It cannot be verified.

14. The architect of the outline, Michita Sakata, director general of the Defense Agency at that time, deemed it very important to have the SDF's defense efforts supported by the public. But he was against the ceiling and tried in vain to make the 1 percent "ceiling" only a "target" figure.

15. Gerald Curtis, "Japanese Security Policy and the United States," *Foreign Affairs*, Spring 1981, vol. 59, no. 4, pp. 852–874.

*Chapter 8*

# THE SOVIET MILITARY BUILDUP IN THE FAR EAST: IMPLICATIONS FOR THE SECURITY OF SOUTH KOREA

*by Young-Sun Ha*

The Soviet Union has substantially increased its military strength in Asia in a buildup that has been under way since the mid-1960s. This buildup was initially stimulated by the Sino-Soviet feud, but as relations with the United States deteriorated in the late 1970s, the pace of Moscow's military modernization efforts accelerated. As a result of this 20-year buildup, Soviet military forces in the Far East now pose a potential threat to nations in the Asia-Pacific region as well as to the United States.

It is important that there should be a balanced and objective understanding of the real meaning of the Soviet military threat in Asia. To this end, this chapter will first sum up current trends in the Soviet military buildup in the Far East—but only briefly since they are discussed in detail elsewhere.[1] Second, it will examine conflicting views on the nature of the threat. Third, major regional aims of the Soviet military expansion will be analyzed. Fourth, the impact of this buildup on the security of the Korean Peninsula will be discussed. Fifth, the South Korean response will be reviewed.

The chapter will conclude with some suggestions about a preferred way of responding to the Soviet military buildup in the region.

## The Soviet Military Buildup in the Far East

Historically, the Far East has been an important area of military concern for the Soviet Union, although it has been of second priority in relation to Europe as a theater of war. During the past two decades, Soviet forces in the Far East have been substantially expanded and improved and are now capable of large-scale offensive as well as defensive operations. The following is a brief summary of the principal aspects of recent Soviet military expansion in the region:[2]

1. Soviet ground forces east of the Urals, including those on the Sino-Soviet border, increased from 150,000 in 1965 to almost half a million men in 1985, organized into 53 divisions. Thirty-nine divisions, some 360,000 men, are in the Far East (roughly east of Lake Baykal), including a division-sized force in the Northern Territories claimed by Japan. Only about 15 percent of these forces are at Category 1 readiness (75 to 100 percent authorized wartime strength), with about 35 percent at Category 2 (50 to 75 percent), and the remaining 50 percent at Category 3 (cadre strength).

2. The Pacific fleet, the largest of the Soviet Navy's four fleets, has grown steadily since the mid-1960s from about 50 principal surface combatants to about 90 today. The 1979 assignment of the *Kiev*-class aircraft carrier *Minsk* to the Pacific fleet highlights the qualitative aspect of the improvements that have taken place, which include the addition of other major surface vessels, including a second *Kiev*-class carrier in 1984. Equally impressive have been the improvements in the Soviet submarine force in the Pacific, which now includes 15 *Delta*-class SSBNs equipped with the SS-N-8 missile (of 8,000 km range) or SS-N-18 missile (7,500 km) and 8 *Yankee*-class SSBNs armed with the SS-N-16 missile (1,600 km), in addition to some 90 attack submarines.[3]

3. The Vladivostok-based naval infantry division has increased to 9,000 troops in three regiments, with the latest infantry combat vehicles, 122 mm self-propelled cannons, and new surface-to-air SAM-8 missiles.[4]

4. Soviet Naval Aviation in the region has grown by over 50 percent since the mid-1960s, and long-range naval *Backfire B* aircraft have been deployed since 1980. The tactical aviation fixed-wing force in the Far East has also dramatically increased to well

over 2,000 combat aircraft today. There are also *Backfire* bombers with the Soviet Air Force in the region, making a total when considered with the naval aircraft of some 80 in all. Significantly, over 70 percent of the tactical aircraft are third-generation types (MiG-23, MiG-27, and SU-24) compared to less than 50 percent in 1978. In late 1983, the Soviets began to deploy MiG-31 *Foxhound* interceptors, their first interceptor with a true look-down/shoot-down capability, on Sakhalin Island.[5]

5. The Soviet Union has deployed since 1977 more than 170 SS-20 intermediate-range nuclear missiles at 15 bases in its eastern districts bordering on northeastern China, with two additional bases (18 missile launch sites) under construction in the central USSR.[6]

In sum, during the past two decades, the Soviet Union has rapidly increased its conventional and nuclear forces in the Far East. As a result, they now pose a potential threat to the security of Northeast Asia.

## The Soviet Threat: Myth and Reality

Although there is general agreement about the dimensions of contemporary Soviet military strength in the Asia-Pacific region, there are some disagreements about the nature of the threat this poses. In an interview with a Dutch journalist, Georgi A. Arbatov, the director of the Institute of United States and Canadian Studies in Moscow, commented on the "Soviet threat":[7]

> *You really have to produce an emotion if you intend to impose a dangerous and costly arms race on your nation. Only when you scare people to death will you get your hundreds of billions of dollars for "defense." And nothing will scare the public more effectively than [the argument], "the Russians are coming."*

Arbatov's statement is a typical Soviet response: Soviet government officials and journalists have repeatedly asserted the "defensive" nature of their military buildup in the Far East. On April 2, 1983, Soviet Foreign Minister Gromyko said that SS-20 nuclear missiles were being deployed in Asia to counter U.S. nuclear delivery systems in Japan, South Korea, the Indian Ocean, and the Persian Gulf. He further commented that, as these American weapons have within their range the entire Soviet Union, the Soviets have the right, for defensive purposes, to have something to counter these weapons.[8]

In an interview with a Japanese newspaper in May 1983, Viktor G. Afanas'yev, Chief Editor of *Pravda*, strongly refuted the argument of a Soviet military threat to Japan. He asserted that, as the Soviet Union is now facing many domestic and international problems, Moscow does not want its relations with Japan to deteriorate. As for nuclear weapons in the Far East, he argued, they are there to counter American nuclear expansion in Northeast Asia. He used as an example the *Enterprise* carrier battle group, armed with nuclear weapons, aircraft equipped with nuclear weapons, U.S. military forces in Japan and Korea, and the militarization of Japan.[9]

In his talk with the Japanese newspaper *Asahi Shimbun* in November 1983, Lev. N. Tokunov, Chief Editor of *Izvestia*, said:[10]

> On the pretext of a Soviet threat, the United States is planning to take various actions in Northeast Asia. However, there is no Soviet threat to Japan and any other countries in the region. The U.S. Pacific fleet is twice as strong as the Soviet Pacific fleet. In addition, the United States is planning to establish military predominance over the Soviet Union throughout the world.

A similar argument can be found in a February 1984 *Asahi Shimbun* interview with Ivan I. Kovalenko, Deputy Chief of the International Department of the CPSU Central Committee.[11] Acknowledging the existence of SS-20s in the Far East, he asserted, ". . . as they are deployed only for defensive purposes, they do not aim at Japan." And, he added, "They aim at U.S. nuclear weapons in the region." He further commented that, as the United States does not make serious efforts to control intermediate-range nuclear weapons in the region, the real threat is from the United States.

The American government has responded strongly on the issue. Testifying before the House Foreign Affairs Subcommittee on Asian and Pacific Affairs on October 19, 1983, James A. Kelly, Deputy Assistant Secretary of Defense for East Asian and Pacific Affairs, said:[12]

> As two results of the Soviet offensive buildup, first, Soviet military forces in the Pacific for the first time pose a significant direct threat to U.S. forces, territory and lines of communication. . . . Second, like our European allies, our Pacific friends and allies must increasingly weigh the benefits of cooperation against real risks of thereby becoming Soviet targets. At the same time, those who would aid or yield to the Soviets and their hegemony must face the risk of Brezhnev Doctrine intervention as in Afghanistan should they try to change their minds. Soviet power projection capability poses a real and growing threat.

In sum, the Soviet Union argues that its Far Eastern military buildup is mainly to counter U.S. nuclear expansion in Northeast Asia, and that as the present military balance in the region still favors the United States, the basic nature of the buildup is "defensive." The United States strongly repudiates the Soviet explanation, and instead argues that the Soviet military forces in the Asian theater are now strong enough to pose a significant direct threat to security in the region. In such a situation, it is difficult to arrive at an objective evaluation of the military balance in the region. It is likely that both superpowers have exaggerated their arguments, so that the region is faced with both myth and reality.

## Soviet Regional Objectives

In the Far East, as elsewhere, the Soviet leaders see their growing military power as a key means of accomplishing political and economic, as well as military, objectives. These military aims have to be seen against the background of the historical evolution of the military order in Northeast Asia set in a global perspective.

After the end of World War II, the United States emerged as the predominant military and economic power in the world; and in the immediate postwar era it tried to establish and maintain a world order congenial to its political and economic interests. In 1947, facing a strong Soviet challenge, the Truman administration adopted what has become known as the Truman Doctrine, which was primarily focused on political and economic containment of the Soviet Union in Europe. However, following the victory of the communist revolution in China and the explosion of the first Soviet atomic bomb in 1949, the United States began to shift away from dependence on a Eurocentric and nonmilitary containment to a remobilization of its military power for the tasks of global containment of the Soviet Union. In the midst of the Korean War, the United States stepped up its efforts to construct a global alliance system and develop its strategic forces. In Northeast Asia, both Japan and South Korea were included in its regional military alliance system in order to maintain regional order.[13]

During the 1950s and the early 1960s, with only minor changes, the United States maintained the basic structure of international military order in the region. The Soviet Union, however, faced with growing tension with China but also seeing the erosion of American predominance in Asia in the late 1960s, began to make serious efforts to expand its own military capability in the Far East. Moscow has therefore worked to achieve a military balance with and, if possible, superiority over the United States in the region; to contain China's growing strength; to neutralize the buildup of Japan's armed forces; and to give military assistance to North Korea and Vietnam. A major aim of this military expansion has been to increase Soviet political influence over the countries in the region: as Moscow's power projection capability has grown, more emphasis has been placed on the role of military forces as a political instrument.

In June 1969, Soviet President Brezhnev proposed an Asian Collective Security System for the development of an Asian political order under the leadership of the Soviet Union and for the containment of China.[14] The proposal never gained much international support. On the other hand, the United States, compensating for the decline of its military power in the region, endeavored to develop an American-led political order in Northeast Asia with the help of Japan and China. As a result, in August 1978, Japan and China concluded their Peace and Friendship Treaty, and in January 1979 the United States established normal diplomatic relations with China. The Soviet Union continued to reinforce its military strength in the region as a political warning against closer relations among the United States, Japan, and China.

The buildup of Soviet military forces in the Far East is also related to the growing economic importance of the region. The development of Siberian resources has assumed increasing significance for the growth of the Soviet economy in recent years, both as a source of raw materials and of exports.

## The Impact on the Korean Peninsula

The Soviet military buildup has emerged as one of the most important factors influencing the stability of Northeast Asia and the security of the Korean Peninsula. During the past two decades, there has been an intense arms race on the peninsula. As shown in Table 8–1, North Korea has strengthened its already significant military capabilities, doubling its army to the level of 700,000 to 800,000 men and more than doubling its inventory of major ground force weapons systems.[15] In particular, a force of more than 20 brigades of ranger/commandos and other special operation forces trains intensively and would become the vanguard of an attack across the Demilitarized Zone (DMZ) as it was landed by sea and air deep into the rear areas of South Korea. The North Korean Air Force has further increased its numerical superiority over the ROK (Republic of Korea) Air Force, with the addition of between

**Table 8–1 The Military Balance on the Korean Peninsula**

| | North Korea | | South Korea | |
|---|---|---|---|---|
| | *1975* | *1984* | *1975* | *1984* |
| Army | 410,000<br>1 tank division<br>3 motorized divisions<br>20 inf. divisions<br>3 independ. inf. dvs.<br>3 SAM brigades<br>1,130 tanks | 700,000<br>2 arm. divisions<br>3 motorized inf. divs.<br>34 inf. divisions<br>5 arm. brigades<br>9 inf. brigades<br>Spec. Forces (100,000)<br>2 indep. tank regiments<br>120 art. battalions<br>82 rocket battalions<br>6 SSM battalions<br>5 river crossing regiments (13 bns.)<br>2,825 tanks | 560,000<br>23 inf. divisions<br>2 arm. brigades<br>40 art. battalions<br>1 SSM battalion<br>2 SAM battalions<br>1,000 tanks | 540,000<br>2 mech. inf. divisions<br>20 infantry divisions<br>4 airborne brigades<br>2 spec. force brigades<br>2 anti-aircraft artillery brigades<br>2 SSM battalions<br>2 SAM brigades<br>1 army aviation brigade<br>1,200 tanks |
| Navy | 17,000<br>8 submarines<br>15 sub. chasers<br>18 fast patr. boats<br>54 mtr. gunboats<br>90 torpedo boats | 33,500<br>21 submarines<br>4 *Najin* frigates<br>24 ex-Sov. fast attack craft<br>33 lrg. patrol craft<br>107 landing craft | 40,000 incl. marines<br>7 destroyers<br>9 destroyer escorts<br>15 coastal escorts<br>22 patrol boats<br>10 coastal minesweepers<br>20 landing ships<br>60 amphibious craft | 49,000 incl. marines<br>11 ex-U.S. destroyers<br>8 frigates<br>3 ex-U.S. corvettes<br>8 fast attack craft<br>23 lrg. patrol craft<br>4 coastal patrol craft<br>8 coastal minesweepers,<br>1 minesweeping boat<br>33 ex-U.S. landing ships<br>22 S-2A/F ASW ac |

**Table 8–1** (continued)

|  | North Korea | | South Korea | |
| --- | --- | --- | --- | --- |
|  | 1975 | 1984 | 1975 | 1984 |
| Air Force | 40,000 | 51,000 | 25,000 | 33,000 |
|  | 588 combat aircraft | 740 combat aircraft | 216 combat aircraft | 440 combat aircraft |
|  | 70 Il-28 | 70 Il-28 | 36 F-4C/D | 260 F-5A/B/E |
|  | 28 Su-7 | 20 Su-7 | 100 F-86F | 70 F-86F |
|  | 300 MiG-15/-17 | 290 MiG-15/-17 | 70 F-5A | 72 F-4D/E |
|  | 150 MiG-21 | 160 MiG-21 | 10 RF-5A | 24 OV-10G |
|  | 40 MiG-19 | 200 MiG-19 |  | 10 RF-5A |
|  |  |  |  | 20 S-2A |
|  |  |  |  |  |
| Population | 16.5 mn. | 19.6 mn. | 36.7 mn. | 41.6 mn. |
| GNP | $10.1 bn. | $19.1 bn. (1983) | $28.0 bn. | $76.6 bn. (1983) |
| Military Expenditure | $1.24 bn. | $2.0 bn. (1984) | $1.33 bn. | $4.3 bn. (1984) |

*Sources:* The International Institute for Strategic Studies, *The Military Balance,* 1975-1976 and 1984-1985; U.S. ACDA, *World Military Expenditures and Arms Transfers 1970-1979.*

25 and 50 F-7 fighters (Chinese-built copies of the MiG-21), bringing its total inventory of fighters and bombers to well over 700. The North Korean Navy has a highly versatile force of over 500 combatant vessels, and continues to strengthen its capability for interdicting shipping and offensive minelaying in the approaches to South Korean ports.

In parallel with North Korea's military buildup, South Korea has made serious efforts at modernizing its military forces with its first (1976–1981) and second (1982–1986) Force Improvement Plans.[16] In 1984, the South Korean defense budget was set at $4.4 billion, equal to some 6 percent of GNP and 33.2 percent of the national budget.

In addition, U.S. forces in Korea have been recently strengthened in accordance with President Reagan's program to restore American military strength in the Pacific.[17] First, the 2nd Infantry Division has received new long-range artillery, including 155 mm howitzers, new *Cobra* helicopters armed with antitank missiles, *Stinger* SAMs and M-60 tanks. Second, the U.S. Air Force (USAF) in Korea has undergone significant improvement with the assignment of 48 F-16 fighters and 18 A-10A antitank aircraft, as well as the replacement of F-4D with 36 F-4E fighters.

The United States has also strengthened its naval and air forces in Northeast Asia and the Pacific. The Pacific fleet improvements include the *Nimitz*-class carrier *Carl Vinson*, *Perry*-class guided-missile frigates, more *Los Angeles*-class nuclear-powered attack submarines (SSNs), and *Spruance*-class destroyers. Two *Trident* ballistic-missile submarines (SSBNs) are now operational, as is the battleship *New Jersey*, which has been fitted with cruise missiles. F-14s have replaced many F-4s on the carriers. The USAF B-52 squadron based on Guam has been reequipped with more modern B-52Gs that are capable of carrying nuclear weapons and short-range attack missiles (SRAMs). In Japan, USAF F-4s have been replaced with F-15s, and some 48 F-16 fighters are to be deployed at Misawa Air Base in northern Japan over a four-year period beginning in 1985.[18]

Both superpowers have thus substantially improved the quantity and quality of their military forces in the region. In the short term, as Figure 8–1 shows, these efforts have probably contributed to the maintenance of a military balance in Northeast Asia. However, in the long term, a continuing arms race between the United States and the Soviet Union in Northeast Asia potentially risks a strategic deterioration which might lead to the disruption of the precarious military balance on the Korean Peninsula. Since the Soviet Union has a nuclear balance with the United States and

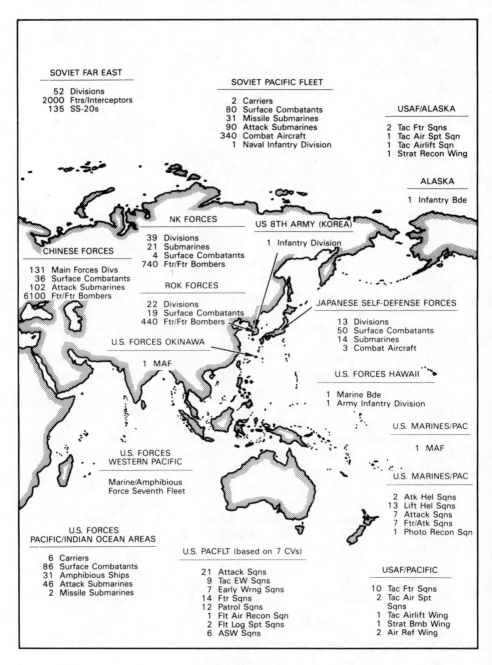

**SOVIET FAR EAST**

  52 Divisions
2000 Ftrs/Interceptors
 135 SS-20s

**SOVIET PACIFIC FLEET**

  2 Carriers
 80 Surface Combatants
 31 Missile Submarines
 90 Attack Submarines
340 Combat Aircraft
  1 Naval Infantry Division

**USAF/ALASKA**

2 Tac Ftr Sqns
1 Tac Air Spt Sqn
1 Tac Airlift Sqn
1 Strat Recon Wing

**ALASKA**

1 Infantry Bde

**NK FORCES**

 39 Divisions
 21 Submarines
  4 Surface Combatants
740 Ftr/Ftr Bombers

**US 8TH ARMY (KOREA)**

1 Infantry Division

**CHINESE FORCES**

 131 Main Forces Divs
  36 Surface Combatants
 102 Attack Submarines
6100 Ftr/Ftr Bombers

**ROK FORCES**

 22 Divisions
 19 Surface Combatants
440 Ftr/Ftr Bombers

**JAPANESE SELF-DEFENSE FORCES**

13 Divisions
50 Surface Combatants
14 Submarines
 3 Combat Aircraft

**U.S. FORCES OKINAWA**

1 MAF

**U.S. FORCES HAWAII**

1 Marine Bde
1 Army Infantry Division

**U.S. MARINES/PAC**

1 MAF

**U.S. FORCES WESTERN PACIFIC**

Marine/Amphibious
Force Seventh Fleet

**U.S. MARINES/PAC**

 2 Atk Hel Sqns
13 Lift Hel Sqns
 7 Attack Sqns
 7 Ftr/Atk Sqns
 1 Photo Recon Sqn

**U.S. FORCES PACIFIC/INDIAN OCEAN AREAS**

 6 Carriers
86 Surface Combatants
31 Amphibious Ships
46 Attack Submarines
 2 Missile Submarines

**U.S. PACFLT (based on 7 CVs)**

21 Attack Sqns
 9 Tac EW Sqns
 7 Early Wrng Sqns
14 Ftr Sqns
12 Patrol Sqns
 1 Flt Air Recon Sqn
 2 Flt Log Spt Sqns
 6 ASW Sqns

**USAF/PACIFIC**

10 Tac Ftr Sqns
 2 Tac Air Spt
   Sqns
 1 Tac Airlift Wing
 1 Strat Bmb Wing
 2 Air Ref Wing

**Figure 8–1   The Military Balance in Northeast Asia**

enough active conventional forces and reserves to mount simultaneous campaigns in more than one theater, it can conduct a more aggressive strategy for conventional conflicts. The Reagan administration, to counter Soviet "flexible aggression" capabilities, has adopted a "simultaneous and multitheater retaliation" strategy instead of a "one-and-a-half wars" strategy.[19] Under these circumstances, both superpowers can more easily raise the threshold of provocation, increasing the repertoire of moves open to them in a crisis. This has a destabilizing effect on the security of lesser powers in the theater. As compared with Western Europe and the Middle East, the Northeast Asia theater—including the Korean Peninsula, which is strategically less important for the United States than these other theaters—runs the risk of becoming the victim of superpower aggressive strategies involving conventional conflicts.

## The South Korean Response

In the midst of the improving Soviet military posture in the Far East, the South Korean government has pursued a dual-track policy of maintaining formally hostile relations with the Soviet Union while quietly promoting conciliatory relations with the same country and with China.

In contrast to the prompt Japanese reaction to Soviet Foreign Minister Gromyko's statement on the deployment of SS-20s in Asia that was noted earlier, the South Korean government did not respond to the statement immediately. On April 15, 1983, testifying before a plenary session of the National Assembly, Minister of Foreign Affairs Lee Bum-suk commented on the issue:[20]

> The Soviet Union has rapidly increased its military forces in the Far East since the early 1970s. The USSR now deploys about one-third of its military forces in the Far East including 108 SS-20s, and Backfire bombers. With a range of 5,000 km, the SS-20 is now posing a threat to South Korea as well as to Southeast Asia. The government is now coping with nuclear issues such as the INF talks in close cooperation with the United States.

On November 9, 1984, Lee Won-kyung, Minister of Foreign Affairs, testified before the National Assembly Foreign Affairs Committee that, as the Soviet Union's deployment of SS-20s in the Far East was a serious threat to the security of South Korea, the government was now carefully watching responses by Japan and China, two countries directly threatened by the SS-20s, and was dealing with the issue in cooperation with the United States.[21] In addition, during a conversation at the Blue House with General John Vessey, Jr., Chairman of the U.S. Joint Chiefs of Staff, President Chun stressed that the communist military buildup on and around the Korean Peninsula was a serious threat to the security of the United States and Japan as well as to that of the ROK.[22] He further said that closer cooperation between South Korea, the United States, and Japan was required to check communist expansion in Northeast Asia.

In parallel with its hostile response to the Soviet military buildup in the region, the South Korean government has nonetheless tried to establish friendly relations with Moscow. On June 29, 1983, outlining the foreign policy objectives "for an advanced Korea" at the National Defense College, Foreign Minister Lee Bum-suk said South Korea needs to maintain friendly relations with the communist superpowers to secure peace on the Korean Peninsula. He further stated that the Republic of Korea would pursue a *Nordpolitik* to "normalize relations with the Soviet Union and Mainland China."[23] Shortly after the Soviet attack on a Korean civilian airliner on September 1, 1983, and the North Korean terrorist attack in Burma on South Korean cabinet ministers and officials in the following month, Foreign Minister Lee Won-kyung reaffirmed that the government has no plan to change its open-door foreign policy toward the major Communist countries. He further added that the open-door policy, including *Nordpolitik*, should be carried out from a longer-term perspective.[24]

## Conclusions

The preceding analysis shows that the Soviet Union's military forces in the Far East have been substantially strengthened and now pose a potential threat to the security and peace of Northeast Asia. Although there are conflicting views on the nature of the threat posed by Soviet military power in the region, it is likely that Moscow has built up its military strength in Asia for the purpose of developing a framework of regional order in which the Soviet Union rather than the United States is the predominant power. For the security and peace of South Korea, the Soviet buildup is likely to have a destabilizing effect by intensifying the arms race with the United States. In response, South Korea has pursued its dual-track policy of traditionally hostile relations combined with conciliatory gestures toward the Soviet Union.

These South Korean efforts have not been sufficient to date to decrease the Soviet threat to the peninsula. What is needed in addition is a more sophisticated politico-military response by the United States to the Soviet military buildup in the region— something that would reinforce China's presently more accommodating posture toward Moscow. For this purpose, first of all, the Reagan administration should give greater emphasis to political responses to the Soviet threat. Without an improvement in diplomatic relations between the two superpowers, the present nuclear arms race in the region is unlikely to be restrained. At the same time, the United States has to maintain in a nonprovocative manner the strategic balance with the Soviet Union in the region to establish a framework for political solutions to issues of peace and security in Northeast Asia.

## Endnotes

1. See, in particular, Chapter 3 by Harry Gelman, Chapter 4 by J. J. Martin, and Chapter 5 by Yao Wenbin.
2. U.S. Department of Defense, *Soviet Military Power 1984* (Washington, D.C.: U.S. Government Printing Office, 1984); *Asian Security 1979–1984* (Tokyo: Research Institute for Peace and Security, 1979–1984); James A. Kelly, "Soviet Asian Forces, A World Threat," statement prepared for delivery to the House Foreign Affairs Subcommittees on Asian and Pacific Affairs, and Europe and the Middle East, October 19, 1983.
3. *The Military Balance 1984–85* (London: International Institute for Strategic Studies, 1984).
4. *Sankei Shimbun,* January 11, 1984.
5. *Defense of Japan 1984* (Tokyo: Japan Times, Ltd., 1984), pp. 31–32; *Sankei Shimbun,* December 10, 1983.
6. *Soviet Military Power 1984,* p. 5.
7. Georgi A. Arbatov and Willem Oltmans, *The Soviet Viewpoint* (New York: Dodd, Mead & Company, 1983), p. 107.
8. *Asahi Shimbun,* April 3, 1983; *International Herald Tribune,* April 4, 1983.
9. *Asahi Shimbun,* May 11, 1983.
10. *Asahi Shimbun,* November 13, 1983.
11. *Asahi Shimbun,* February 5, 1983.
12. Kelly, "Soviet Asian Forces, A World Threat," pp. 6–7.
13. Samuel P. Huntington, *The Common Defense: Strategic Programs in National Politics* (New York: Columbia University Press, 1961), pp. 47–64; George Modelski, "United States Alliances: Obsolescence of the 'Korean' System?" *World Affairs,* vol. 139, no. 2 (Fall 1976), pp. 75–86; Robert Jervis, "The Impact of the Korean War on the Cold War," *Journal of Conflict Resolution,* vol. 24, no. 4 (December 1980), pp. 563–92.
14. *Asian Security 1981,* pp. 38–40.

15. Robert W. Sennewald, "General Sennewald's Statement to the House Armed Services Committee," *U.S. Policy Series No. 4* (Seoul: USIS, April 1983), pp. 11–12.

16. *Ibid.*, pp. 15–16; Richard P. Cassidy, *Arms Transfer and Security Assistance to the Korean Peninsula 1945–1980: Impact and Implications*, Unpublished M.A. Thesis, U.S. Naval Postgraduate School, Monterey, California (1980), pp. 118–24.

17. Sennewald, "General Sennewald's Statement to the House Armed Services Committee," p. 15; The International Institute for Strategic Studies, *The Military Balance 1984–1985* (London: IISS, 1984); *Asian Security 1984*, p. 33.

18. Kelly, "Soviet Asian Forces, A World Threat," p. 9; *Asian Security 1984*, pp. 32–34; *Asian Security 1983*, p. 240.

19. U.S. Department of Defense, *Annual Report to the Congress Fiscal Year 1983*, pp. I/15–I/17; *Fiscal Year 1984*, pp. 35–36; *Fiscal Year 1985*, pp. 37–38.

20. *Chosun Ilbo*, April 16, 1983.

21. *Chosun Ilbo*, November 10, 1984.

22. *Korea Herald*, November 24, 1983.

23. *Korea Herald*, June 30, 1983; On the history of the *Nordpolitik*, see Sung-joo Han, "South Korean Policy Toward the Soviet Union," in Sung-joo Han (ed.), *Soviet Policy in Asia: Expansion or Accommodation?* (Seoul: Panmun Book Company, Ltd., 1980), pp. 315–37.

24. *Korea Herald*, October 27, 1984.

*Chapter 9*

# ANZAC* PERSPECTIVES
# ON SOVIET POWER
# IN THE PACIFIC

*by Tom Millar*

## Australian Views on Regional Security

There is a long history to Australian fears of attack from the country now called the Union of Soviet Socialist Republics. The war on the Crimean Peninsula in 1854–1856 between Britain and France, on the one hand, and Russia on the other, aroused considerable apprehension in the Australian colonies, especially in New South Wales and Victoria. Gold had recently been discovered in considerable quantity, bringing a rush of immigrants and a sense of vulnerable affluence. What would be more natural than to assume that Russia, with its Pacific fleet and engaged in a war against England, would attack the latter's remote, rich colonies?! The colonial governments accordingly constructed port defenses, enlisted volunteers, and in Victoria's case, raised a small navy. These actions were based on misunderstandings by colonial politicians who viewed the world through European images, but they consti-

---

*The term "ANZAC," an acronyn for the Australia-New Zealand Army Corps, originally referred to the joint military force sent to Gallipoli in World War I. In common usage, ANZAC is either a noun or an adjective applicable to the two countries. The term is not meant to imply that the two peoples have identical perspectives or that the two governments have identical policies, which they do not; but they share a high degree of commonality in many areas.

tuted the first moves toward self-defense and may have hastened the British decision to withdraw garrison troops, completed in 1870. The Australian colonies continued to follow, with a sense of direct interest and occasional alarm, the vicissitudes of Anglo-Russian relations during the rest of the century.

Fifty years after the Crimean War, more sophisticated Australian politicians viewed another conflict—that between Russia and Japan—with less immediate but greater long-term apprehension. In December 1901, the newly federated Australia, united but still colonial in many of its attitudes, had already passed restrictive immigration legislation designed primarily to keep skilled Japanese out of the continent. Asian Japan's defeat of European Russia, narrow though the margin of victory was eventually shown to have been, sent shock waves throughout the white empires with possessions in the Pacific, including the United States. Australian Prime Minister Alfred Deakin, showing in this, as in other matters, more prescience than most of his compatriots, sought reassurance from the United States. He arranged for Theodore Roosevelt's "Great White Fleet" to visit Australian ports in 1908, which it did to unparalleled scenes of national euphoria. Deakin's further attempt to establish a Monroe Doctrine for the Pacific was less successful, but it anticipated by 30 years the alliance of World War II and by 40 years the 1951 ANZUS (Australia-New Zealand-United States) defense pact, on which the two antipodean partners have based their security for a third of a century.

Security against what, or whom? Percy Spender, the Australian Foreign Minister in the 1949 conservative (Liberal and Country Parties) government of Robert Menzies, took the initiative in the 1950 negotiations with John Foster Dulles that led to the formation of ANZUS. His vehement concern was to protect Australia against a Japan that would be entitled, under the forthcoming peace treaty, to rearm—albeit in what was called "self-defense." Fear of a rearmed Japan was the leverage Spender successfully used to get the United States to underwrite Australian security. Formation of ANZUS, as a way of ensuring Australian agreement to a peace treaty with Japan, was rational to an American administration reluctant to go on paying for Japan's security while fighting a war in Korea. It was also desirable to an Australian electorate with bitter memories of the Pacific war against imperial Japan. Yet, Spender was, in fact, far more exercised by the growth of communist power in Europe and Asia as well as within the trade union movement in Australia. The Menzies government and many other Australians concurred with Western views that there was an international communist conspiracy based in Moscow, intent on taking over the world and well on the way to doing so. The new conservative (National) government in New Zealand shared these fears, which were reinforced by the anti-Soviet policies of its old imperial partner (Britain) and its new American ally, as well as by the confidential information on security issues these two governments provided. Australia and New Zealand became part of the Western alliance system, established and still retained as the bulwark against Soviet military expansionism. In Australia, particularly, the perceptions of that expansionism played on the historic sense of vulnerability. Partnership in the alliance reinforced the ingrained sense of dependence on what Menzies called "great and powerful (or, on other occasions 'powerful and willing') friends."

Fear of its vulnerability and assertion of its dependence remain the foundations of Australian foreign and defense policies, but the superstructure has been adjusted to changing patterns of perceived power in the region: the exaggerated sense of the rise and decline first of Indonesia and then of China and Vietnam as "threats" to Australian security. Throughout the entire post–World War II period, however, the one continuum of danger has been the Soviet Union as inspirer of communist activity at all levels, as an ally of China (the Sino-Soviet split took a long time to become visible to Australian politicians), and supplier of Indonesia's and Vietnam's military materiel. An Australian foreign minister in the late 1960s who declared that Australia should not panic at the sight of Russian ships in the Indian Ocean—a not unreasonable proposition—lost his seat at the subsequent election and thus his cabinet post. In New Zealand, with some exceptions, the Soviet threat—indeed, all discussion of external danger—has tended to be played in lower key.

Conservative parties have held power in Australia for all but 7 of the 37 years since the communist takeover of China. They have committed the country to anti-communist conflicts in Korea, Malaya, Malaysia, and Vietnam. The Whitlam (Labor) government of 1972 to 1975 shifted the emphasis of Australian foreign policy. It recognized the People's Republic of China, the German Democratic Republic, the Democratic People's Republic of Korea, and the Socialist Republic of Vietnam. It also acknowledged Soviet sovereignty over the Baltic states. None of these actions, nor a general soft-pedaling of anti-Soviet propaganda, however, earned it any credit in Moscow, partly because of Whitlam's euphoric acceptance of Mao Zedong's China on Mao's terms. The Fraser conservative government of 1975 to 1983 withdrew recognition of Soviet authority in the Baltic states and condemned assertive Soviet policies, especially the invasion of Afghanistan in December

1979. The government discouraged but did not prevent Australian athletes from taking part in the 1980 Olympic Games in Moscow. It imposed constraints on cultural exchanges and on Soviet cruise ships operating from Australian ports, but trade continued without interruption or hindrance. The cultural exchange and ship bans were eliminated by the Hawke Labor government, in office since 1983, but in all other significant respects that government has sustained the foreign policies of its conservative predecessors.

In 1980–1981, the Australian Parliament's Joint Committee on Foreign Affairs and Defence produced an assessment of the threats to Australia's security.[1] It classified the threats under four headings: (1) the potential for global conflict and its implications for Australia; (2) an invasion of Australia; (3) intermediate-level threats to Australian interests; and (4) low-level contingencies. It considered the Soviet Union in each of these categories. The committee's report, representing a consensus among all parliamentary parties, declared that conventional war between the superpowers was unlikely, because of the probability that it could escalate into nuclear war, and that "on rational calculations nuclear war between the superpowers should be regarded as an unlikely eventuality, given the immense devastation engendered in such a conflict which would negate any conceivable benefit to the belligerents." The report states that Australia's security depends substantially on the global balance between the United States and the USSR and their allies, and any breakdown in that balance would seriously affect Australia. In any global nuclear war, American defense facilities in Australia—especially those at North West Cape, Pine Gap, and Nurrungar[2]—would probably be on the list of Soviet missile targets. However, the committee tended to sympathize with the view of successive Australian governments that the existence of these facilities enhances the capacity of the United States to deter or, if necessary, to engage in a nuclear war.

In a conventional conflict associated with a general war, "Australia's geographical position is such that it is unlikely to become automatically or immediately involved." Only the United States (with no motive) would be *capable* of invading Australia without a large buildup in the area. The Soviet Union would require new bases in Southeast Asia to launch such an invasion. As to intermediate-level threats, the USSR *could* project military power to a distant country, as it had shown itself to be capable of doing in Angola, but it would find an opposed landing—as would be the case in Australia—much more difficult to conduct successfully. The committee concluded that "reassurance as to Australia's security is available only so long as the perilous balance between the super-powers is maintained or alternatively their armaments dismantled, and also so long as we in Australia continue to play our part in contributing to the Western alliance and improving our own self-reliance within our region."

This was a bipartisan assessment during the reign of a conservative parties coalition, but it remains the basic premise of the present Labor government. The Labor Party includes a far-left element missing from the Liberal or National parties and, accordingly, Labor Party leaders have to make occasional gestures or even concessions to the left. It engages in much less anti-Soviet rhetoric, and is liable to kick the United States in the shins or spit in its eye from time to time to demonstrate its independent antipodean and socialist virility. The Whitlam government (1972 to 1975) renegotiated—with much huffing and puffing—the agreement over the North West Cape facility. Cosmetic changes resulted. An Australian was appointed titular joint commander of the site, and flag heights were equalized. On the other hand, Australia was still not given (as it could not be) any control over the messages passed to SSNs and SSBNs that conceivably could initiate a nuclear war; and it now paid hard cash for access by its navy to this facility, which it had used for free the previous 12 years. The Hawke government, not to be outdone, has reviewed the ANZUS treaty, yet to even less noticeable effect. Some years earlier, Hawke, when president of the Australian Council of Trade Unions, had had his fingers burned while trying to negotiate, on behalf of Israel, the release of Jewish would-be emigrants from the USSR, and was under no illusions about the nature of the Soviet system and the strength of its military power.

Although less deferential to the United States and more concerned with preserving Australian sovereign rights, Labor governments—under both Whitlam and Hawke—have taken the view of their conservative counterparts that the facilities at North West Cape, Pine Gap, and Nurrungar, contribute to the American deterrent against a Soviet nuclear first strike: the first by providing more assured retaliation through more accurate signals; the last two by providing intelligence regarding Soviet preparations for and execution of missile launches. Thus, while both conservative and Labor governments appreciate that the existence of the facilities makes them likely targets in the event of a nuclear war—a point that Labor, in opposition, took pains to publicize and in government had to live with—they also have taken the view that the facilities help to make nuclear war less likely. The facilities (or "bases" as they are commonly and incorrectly referred to) are, of course, only part of a much wider network of defense and other relationships linking Australia and the United States.

## New Zealand Security Perspectives

New Zealand has nothing comparable in the way of American defense facilities. Some years ago the United States sought to erect an Omega navigation station in New Zealand, but it ran into such political opposition that the attempt was abandoned and the station was instead erected in Australia's southeastern state of Victoria. Even here it encountered resistance from left-wing trade unions who protested on the grounds—strenuously and probably foolishly denied by government, but not entirely without substance—that it had a defense function alongside its civil ones.

Over the years, New Zealand's strategic perceptions and policies have tended to be similar to those of Australia. In the two world wars, the Korean War, Malaya's "emergency," Malaysia's "confrontation" by Indonesia, and in Vietnam, New Zealand forces operated alongside Australia's, with joint headquarters usually under Australian command. In 1944, in reaction to being left out of the Allies' decisionmaking process for the Pacific, Australia and New Zealand proclaimed in the ANZAC (or Canberra) Pact their own charter, setting out their rights and obligations for the security of their region. The effort was a bit pretentious, and the great powers were not amused; but in subsequent regional institutions—the South Pacific Commission and the South Pacific Forum—the two powers took the leading roles. New Zealand joined in ANZUS and in the 1954 collective treaty that produced the Southeast Asia Treaty Organization (SEATO). Both countries contributed to U.N. peacekeeping in Cyprus, and to the Multinational Force and observers in the Sinai. These policies derived from a common perception of the world strategic situation and their relation to it, a largely common cultural heritage with similar political institutions and social values, and a shared sense of vulnerability. Governments of whatever persuasion in Canberra and Wellington have viewed their two countries as constituting a single strategy entity. As the present secretary of the New Zealand Defense Department has written:[3]

*Both have overlapping if not identical interests in the South Pacific, each is equally dependent for its own prosperity and development on the maintenance of stability in the wider Pacific basin, including the*

*security of lines of communications; the need to avoid being cut off
by adverse developments in Southeast Asia is equally clear to both
countries, as is the importance of a continued constructive approach
to Antarctica.*

In this statement, written before the New Zealand election of July
1984 that changed its government's policy over U.S. nuclear
vessels, Mr. McLean went on to say:[4]

*ANZUS must be weighed against the realities of each partner's
strategic preoccupations within the declared region of interest, the
Pacific. It is a regional affair. The global nuclear confrontation
between the Soviet Union and the United States of course impinges
on the issues of Pacific basin security. The matter of Soviet expansionism in the Pacific could equally be seen as being manifested in a
non-nuclear way through the development of Cam Ranh Bay as
through the installation of SS-20 missiles in East Asia. . . . There is
danger in being so mesmerised by the remote possibility of Armaged-
don as to stumble on much more real and immediate problems
beneath one's feet.*

The fact that New Zealand is "surrounded" by Australia in one
segment and by ocean everywhere else has given it not (as one
might expect) a greater but a reduced sense of vulnerability. World
War II demonstrated that Australia lay between New Zealand and
any likely source of invasion. In Korea, Malaya, Malaysia, and
Vietnam, New Zealand has been a very junior partner. New
Zealand, accordingly, has been much preoccupied with the Australian relationship and with the overall South Pacific neighbor states
and territories in ways that, especially in recent years, have given
it a degree of detachment from the Asian regional conflicts and the
global confrontation that have preoccupied Australia. It is no less
aware of the outreach of Soviet power, and has not shrunk from
what McLean calls "the larger security and defence responsibilities"; it has played its part, as the record shows. But it has done so
less fulsomely than Australia, less vociferously, less in the nature of
"follow my leader."

## Reactions to Contemporary Soviet Power in Asia

Through their direct exchanges, their partnership in ANZUS, and
from the wider Western political and economic network in which
they share, Australia and New Zealand have acquired a very
similar view of the world and its strategic relationships. New
Zealand governments are even less given to public analysis on such
issues than are Australian governments, but except for the nuclear

ship visit issue (commented on below), there is nothing to suggest a significantly different appreciation of Soviet power in the world or in the region. The Australian Foreign Minister, Bill Hayden, gave an address in Sydney in late 1984 on the topic, "The USSR: Image and Reality." He spoke of its rough nuclear parity with the United States, its superiority in conventional arms in Central Europe, and its strong blue water navy and air-lift capability, which enable it to project military power at a distance:[5]

> But while the Soviet Union has great strengths, it also suffers from great weaknesses. It spends between 12-15 per cent of its GNP for military purposes—a proportion 2-4 times as much as most NATO countries . . . Soviet leaders suffer from an exaggerated fear of being encircled, and their greatest fear is of being forced to fight simultaneously on several fronts.

The Soviet Union has not managed to achieve a decisive shift in the balance between West and East, Hayden concluded. It is an "incomplete superpower,"[6] and if power is considered in a wider sense than military strength, the USSR "cannot be regarded as a state capable of dominating the world." It has a vastly inefficient and unbalanced economy, a lagging technological base, stagnating standards of living, endemic corruption, and suffers from general social and cultural malaise. While Moscow is prepared to exploit targets of opportunity for intervention in the Third World, it has a perennial cross to bear in controlling Eastern Europe. Its invasion of Afghanistan was "a gross political miscalculation" which the Australian government condemns in the broadest possible terms. And even in military considerations, "the Soviet Union suffers from the fact that the nuclear strategic dimension of military power is something it cannot ultimately use except in the cause of its own destruction as well as ours." Mr. Hayden and his prime minister, Mr. Hawke, have pressed for the superpowers to negotiate arms control agreements, including a comprehensive test ban treaty, mutual and balanced force reductions in Europe, a continuation beyond 1985 of the provisions of the unratified SALT II Treaty, and a reduction in the nuclear weapons inventories of both sides.

Australia is concerned with three principal aspects of Soviet power in the Asia-Pacific region. The considerable Soviet military strength in its Far Eastern provinces, reported in journals such as *Asian Security* (of the Research Institute for Peace and Security in Tokyo) and *The Military Balance* (of the International Institute for Strategic Studies in London), reflects the Soviet Union's historic paranoia toward China, exacerbated by the border clashes of 1969. This has led the USSR to deploy a quarter to a third of its conventional forces in this region, with a steady improvement in the quality of their armaments, and about a third of its ICBMs, IRBMs, and SLBMs. Missiles on *Delta*-class submarines are capable of reaching the United States mainland from bastion areas within the Sea of Okhotsk. In a gesture of assertive defiance, Soviet troops have occupied the Japanese "Northern Territories," islands adjacent to Hokkaido and in dispute between the two governments.

The USSR thus has deployed to the Asian theater the capacity to virtually obliterate Japan by nuclear weapons, to eliminate the major military facilities and centers of industry and population in China, and to launch a massive conventional attack on either country if, for some almost inconceivable reason, it decided to do so. Soviet policies of intimidation and abuse toward Japan have reinforced the latter's commitment to the Western alliance system, which it supports through American bases and forces on its soil. The Soviet relationship with China, while subject to variations in temperature, is unlikely to move to anything approaching the partnership of the 1950s, so important is the United States to China's "modernization" and so inadequate is the USSR as an alternative source of capital and technology.

Thus, while neither Australia nor New Zealand has any doubts as to the formidable and increasing nature of Soviet military strength in Northeast Asia and the challenge it poses to U.S. power around the Pacific, under present circumstances they see little political support for the USSR anywhere in the region except in Vietnam and North Korea (both liabilities). There is, in contrast, a large group of anti-communist states with treaty links (the United States, Japan, the Republic of Korea, Thailand, the Philippines, Australia, and New Zealand), and a much wider, if informal, coalition of countries opposed to Soviet policies, including China and the ASEAN states. U.S. forces are still, for the most part, qualitatively superior to those of the USSR, including a submarine detection capacity reinforced by a network of acoustic devices across all the key straits between Siberia and the open ocean. It is true that the recent change in the Soviet leadership and possible policy changes in China, Japan, and the United States could produce a different strategic balance in the region, but the forces for movement in that balance are not yet apparent. As part of the process of maintaining the status quo, Australia and New Zealand (until the recent imbroglio) take part in the regular RimPac naval exercises.

Southeast Asia is a different matter. China's none-too-successful attempt to teach Vietnam the lesson that it could not rely on Soviet help in fact taught Hanoi that it needed Moscow's support in the face of Chinese pressures if it were to attain its goals in Indochina. This gave the Russians the leverage they needed to gain access to the former American naval and air bases at Cam Ranh Bay, where they have steadily moved since 1979 to improve the capacity of the bases and install a sophisticated communications and interception facility. This has significantly altered the strategic situation in the region, giving the USSR an air surveillance, interception, and antisubmarine warfare capability ranging from India to well across the Pacific, and reducing by several thousand miles the travel distance for Soviet Pacific fleet vessels to deploy from their bases in the Maritime Provinces into the Indian Ocean, the South Pacific, or Antarctic waters.

With over a third of Australia's trade going north to Southeast and East Asia, and with a further quarter passing through Pacific island territorial zones, this change represents for Australia a significant increase in its strategic vulnerability. This has prompted successive Australian foreign ministers to soften the government's attitude toward Vietnam, even at the expense of breaking solidarity with ASEAN. The Liberal Andrew Peacock withdrew recognition from the Pol Pot regime in Kampuchea, and Labor's Hayden has provided limited aid to Vietnam and engaged in a dialogue with it. The Australian objective—presumptuous, pretentious, or insignificant though it may seem to some to be—is to help wean Vietnam away from total dependence on the Soviet Union. Although Australia would like to see Vietnam withdraw from Kampuchea, it accepts, as probably the best arrangement now available, the present rough balance of forces in Indochina, where Vietnam is restrained by Chinese military pressures and ASEAN political opposition based on the Vietnamese "threat" to Thailand. It does not see any benefit to the USSR (which heavily subsidizes the Vietnamese economy and war effort) in encouraging desperately poor Vietnam to pursue more expansionist policies, or to engage itself in destabilizing activities around Southeast Asia.

The Soviet military capacity in the region is enhanced, above all, by its Vietnamese bases, which bear directly on the situation in the Philippines and the security of ASEAN and China. America's entire strategic deployment in the Western Pacific depends on its air and naval bases at Clark Field and Subic Bay. Were the United States compelled by a revolutionary change in the Philippines to withdraw from the bases, it would have no comparable basing alternatives, and the Soviet position in the area would become relatively much stronger.

## Soviet Efforts to Penetrate the South Pacific

Both Australia and New Zealand have been sensitive to Soviet activities of any kind in the South Pacific. Most of the small island state governments are conservative in approach, and during the period from 1976 to 1980 they rebuffed Soviet offers of economic aid or of compensation for fishing rights within their exclusive economic zones (EEZs). Two (Tuvalu and Kiribati) have loose security agreements with the United States. In the past few years, both Wellington and Canberra have dived hastily into their pockets to avert island acceptance of Soviet or other Eastern bloc approaches, any hint of which tends to send the two foreign offices into a flurry of anxious and generous activity. In an interesting piece of diplomacy, in 1978 New Zealand entered into the first of a series of fishing agreements with the USSR, believing itself more capable than the microstates of resisting Soviet blandishments and intelligence activities. In 1983, Vanuatu opened diplomatic relations with Cuba after attending a meeting of "nonaligned states" in New Delhi, raising media speculation about the possibility of a Soviet base there. No such basing arrangement appears in prospect, and both Australia and New Zealand have taken a relaxed view of the development—at least in public.

In 1984, the Soviet Union sought fishing rights in the EEZs of Fiji, the Solomon Islands, Kiribati, and Tuvalu, along with access to ports for fuel and provisions. In return, it offered help with maritime scientific research. All but Kiribati rejected the offer. Despite opposition in parliament, Kiribati signed such an agreement in August 1985, following a breakdown in its negotiations with the American Tunaboat Association, whose members— backed by partisan U.S. legislation—ignore national boundaries and sensitivities in their pursuit of the migratory species. The Kiribati-USSR agreement gives fishing rights (16 purse seiners for one year) but no access to land-based facilities. There is a license fee of $2.4 million in three installments, based on 10 percent of the value of the upper limit of the estimated catch. It can reasonably be assumed that Soviet motives are commercial, political (to gain influence), and strategic (including opportunities for hydrography and other military-related research), as well as aimed at obtaining rights onshore. Their efforts are unlikely to cease with the Kiribati agreement. Both Australia and New Zealand give modest help in the naval surveillance and intercept capacity within the island states' vast economic zones. Australia will continue its aid ($2.4 million per year) to Kiribati.

## Efforts to Create a South Pacific Nuclear-Free Zone

Although it may seem otherwise, there is no incongruity between the sensitivity of Australia and New Zealand to any kind of Soviet presence in the region and their attitudes to a nuclear-free zone in the region and to Russian ship visits and missile tests. For many years, both states, irrespective of the party in power, have identified with the interests and alarms of the island territories and have protested French nuclear testing in the Pacific. Not unreasonably, thay have also protested Japanese dumping of nuclear wastes in the ocean. The idea of a nuclear-free zone was promoted initially by the New Zealand Labor government in 1974–1975, with the support of Australia and the regional microstates. It was shelved under pressure from the conservative governments that were elected soon thereafter in both New Zealand and Australia, taken up again by Mr. Hawke and his Labor counterpart David Lange, and brought to agreement at a meeting of the South Pacific Forum in Rarotonga, New Zealand, on August 6, 1985.

The "Treaty of Rarotonga," as it is known, and which is open to any member of the South Pacific Forum, was signed subject to ratification by New Zealand, Australia, the Cook Islands, Fiji, Kiribati, Niue, Tuvalu, and Western Samoa. It is a mild but not wholly meaningless agreement. It does not proscribe the passage of nuclear-powered or nuclear-armed vessels; Article 2 reaffirms the rights of states under international law to exercise freedom of the seas. The parties undertake not to make, acquire, or have control over nuclear explosive devices nor to encourage their acquisition by any state (Article 3); not to supply fissionable material to any state except under International Atomic Energy Agency safeguards (Article 4); to prevent the stationing or testing of any nuclear device on its territory (Articles 5 and 6); and not to dump radioactive wastes and other radioactive matter at sea anywhere within the South Pacific Nuclear Free Zone (see Figure 9-1), nor to allow such dumping within its territorial sea. Draft protocols not yet adopted will open the treaty to acceptance by nuclear weapon states.

Some members of the forum, including New Zealand, would have preferred a stronger treaty. Some refused to sign for that reason; others either abstained or went along with the treaty because it was all that was politically achievable among the group or credible to the world at large. Its major effect is to increase pressures against the dumping of nuclear wastes at sea; but, as the

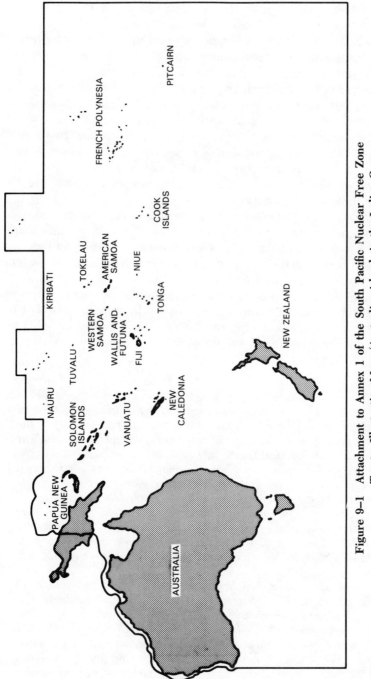

**Figure 9–1  Attachment to Annex 1 of the South Pacific Nuclear Free Zone Treaty: Illustrative Map. (Australian islands in the Indian Ocean, which are also part of the South Pacific Nuclear Free Zone, are not shown.)**

positive Soviet reaction to the treaty suggests, it may stimulate efforts elsewhere to establish nuclear-free zones.

New Zealand, of course, has gone much further than the terms of the treaty. In early 1985, under pressure from the left wing of the party, the Labor government decided to ban visits to New Zealand ports by any nuclear-powered or nuclear-armed vessels. This ban puts no new constraints on the USSR, but it does affect the United States and (more rarely) the United Kingdom, both of which strongly objected to the treaty, as did Australia (privately). The United States, demonstrably upset by the decision, has suspended most of the operations of the ANZUS treaty as they relate to New Zealand, and has under consideration much more directly damaging economic sanctions.

The New Zealand policy is based primarily on domestic considerations, including a good deal of ignorance about the difference between nuclear-armed and nuclear-powered vessels, and an uninformed fear that the presence of either in New Zealand waters would constitute a nuclear target. A majority of the electorate supports the government in excluding nuclear weapons, but an even greater majority wants the country to remain in ANZUS. Prime Minister David Lange put his case for the no-visit policy to the U.N. Conference on Disarmament in Geneva on March 5, 1985:

> *New Zealand is a fortunate country. It faces no external threat. Incursions by outside interests into the South Pacific are best met at this time not by military presence but by economic and social development and by friendly association. . . . The security of the South Pacific is neither threatened nor guaranteed by nuclear weapons. New Zealand would betray its own best interests and the interests of the region as a whole if it played any part in allowing a nuclear confrontation to develop in the region. That would be to acquiesce in the process of escalation which has brought us all already to the brink of the precipice. New Zealand has chosen to resist that process of escalation. Two factors have guided its course of action. The first is the longstanding public concern in New Zealand about nuclear weapons [notably, France's testing program].*
>
> *The second factor which allows New Zealand to exclude all nuclear weapons from its territory is the fact that New Zealand is not and never has been part of any nuclear strategy. No nuclear weapons have ever been based or stored in New Zealand. New Zealand has not assisted and does not assist in any system of nuclear defence. The ANZUS alliance . . . imposes no specific military obligations on its members. . . . Our action has not altered for one moment the balance of strategic power. . . .*

*We do not ask to be defended by the nuclear weapons we exclude and we do not ask any nuclear power to deter any enemy of New Zealand by the threatened use of nuclear weapons against that enemy. Any such proposition is simply irrelevant to the strategic circumstances of the South Pacific and to introduce it would be to submit to the compulsive competitiveness which has characterised and sustained the arms race.*

These arguments, which have wide emotional appeal among those opposed to nuclear war, beg the whole question of New Zealand's responsibilities within the Western alliance and its dependence for ultimate protection upon the United States' military capacity *including nuclear deterrence*. Lange sees his action as a small contribution to arms control. It is nothing of the sort, for the reasons he gives—New Zealand is irrelevant to the West's nuclear strategy. But New Zealand is not irrelevant to the politics of the Western alliance, and it is this consideration that he ignores and which the United States, with other allies in mind, has chosen to emphasize. The outcome seems likely to be the formal exclusion of New Zealand from ANZUS, at least until there is a change of government in Wellington. New Zealand's defiance of the U.S. has struck some responsive chords in Australia, although not so strongly as to affect policy, and must have been welcomed in the Soviet Union.

In Australia, similar potential forces have operated, though in different forms, upon the Labor government. In 1983, Prime Minister Hawke agreed to assist in the testing of U.S. MX missiles off the Tasmanian coast. He took only a few of his Cabinet colleagues into his confidence. In 1985, as the time of testing approached, the matter became public and Hawke, counting heads among his party, withdrew the offer. Australia has also not been prepared either to support the strategy or to take part officially in the research phase of President Reagan's Strategic Defense Initiative. There is an anti-U.S. element in these decisions; but, as with New Zealand, there is also an emotional feeling that the United States—especially the Reagan administration—has been altogether too combative in its approach to dealing with the USSR, too demanding of unquestioning loyalty from its allies, and too reluctant to explore the possibilities of nuclear arms reductions in a world seen to be moving steadily toward the brink of its own annihilation. Both conservative and Labor governments in Australia mask these sentiments within the pragmatism of alliance policies. Fear of the Soviet Union, or of some subsequent enemy out of Asia, is greater than the fear of nuclear war. In New Zealand, the reverse has come, briefly perhaps, but genuinely to hold the minds of a majority of voters.

## Endnotes

1. Parliament of the Commonwealth of Australia, Joint Committee on Foreign Affairs and Defence, *Threats to Australia's Security, their Nature and Probability*, Canberra, Australian Government Publishing Service, 1981.
2. The facility at North West Cape is for naval communications, especially with submerged nuclear-armed submarines in the Indian and Western Pacific Oceans. Pine Gap and Nurrungar are ground stations for satellites engaged in gathering intelligence and monitoring Soviet nuclear missile activities, and thus, in the committee's view, play a vital part in the U.S. verification program for the SALT agreements.
3. Denis McLean, "New Zealand's Strategic Position and Defence Policies," in Desmond Ball (ed.), *The ANZAC Connection* (Sydney, London and Boston: George Allen & Unwin, 1985), p. 7.
4. *Ibid.*, p. 8.
5. Address to the Australian Institute of International Affairs, Sydney, 25 October 1984, *Australian Foreign Affairs Record*, October 1984, pp. 1077–84.
6. This phrase is used by Paul Dibb in a forthcoming book on the USSR to be published by the International Institute for Strategic Studies, London.

*Part Three*

# REGIONAL CONFLICT CONTINGENCIES

*Chapter 10*

# PROSPECTS FOR A NEW KOREAN WAR: IMPLICATIONS FOR SECURITY IN NORTHEAST ASIA

*by Fuji Kamiya*

### The North Korean Enigma: Militancy or Conciliation?

Predicting what developments are likely to occur in Korea in the coming decade, or what the current signs of change in both the North and South might lead to are not easy tasks. There is, in particular, a dearth of essential information about North Korea. For example, it is unclear what intentions lay behind the terrorist assault on the South Korean leadership in Rangoon in October 1983, or the now-familiar North Korean proposal for a tripartite (North Korea-United States-South Korea) peace conference. There is no doubt that the biggest domestic political issue inside North Korea concerns the hereditary transfer of power from President Kim Il Sung to his son, Kim Jong Il; but there is not enough information available to enable outside observers to judge with confidence how this succession is being played out in the North and whether or not it is meeting hidden opposition from Communist Party or military leaders. Thus, with the northern half of the peninsula enshrouded in mystery, it is difficult to forecast with reasonable accuracy the future of one half of the complex Korean equation.

In order to assess the consequences of renewed conflict in Korea for regional security, however, we will begin by analyzing the terrorist bombing in Rangoon, where South Korean President Chun Doo Hwan narrowly escaped the violent fate of his aides when he was unexpectedly delayed on his way to a ceremony at the Burmese war memorial. Had he been killed, as the North Korean plot intended, what would have been the consequence? Two possibilities come to mind. First, the Republic of Korea (ROK) might have fallen into a state of shocked confusion, leading to a political crisis in the South. Perhaps this, more than anything else, was what the North Koreans hoped to achieve. Alternatively, the ROK might have struck back at the North immediately, under the leadership of the military; that is, the South might have launched military action in retaliation for North Korea's act of terrorism.

What did North Korea intend to do had the second possibility— an armed reprisal from the South—materialized? Had the Kim Il Sung leadership taken adequate measures beforehand to protect itself against such action? Or did they have some other alternatives to fall back on? We are, as already mentioned, too poorly informed to answer these questions properly. It is possible, however, that the North might have met South Korean military action with military force of its own, and such action and reaction might have escalated into a second all-out Korean war.

Judging from world reaction to the bombing in Burma and the recent atmosphere of the North-South dialogue that has resumed since September 1984, it is not likely that the leadership in Pyongyang will soon venture another assassination attempt like Rangoon. But then the Rangoon incident itself was something unimaginable by ordinary standards, something inconceivable to outside observers. It seems that such a possibility cannot be ruled out, in which case the danger of resulting armed conflict between North and South Korea cannot be ruled out either.

In the 1960s and 1970s, it may be said, such renewed warfare on the peninsula seemed very unlikely. In the 1980s, the possibility of such conflict seems to have increased somewhat—although not greatly. The relationship between the two Korean states seems to have become less stable than it was. When considering the future of Korea, therefore, the four major powers with interests on the peninsula—China, the Soviet Union, the United States, and Japan—should be prepared to react to the possibility of renewed armed conflict even if its likelihood is not great.

Further complicating any assessment of the plot in Rangoon is

the accompanying North Korean proposal for a tripartite conference. It is obvious that the Rangoon bombing reflected an extremely radical, militant policy aimed at physically destroying
President Chun and his government. In contrast, the North's
tripartite proposal suggests an attitude of flexibility and accommodation, for Pyongyang has until now opposed Seoul's participation
in such talks, insisting instead on bilateral negotiations between
Pyongyang and Washington.

How should the apparent contradiction between these two
attitudes—militancy and conciliation—be explained? Various interpretations are possible, especially when they are made in
conjunction with the pending transfer of power from North Korean
President Kim to his son. One is that, although the transfer of
power has been making slow but steady headway, there may be
conflicting policy lines or factions inside the North Korean leadership. This interpretation suggests that the flexible stance discernible in the tripartite proposal can essentially be identified with one
group, and the radical, aggressive approach of the terrorism in
Rangoon, with another. These two would thus appear to be at
odds. From the same viewpoint, it may be suggested that the
radical or aggressive leadership group was in the predominant
position until the Rangoon incident, but that the failure of the
attack and the unfavorable consequences of the incident for North
Korea led the flexible group to become dominant, which resulted
in the proposal for a tripartite conference and the positive attitude
toward a North-South dialogue.

In contrast, a different school of thought holds that there may
not be such a division of groups within the North Korean leadership, and that aggressive and conciliatory policies are but part of a
"dialectical" communist approach to dealing with the capitalistic
South. Pyongyang has been consistent over the years in its efforts
to divide Washington and Seoul. It has never trusted President
Chun or his regime, or regarded the authorities in Seoul as a
legitimate negotiating party. For the past four years, North Korea
has regarded Chun Doo Hwan and his colleagues as enemies to be
destroyed, as they did the Park Chun Hee government in the
years before. Therefore, it was not unreasonable in Pyongyang's
eyes—though objectively it is unjustifiable—to go to such extremes as it did in Rangoon to eliminate the Chun government.

North Korea has also insisted for years that the withdrawal of
the United Nations forces—that is American forces—from the
peninsula is a prerequisite for Korean peace and reunification.
Within the framework of this policy, Pyongyang's attitude toward
the United States has been militant at times, and at other times

relatively flexible. Pyongyang's current proposal for a tripartite peace conference may be seen as a new, flexible phase in its unremitting efforts to achieve a complete U.S. troop withdrawal from the South. The peace proposal and the terrorist plot thus can be seen as two sides of the same coin. Reading the Korean Workers' Party organ, *The Rodong Sinmun,* for example, one can find little evidence of conflict between two policy lines.

The second view just described presupposes an integrated North Korean policy toward the South that combines contradictory elements of militancy and conciliation. The idea that the aggressive and conciliatory aspects of Pyongyang's policy are not really contradictory, and that it is incorrect to assume a conflict between Kim Il Sung and Kim Jong Il or other elements within the leadership, gives much food for thought.

To sum up, the contradictory soft-hard lines seen in North Korean behavior can be interpreted in two different ways: one way sees the leadership as having "two heads"; the other way sees "two faces but one head." While the former interpretation had been widely shared, recently the latter view of a dialectical or two-faced policy has gained greater acceptance. This author's view is that although the two North Korean actions contradict each other in their methods, the underlying objective of national reunification is common to both.

## The North's Proposal for Tripartite Talks

Pyongyang's proposal for a tripartite conference can be explained as well in terms of a combination of hard and soft lines of policy. The North, as pointed out above, has been trying for years to get the United States to withdraw its forces from the South; and it has called, therefore, for direct talks with the United States. But Washington, especially the Reagan administration, has made it clear that it will not negotiate behind Seoul's back. Therefore, Pyongyang has put forward the tripartite proposal in order to meet American objections.

A proposal for tripartite talks has been made before: in June 1979, during President Carter's visit to Seoul, the United States and the ROK jointly proposed three-way talks with North Korea. However, what Pyongyang means by a tripartite conference is very different from what Washington or Seoul have had in mind. Specifically, Pyongyang proposes a conference with Washington in which Seoul's participation is subsidiary to that of the United States, which it wants to be the primary interlocutor.

North Korea has put forward the proposal three times now—twice unofficially. The first time was in October 1983, immediately before the Rangoon incident, when Chinese leaders conveyed the proposal to Washington. The second occasion was in December of that same year, when North Korea again requested China to transmit it to the United States, which was done by Premier Zhao Ziyang when he visited Washington in January 1984. China has thus been a consistent channel in conveying North Korean proposals to the United States.

Finally, on January 10, 1984, the North Korean Supreme People's Assembly and Central People's Committee held a joint session, during which they adopted a proposal for a tripartite conference, which was conveyed in a letter to the U.S. Congress, also dated January 10. There is one subtle difference in wording between Pyongyang's proposal in this letter and the proposal made directly to Seoul. The former only talks of allowing the South Korean authorities to participate in the talks between "us [North Korea] and United States," while the latter says that "The Republic of Korea should participate on an equal footing" in the proposed talks between North Korea and the United States. Both were a step forward from the old North Korean stand, which was that if Seoul participates in a Pyongyang-Washington conference, it should do so as an observer. What is notable is that Pyongyang now agrees to Seoul's participation on "an equal footing."

Even if this adjustment in position is taken at face value, there is no denying that Pyongyang still considers talks with Washington as central, with Seoul taking part as a third or subordinate party. At present, there seems to be little chance that this modified proposal will be accepted by Washington or Seoul. This is particularly true when one considers the fact that Seoul interprets Pyongyang's move as a way to improve its external relations after the unfavorable international reaction to the bombing in Rangoon. Long considered to be a doctrinaire and self-isolated society, North Korea's reputation in the world was further and seriously impaired when it brought this international disgrace upon itself. As seen from Seoul, North Korea is merely launching a false peace offensive with its calls for a tripartite meeting. In view of such deep distrust, the North Korean proposal is unlikely to lead to any important new development in the near future.

Is Pyongyang's proposal really nothing more than a false peace offensive to cover up its damaged reputation after Rangoon? Perhaps not. Perhaps it is part of a carefully formulated, deliberate foreign policy. The peace proposal may be necessitated by a change of situation in which North Korea is no longer in a stronger position relative to the South. Pyongyang may be making a concession in proposing a tripartite conference—even though the concession is not substantial enough to satisfy Seoul or Washington—for several reasons. The first may have to do with the fact that a series of events of international significance are taking place in Seoul. The Inter-Parliamentary Union (IPU) convention was held in the South Korean capital in October 1983, as was an International Monetary Fund (IMF) world convention in 1985. The Asian Games will be held in South Korea in 1986, and the Olympics will convene in Seoul in 1988. These events highlight the growing international acceptability of the ROK and the relative isolation of the North.

Another incentive for flexibility on Pyongyang's part is that relative to the South, North Korea is suffering from economic stagnation and sees the North-South economic gap steadily widening. Although economists refrain from making firm judgments about the North's economic condition due to the lack of reliable information, it is known that Pyongyang has postponed its repayment of foreign loans three times. Foreign observers generally agree that there is serious economic stagnation in the North. For example, the Japanese Ministry of Finance's *Monthly Report on International Politics and Economy* (January 1985) states that the North Korean economy "seems to be still inactive," judging from the fact that Kim Il Sung did not refer to the economic achievements of the previous year in his New Year statement in January 1984, nor to the progress of the second seven-year plan, which was to conclude at the end of 1984. Kim's silence suggests that there are increasing difficulties in meeting the plan's targets. Since the country's economic performance continued to be kept secret in 1984, one economist judges that the economy has come to a halt both financially and technologically, and that the Joint Venture Law announced on September 8, 1984 was one measure designed to help break the North out of its isolation and economic stagnation. In other words, North Korea is gradually being forced to introduce an open-door economic policy on the order of the dramatic example set by China, which is now making steady progress in its national development.

The North Korean domestic political situation provides another of the reasons for a policy of greater flexibility. At the moment, North Korea is politically unstable, due to the transition of power from President Kim Il Sung to his son Kim Jong Il. From the viewpoint of securing its authority, the Kim family's regime is in need of certain justifications for the hereditary succession. One of the possible justifications would be the need for continuity in leadership and policy in bringing about economic progress through an "open-door" approach to development, particularly if such a policy is required by economic necessity.

Pyongyang fears that it may become impossible to narrow these growing economic and international gaps between North and South unless it takes some new action now. Out of this fear came, on the one hand, the idea—a terribly erroneous one—of the Rangoon plot to throw the South into confusion, and, on the other, the more flexible approach symbolized by the tripartite proposal.

As just pointed out, such a proposal cannot be expected to be accepted immediately while such distrust of North Korean motives endures. But it cannot be said that absolutely no possibility exists for some new developments arising from Pyongyang's more conciliatory attitude.

It appears that China, which is the country with the closest relations with North Korea, has advised Pyongyang to adopt a more realistic policy. Chinese leaders may even be putting some pressure on the North to be more flexible because of their own desire to keep the neighboring area stable. China made a complete foreign policy turnaround while Mao Zedong was still alive, from a posture of antagonizing the United States and the West to a policy of normalizing relations with them. Similarly, North Korea may be able to institute a basic policy change under Kim Il Sung's leadership, for his great authority makes it easier to change long-held policies of international self-isolation and hostility toward the South and the United States. To show such flexibility might be much more difficult after Kim Jong Il takes over, for he will lack his father's power and legitimacy. Rather, the younger Kim is more likely to strengthen the militancy of North Korea's foreign policy and make the country all the more autarkic.

## South Korea: A Future Succession Crisis?

The Fifth Republic under President Chun Doo Hwan celebrated its third anniversary in March 1983. Looking back on his regime since that time, one characteristic trend can be noted: it has been highly successful in foreign relations but less so in the domestic arena.

Following his assumption of office, President Chun immediately opened a solid channel of communication with President Reagan in Washington. Together with Premier Nakasone in Tokyo, he repaired the Japan-South Korean relationship, which had been strained by the Japanese textbook issue and the Korean request for large loans from Japan. Things are now going very smoothly between Seoul and Tokyo. President Chun also visited Southeast Asia and Africa, and he was making overtures to the nonaligned camp—in part by stressing a new policy toward the North—when the Rangoon incident temporarily forced him to pull back. Nevertheless, he has eagerly sought ways of improving relations with the communist world, especially with China at official levels, while sustaining his approach to the nonaligned nations. This series of foreign policy moves has evidently brought improved world recognition for the ROK, as reflected in the choice of Seoul as the site of the 1988 Olympics. It can also be argued that the South Korean government benefits from signs of progress in the North-South dialogue; but in any event it cannot lightly dismiss North Korean proposals for improved contacts, such as the Red Cross talks, without weakening its foreign support.

In the domestic arena, in contrast, the Chun government seems to have been less successful. In the March 1981 congressional elections, the first under the regime, the ruling Democratic Justice Party (DJP) garnered 35.6 percent of the total vote. In the second congressional election, in February 1985, the DJP gained a plurality of the seats, but for the regime the outcome was far from victorious. The New Korea Democratic Party (NKDP), an opposition party created just before the elections, drew unexpectedly high support, an outcome that gained greater public attention than the fact that the DJP had sustained its predominant position.

The NKDP continued to make advances. In March 1985, it absorbed most of the members of the Democratic Korea Party (DKP), which had lost ground, to become the second opposition party—thus creating a virtual two-party system in South Korea. Moreover, the DJP vote was 35.5 percent of the total cast, while the votes for the NKDP and DKP were 28.7 percent and 19.3 percent, respectively. Since the NKDP and DKP have become practically integrated, the total vote for the main opposition exceeds that for the ruling party, and so the number of seats should be reallotted accordingly. This is the general mood of the public. Not many think that the DJP or President Chun gained confidence as a result of the election outcome.

President Chun, quite frankly, does not enjoy broad domestic political support, and something needs to be done to improve this difficult situation. A positive attitude on the part of his administration toward the North-South dialogue is said to be one of the measures under consideration to increase his popularity. It seems that domestic politics provides an incentive for progress in North-South relations for leaders in both Pyongyang and Seoul.

Under the ROK's political system, the governing party will, of course, be able to maintain a stable majority in Congress; but some measures should be taken to increase popular support. The basic problem concerns the legitimacy of the Chun regime, which is essentially the same in character as its predecessor, that of former President Park Chun Hee. The Chun regime seized power by a military coup and then maintained its authority by shedding uniforms and transferring power to a civilian government. Consider how these two leaders emerged, one in the early 1960s and the other 20 years later. From the beginning of his rule, President Park was more or less a legitimate leader in the eyes of the public; in contrast, President Chun has not elicited the same degree of popular support. There is a hidden gap here that is really very important and may not be easily overcome.

The ROK will probably continue to be troubled by public opposition and face periodic, antigovernment activities by students and other groups. Since the founding of the Fifth Republic, a number of instances of economic irregularities and corruption have come to light, including several widely reported cases implicating members of the president's own family. If such scandals continue to crop up, President Chun may find himself in an increasingly awkward position. But then, there are brighter aspects of his rule as well. Chun has been very skillful in filling important posts in his regime, which now includes few persons who might threaten any time soon his position as national leader. In the contemporary political world of South Korea, no potential successors to Chun can be seen, indicating that political stability is likely to remain fairly high for the time being.

Assuming that President Chun will use this period of stability to maintain his power, the key question becomes: Who will succeed him? Under the present constitution, a president can serve only one term of seven years. This is a fairly long tenure, even though it is limited to one term. President Chun has declared repeatedly that he will leave office after serving out his seven years and thus establish a good example of the peaceful transfer of power in a democracy.

One must recall, however, that President Park used to say the same thing but then remained in power by changing the constitution. About half the people in the South seem to feel that President Chun will not leave office after a single term, regardless of what he says now. It is true that the constitutional provision against presidential reelection is very carefully worded, so that even if it is amended by an incumbent president to permit reelection, the new rule would not apply to him, so that he would have to step down when his term expires. On the face of it, then, one may reasonably assume that the reelection of President Chun is very unlikely. Many ROK citizens, however, still have a hunch that he might resort to some procedural device to make the unlikely possible.

In the ROK, this subject of the succession is, and will remain, something close to a political taboo that cannot be readily discussed openly. Whether or not the constitutional provision is observed will have a great influence on the future of democracy in the country. If President Chun keeps his repeated public pledge and retires at the end of his term, his action may go down in history as one of his greatest achievements. If, on the other hand, Chun retracts his pledge and gets himself reelected on one excuse or another, such as the need to make a success of the 1988 Olympics in Seoul, the future of democracy in the South would be seriously threatened. This question, along with the uncertain legitimacy of the regime, needs close attention when assessing future political developments in the ROK. And stability in the South, or lack thereof, will have an important bearing on the future of relations between North and South Korea.

## The North-South Exchanges

The North made a major conciliatory move toward the South in the autumn of 1984 by offering to supply relief goods to flood-stricken areas of the ROK. And a new round of North-South talks was launched in November 1984, the fourth in the series since the "North-South Joint Communiqué" was issued on July 4, 1972.

The first round in the series was conducted by the "North-South Coordinating Committee" as created by the above-mentioned Joint Communiqué, with talks alternating between Seoul and Pyongyang. At one point, public enthusiasm for North-South reconciliation rose so high that some even expected reunification in the near future. However, as early as June 23, 1973, President Park Chung Hee's plan for simultaneous membership of the North and the South in the United Nations clashed with President Kim Il Sung's proposal for a Confederal Republic of Koryo. Using the Kim Dae Jung incident as an excuse, the North broke off talks with the Park government.

President Park's call for a North-South summit meeting on January 19, 1979, led to preliminary contacts for the second round of talks. While these contacts were characterized by the South as "administrative preliminaries," the North insisted on calling them a stepping-stone to the establishment of an "all-nation" consultative organization. Such differences in positions were reflected in the names used for each of the representatives: "Representative for the North-South Coordinating Committee" for the South; and "Representative for the Democratic Front for National Unification" for the North. After holding three unproductive sessions, this round of talks came to an end.

The third round was initiated through letters sent by North Korea to 12 prominent leaders of the South, including State Minister Shin Hyon Hwack. The letters called for reunification talks in January 1980. The South, having insisted on a high-level North-South meeting, agreed to hold only a summit meeting of the premiers of each side, and preliminary sessions were started in February 1980. These sessions, which lasted for six months, failed to produce agreement on even the agenda or the timing of a summit meeting; they ended with the tenth session on August 20.

The fourth round was started at Panmunjom on November 15, 1984, after a four-year interval, amid both domestic and international attention. The early stages of this round gave rise to some optimism, not only among foreign observers but even in the South, where public opinion is usually very skeptical about North Korean intentions. For example, one of the major papers in the South, the *Dong-a Ilbo*, suggested on November 16, 1984, that judging from the unexpectedly flexible posture of the North shown in the first round of economic talks, North Korea might be planning to establish economic ties with the South on the basis of separating economic issues from politics. It also suggested that in order to facilitate a constructive outcome from the talks, a barter trade system, which is relatively easy to arrange, should be introduced first.

North Korea may have been attempting to induce political confusion in the South by its combination of hard and soft lines in dealing with ROK authorities: it started talks and then stopped them from time to time. It postponed a second round of economic talks in late 1984, citing as justification the shooting incident at Panmunjom on November 23, in which a Soviet citizen defected across the border. On January 9, 1985, the North announced an indefinite postponement of both economic talks and Red Cross talks, using the U.S.-Korean joint military exercise *Team Spirit 1985* as an excuse. Some South Koreans, sobered by their experiences with the North, were very cautious about the future of the talks, judging that they could not be very promising if the North was ready to use *Team Spirit 1985* as an excuse for increasing tensions with the South. But in May 1985, both the economic and Red Cross talks were reopened.

There is place for both optimism and pessimism in viewing the future of North-South talks; no decisive judgment can be made at this point. The South Korean government's assessment that the proposal by the North for tripartite talks is only a tactical maneuver should not be accepted too readily; a more flexible interpretation must be kept open as well. However inflexible it may seem today, the North will be forced to change in some way in the future. When dealing with North Korea, the United States, South Korea, and the West should endeavor, by various means, to stimulate, encourage, and promote the potential for major changes in the Kim Il Sung regime. In other words, it should be their basic policy to give North Korea a significant incentive to make a substantial change for the better in its foreign policy stance and in its approach to dealing with South Korea.

## The International Environment Affecting Korea

Not much change is expected to occur in the international forces that play upon the Korean Peninsula. The four major powers with interests in the area—the United States, China, the Soviet Union, and Japan—will continue to have strong incentives to see stability maintained on the peninsula and to encourage peaceful approaches to dealing with North-South differences. The status quo best serves their interests. Any rash attempt to radically alter the North-South balance would dangerously affect prospects for peace and stability. This is why there need be relatively little anxiety about outside powers upsetting the present situation in Korea despite the unresolved tension and animosity between Pyongyang and Seoul and recent signs that the Soviet Union is increasing its military assistance to the North.

As indicated earlier, however, the expectation that there will be no major change in the international environment affecting Korea does not totally rule out internal developments that could lead to armed clashes between North and South. And if clashes should break out, the four external powers would find it difficult to avoid being drawn into the resulting turmoil. Hence, it is up to them to minimize prospects for a major shift in the military balance on the peninsula and to encourage political stability through the North-South dialogue. Because of the wide regional impact of renewed warfare in Korea, it is very important for the external powers to develop means for joint crisis management. Otherwise, they may be dragged into trouble against their will should hostilities again escalate between North and South.

At the end of the 1960s, this author proposed the conception of so-called "cross recognition" to be achieved by North and South Korea—that is, the major supporters of each of the two Korean states would recognize the other in return for the supporters of the other recognizing their client. However, the concept was too bold to gain much support at that time. Today, however, "cross recognition" is basically a most important and appropriate framework for putting down roots of peace and stability into the complex Korean Peninsula and regularizing dialogues and negotiations between North and South Korea.

Regrettably, the situation inside and outside the peninsula today has not yet matured enough to enable us to attain this goal. There are, however, new opportunities for expanding "cross relationships." An example is the recent informal yet practical relationship that has developed between China and South Korea; it corresponds to a similar relationship between Japan and South Korea.

Finally, on the subject of nuclear proliferation on the Korean Peninsula, this author does not believe that the possibility is as great as some outside observers claim. For many years now, the Soviet Union and the United States have strictly refrained from offering their newest weapon systems and advanced technologies to their allies on the Korean Peninsula. This is because the United States and the Soviet Union are concerned about a renewal of military conflict on the peninsula. On the other hand, both nations have continued to make commitments and provide assistance to their Korean allies in order to reassure them about their security. Neither basic posture of the United States or the Soviet Union is likely to change in the future.

South Korea, which has proceeded to develop a nuclear power-generating capability, can be said to be a step ahead of North Korea in terms of understanding nuclear technology. However, if South Korea ever attempted to develop nuclear weapons, this would be a self-destructive action that would lead to the collapse of the alliance between the United States and the ROK.

In continuity with the past, North Korea's future foreign policy will stress an "independence" line that avoids leaning exclusively toward either the Soviet Union or China. Also, it is this author's view that North Korea will not attempt to develop nuclear weapons in the foreseeable future, although reinforcing its conventional military power will remain Pyongyang's most important policy objective.

*Chapter 11*

# INDOCHINA, 1982–1985: PEACE YIELDS TO WAR

*by Karl D. Jackson*

Irony and unpredictability characterize the involvement of major outside powers in the post–World War II history of Indochina. Some observers have contended that 40 years of bloodshed could have been avoided if the United States had "simply" sided with Ho Chi Minh against the French. This post hoc assertion remains forever secure from contradiction because, unlike other prognostications about what would bring peace and stability to Indochina, "the lost revolution" thesis can never be tested by events.

Instead of aligning itself with Ho, in fact, the United States followed the logic of containment and provided limited backing for France's effort to reestablish its colonial authority. U.S. military assistance, in the name of anti-communism, underwrote the French war effort, but in the end the United States decided not to save the French army at Dien Bien Phu. Inaction in this instance should have been a clear indication that the United States did not consider Indochina an appropriate arena for expending major resources to contain communism in Asia. In 1954 few would have predicted that the United States itself would eventually reverse course and expend in excess of $100 billion and over 50,000 American lives to contain communist expansion in Laos, Cambodia, and South Vietnam.

In the late 1950s and early 1960s, U.S. policy was driven by the image of China on the march—a China allied to the Soviet Union and a radical member of the international communist movement.

Beijing had asserted full control over Tibet in 1959, attacked India in 1962, and was actively supporting North Vietnam's efforts to take over South Vietnam. First President Eisenhower, then Presidents Kennedy, Johnson, Nixon, and Ford, carried forward a policy that originally had been designed to contain Chinese expansion in Southeast Asia. Only in the early 1970s did it become apparent that the United States, through political normalization, could live with China, and that North Vietnam had aligned itself not with China but with the Soviet Union. Policies made in the 1960s on the assumption that China was the enemy lost much of their geopolitical rationale as Beijing, now hostile to the Soviet Union, moved toward normalization of relations with the United States and Vietnam became increasingly dependent on the Soviets.

In the 1960s few would have foreseen the ripening relationship between the politburos in Hanoi and Moscow and that China—after having supplied more assistance to Vietnam than to any other nation—would find itself odd man out when the war's 1975 denouement featured Soviet tanks rather than China's people's war.

The final turnabout came after the victory of 1975. The Vietnamese yen to dominate all of Indochina—whether through an Indochina Federation or its pseudonym of "militant solidarity" among the peoples of Indochina—was out of step with China's perception of its own national interests. By late 1975, the Chinese, who had served as the arsenal of victory at Dien Bien Phu and in the early stages of the war against the Americans, found themselves ever more closely aligned with Pol Pot, supplying arms and advisers, backing a xenophobic regime in an armed conflict with its former ally Vietnam. After Vietnam signed a friendship treaty with the Soviet Union on November 3, 1978, invaded Cambodia on December 25, 1978, and drove Pol Pot from Phnom Penh during the first week of January 1979, China felt it had no option but to "teach Vietnam a lesson." China's limited incursion into Vietnam was short-lived but bloody, with both sides absorbing heavy losses.

Thus, in less than four years, China had come full circle to attack with massive armed force the same socialist Vietnam that it had assisted in defending. The United States, having withdrawn from Indochina in psychological tatters in the early 1970s, witnessed a Communist China and Communist Vietnam engaging each other in meat-grinder battles for the mountain passes of northern Vietnam. Following the withdrawal of Chinese troops from Vietnam in the spring of 1979, the United States and Vietnam's new foe (China), in concert with ASEAN, settled down to a prolonged diplomatic and military effort to contain Hanoi's ambitions and restore Cambodia's sovereignty to the Khmer.

The years 1983 to 1985 present an interesting case study in the international relations of Southeast Asia: peace and war alternated regularly during that three-year period, but as seems so normal in the history of Indochina, war ultimately predominated. As 1982 ended, peace was in the air with behind-the-scenes diplomatic activity dotting the international landscape from Belgium and Romania to the Non-Aligned Conference.[1] However, these peace feelers rapidly withered with Hanoi's January-April 1983 dry season offensive and the harsh rhetoric of Soviet and Vietnamese pronouncements on the Kampuchea problem. With the rain in mid-1983, the pace again changed. The resistance forces of the Coalition Government of Democratic Kampuchea (CGDK) became substantially more active, breaking out of the western border areas and spreading to broad sections of the Cambodian interior. Recruiting prospects exceeded military resources, and even the Khmer Rouge enjoyed a renaissance. With the end of the rains in December 1983, the military momentum did not follow the usual pattern of reverting back entirely to Vietnam. Instead, the dry season was distinguished by continued pressure by the insurgents.

In the midst of these untoward events, Vietnam turned its diplomatic face toward peace. The Indochina foreign ministers, at their eighth joint conference, were slightly more forthcoming in their proposals of January 1984. From January until the last few days of March 1984, "no news" was still "news" on the Thai-Kampuchean border; and it briefly seemed to many, including this author, that there was a very slight chance that there would be no dry season offensive comparable to those conducted by Vietnamese forces in Cambodia in previous years, and that this military hiatus might be the harbinger of a true peace effort. In retrospect, however, it is clear that the "pause" of 1983–84 was a manifestation of Hanoi's "fight-talk" strategy.

Each year signs of peace are planted in the Western media by Hanoi during the rainy season, and the peace feelers endure tantilizingly until they come to a crashing halt in the annual dry season offensive in February-April. We attempt here to portray the process by which annual peace feelers gave birth to war in the late spring of 1984. The same process could be seen at work in mid-1985 as Vietnam played on American political sensitivities regarding servicemen missing in action (MIAs) in an attempt to extract de facto political recognition from Washington.

The important thing to recognize is that the pattern is perennial and probably will endure until significant political transformations occur in Hanoi, Bangkok, and/or Beijing. Otherwise, stalemate at ever higher levels of conflict will probably continue, punctuated by peace offensives not unlike the ones described here. The single most remarkable aspect of "fight-talk" diplomacy is that seemingly obvious ploys continue to be interpreted as genuine moves toward an overall settlement in spite of the repeated reluctance of Vietnam to deviate from its 40-year-long campaign to dominate all of Indochina. With the exception, perhaps, of the Thai foreign ministry, the world has manifested remarkable tolerance in giving Vietnam the benefit of the doubt, interpreting each spring's newly mellowed rhetoric as evidence of something other than a public relations shroud draping the body of imperial conquest.

## The Diplomatic Minuet, 1982–1985

Over the past three years, the fifth, sixth, seventh, eighth, ninth, and tenth conferences of the foreign ministers of the Lao People's Democratic Republic (LPDR), the People's Republic of Kampuchea (PRK), and the Socialist Republic of Vietnam (SRV) have presented proposals aimed at drawing the countries of ASEAN, the Association of Southeast Asian Nations—Brunei, Indonesia, Malaysia, the Philippines, Singapore, and Thailand—into a discussion of how to stabilize the current situation in Kampuchea. The following were the key provisions of the Sixth Indochina Foreign Ministers Conference in July 1982:

1. "Total withdrawal of Vietnamese troops from Kampuchea when that threat ('the threat from Beijing ruling circles acting in collusion with American imperialists and other reactionary forces') disappears."
2. A "safety zone" along the Thai-Kampuchean border in which only PRK troops would be allowed in the Kampuchean side of the zone and only Thai troops in the Thai portion. Thailand would be responsible for removing all anti-Heng Samrin combatants and refugees from its side of the safety zone. Vietnamese troops would remain in all of Kampuchea except the proposed safety zone.
3. A nonaggression pact with Thailand to ensure that "the presence of Vietnamese troops in Kampuchea in no way threatens Thailand's security."
4. A "partial withdrawal of Vietnamese troops from Kampuchea" provided that Beijing stops using Thai territory to help "the Khmer reactionaries," Pol Pot "and other reactionary Khmer forces" are disarmed, and anti-Heng Samrin factions cease to be supplied with weapons and food.

5. Recognition of a role in the settlement for the United Nations if it withdraws recognition for the "Pol Pot or disguised Pol Pot clique" and leaves the Kampuchean seat vacant.

6. A regional conference between the ASEAN and Indochina countries and a subsequent international conference, including the ASEAN and Indochina countries, Burma, the Soviet Union, China, the United States, France, Great Britain, and India.[2]

On September 15, 1982, this proposal was restated and clarified in a letter from the PRK Foreign Minister Phoune Sipaseuth to the ASEAN ministers for foreign affairs. The basic notion was that Thai national security concerns could be satisfied by:

1. A nonaggression treaty.
2. A partial withdrawal of Vietnamese troops from Kampuchea.
3. A safety zone from which Vietnamese troops would be excluded along the Thai-Kampuchean border.

The letter made clear that Vietnamese national security concerns would require:

1. Nonaggression pacts with China and Thailand.
2. The right to station SRV troops up to the edge of the "safety zone" (presumably a few kilometers from the Thai-Kampuchean border).
3. Withholding sanctuary in Thailand from Pol Pot and "other reactionary forces."
4. Removal "far from this border" of all refugees.[3]

The February 20–21, 1983 summit meeting of the Indochina foreign ministers in Vientiane contained no major innovations. The rhetoric continually emphasized the unity of Indochina and invoked the imagery of the Indochina Communist Party and devotion to Ho Chi Minh "who persistently built and nourished the special solidarity among the three nations throughout his life."[4] While conference proceedings avoided the words "Indochina Federation" there are multiple references to "the special solidarity among the three peoples" as "a law of revolutionary development." Rather than putting forth a new position on the Kampuchean problem, the conference emphasized "closer solidarity and cooperation in all fields" among "the three peoples of Indochina." All three parties pledged:

1. "Solidarity and cooperation" in national construction and defense.
2. To resolve all problems through negotiations.

3. To develop long-term cooperation in all fields.
4. To resist "any manifestation of big power chauvinism and narrow-minded nationalism" through "the traditional friendship and special relationship among" the three peoples.[5]

The conference's major innovation was relabeling the Vietnamese troops serving in Kampuchea as "volunteers." This cosmetic change may have been designed for its impact on the Summit of the Non-Aligned Movement. The communiqué stated:

*All volunteers from the Vietnamese army would be withdrawn from Kampuchea after the threat by reactionaries among the Beijing ruling circles and other reactionary forces as well as the use of Thai territory against the People's Republic of Kampuchea and all support for the Pol Pot clique and other Khmer reactionaries have ceased completely and peace and security of Kampuchea, particularly along the Kampuchean-Thai border, are assured.*

In addition, Vietnamese "volunteers" would be withdrawn each year if security considerations permitted. Finally the communiqué told anti-Heng Samrin forces that they could return to the polity and enjoy full rights if they abandoned "Pol Pot and other Khmer reactionary forces . . . and respect the Constitution of People's Republic of Kampuchea."[6]

In effect, the July and September 1982 proposals and the February 1983 pronouncements assumed that the Kampuchean crisis was a border problem and Vietnam should be allowed to maintain its chosen regime in Phnom Penh while continuing to station in Kampuchea whatever number of troops it deemed reasonable with the exception of a narrow "safety zone" on the Thai border. Accepting the Vietnamese proposals would have meant recognizing the right of Vietnam to invade Kampuchea, change its government, and station Vietnamese troops in Kampuchea near the border. These proposals were tantamount to requesting that ASEAN (and presumably other powers) recognize the legitimacy of Vietnamese suzerainty over what had been a sovereign nation prior to the Vietnamese invasion of December 25, 1978. Furthermore, there were no provisions for establishing a legitimate government—that is, a government that would be acceptable to the majority of surviving Cambodians at home and abroad. Even if we put aside any concerns for maintaining Kampuchean sovereignty and self-determination, and consider only *realpolitik*, the proposals offered were extremely disadvantageous to Thailand. They proposed that Thailand help Vietnam extinguish the anti-Vietnamese/anti-Heng Samrin rebellion and allow a de facto expansion of the Vietnamese sphere of military power to within a few kilometers of the Thai border. In return, Vietnam would sign a treaty of nonaggression, establish a "safety zone" (chiefly benefiting Vietnam and the PRK), and withdraw an unspecified portion of Vietnam's occupational force.

The Seventh Indochina Foreign Ministers Conference was held in Phnom Penh on July 20, 1983. Its tone differed only marginally from the earlier pronouncements. The communiqué repeatedly referred to the issue as "the Kampuchean-Thai border" question. The conference reiterated the optimism of earlier conferences: "all hopes to weaken and divide the peoples of Indochina and all attempts to discredit these countries are doomed to a lamentable failure."[7] Further, the conference rejected the formulations of the U.N.'s 1981 International Conference on Kampuchea (ICK), condemned China and the United States, and dismissed Thai Foreign Minister Sitthi Sawetsila's proposal for a 30-kilometer withdrawal of Vietnamese forces as "absurd" and "an act of bad faith."[8]

However, at the same time the Seventh Indochina Foreign Ministers Conference dropped hints of reasonableness. It noted "positive results" from talks between Nguyen Co Thach and Sitthi Sawetsila and accepted the "5-2 formula" originally advanced by Malaysian Foreign Minister Ghazali Shafie in his discussions with Vietnamese Foreign Minister Nguyen Co Thach in New Delhi in March 1983. The Heng Samrin government in July 1983 agreed that talks could begin between the five ASEAN countries and two of the Indochina countries, Vietnam and Laos, without Kampuchean representation.[9]

Unfortunately, Vietnam's concession came too late because ASEAN had long since abandoned Ghazali Shafie's proposal. Nonetheless, accepting the 5-2 proposal was interpreted as a sign of at least marginal flexibility because, without this concession, sitting down to negotiate with the three Indochina countries would have involved ASEAN's de facto diplomatic recognition of the regime placed in power in Phnom Penh by the Vietnamese army.

The Eighth Indochina Foreign Ministers Conference was held in Vientiane on January 28–29, 1984; at the time it appeared to represent a milestone in the gradual transformation of Vietnam's position on the Cambodian conflict. In tone the Eighth Conference seemed markedly less optimistic about the evolution of events inside Kampuchea. Absent was the formalistic prattle about "new successes" and the "more and more stable" situation. The attacks on China for hegemonism, on America for imperialism, and on Thailand for backing reactionaries were reminiscent of earlier conferences. However, the Eighth Conference reaffirmed acceptance of the 5-2 formula, explicitly included the PRC as a negotiat-

ing party to any settlement,[10] and stopped trivializing the Kampuchea problem by calling it "the Kampuchean-Thai border problem.
. . ."[11] Furthermore, the Indochina foreign ministers indicated a
glimmer of flexibility by forecasting "five possible directions" in
which the situation in Southeast Asia might evolve:

1. An "overall solution" based on "the withdrawal of all foreign
   armed forces from the region," an end to external intervention, and the establishment of ZOPFAN.
2. "A partial settlement involving the three Indochinese countries and China aimed at the total withdrawal of Vietnamese
   forces from Kampuchea paired with a termination of the
   Chinese threat," and halting utilization of Thailand by Pol Pot
   and "other Khmer reactionaries."
3. "A partial settlement involving the three Indochinese countries and Thailand on the basis of equal security for both sides
   and the setting up of a safety zone on both sides of the
   Kampuchea-Thai border."
4. "A framework agreement on principles" aimed at "checking
   the danger of escalation."
5. "The continuation of the present situation."[12]

Previous proposals by the Indochina foreign ministers had contained most of these elements. The one exception was the explicit
recognition that the present situation might endure rather than
lead inevitably "to new and still greater victories." In fact, *Nhan
Dan's* editorial on the January 1984 conference actually admitted
that the actions of China, Thailand, and "some ruling circles in
other ASEAN countries" have "rendered the situation tense and
deadlocked."[13] What had once been "irreversible" had two years
later been explicitly recognized as "deadlocked." Admitting the
situation is deadlocked is a far cry from earlier Vietnamese protes-
tations that "there is no Kampuchean problem" and rhetoric about
"irreversibility."

The gulf between the negotiating positions of the Indochina and
ASEAN countries is illustrated by comparing the proposal of the
Indochina foreign ministers with the position of the U.N. International Conference on Kampuchea (ICK) of July 1981, which endorsed (1) a "ceasefire by all parties" and "withdrawal of all foreign
armed forces in the shortest time possible"; (2) "appropriate arrangements to ensure that armed Kampuchean factions" cannot
disrupt or control election outcomes; (3) "a United Nations peacekeeping force" to ensure "law and order"; and (4) "the holding of
free elections under United Nations supervision, which will allow
the Kampuchean people to exercise their right of self-determina-

tion and elect a government of their own choice." Whereas specific proposals by the Indochinese foreign ministers concentrated almost exclusively on creating a climate conducive to the pacification of Kampuchea, ASEAN sought to maximize Cambodian sovereignty as well as to halt the hostilities.

The ICK proposal is unrealistic, if taken at face value, because it contains no provisions for disarming the Khmer Rouge or for providing a military force capable of containing or eliminating Khmer Rouge elements who are unwilling to submit to the authority of the interim administration that might result from the international negotiation. Any diplomatic solution returning Cambodia to the Khmer Rouge would be unacceptable to the United States, the Soviet Union, and world opinion, in addition to being inimical to the legitimate national security interests of the SRV.

In late 1983 and early 1984, the ASEAN countries also took pains to demonstrate flexibility on the Kampuchean problem. In May 1983, in response to Vietnam's annual "troop withdrawal" (that is, troop rotation), the Thai foreign minister stated his willingness to go to Hanoi to negotiate if PAVN units withdrew 30 kilometers from the Thai border.[14] This was rejected out of hand by Vietnam as a transparent attempt to provide a rear base for the Khmer Rouge.

In his address to the United Nations General Assembly on October 3, Sitthi Sawetsila outlined a slightly expanded set of ASEAN proposals:

1. Withdrawal of Vietnamese troops from the immediate border area.
2. Insertion of a U.N. peacekeeping force or observer group to keep the peace along the border.
3. "International economic assistance" to aid "the uprooted Kampucheans."
4. "An international conference for the reconstruction and rehabilitation of Kampuchea after the withdrawal of all foreign forces."[15]

The only entirely new element here is the idea of an international conference for reconstruction. However, like the Vietnamese proposal of January 1984, the UNGA proposal marked a slight softening in tone and detail.

For a moment only did Southeast Asia feel the spell of a possible peace. The entire effort disintegrated during Nguyen Co Thach's March 11-13, 1984 visit to Jakarta.[16] Indonesia had done everything possible to draw Vietnam out. During General Murdani's

February 1984 visit to Vietnam, every effort was made to emphasize the commonalities between Vietnam and Indonesia, namely anticolonialism and fear of China. In what is perhaps the most pro-Hanoi statement by any ASEAN official in recent years, General Murdani stated:[17]

> *Some countries said that Vietnam is a danger to Southeast Asia, but the Indonesian Army and people do not believe it.*

General Murdani was trying to encourage Vietnamese flexibility by providing Hanoi with a sympathetic ear within ASEAN. The ultimate goal of Murdani's February 1984 visit was similar to his previous trips to Hanoi: to find evidence that Vietnam had at last come to accept the necessity of compromise with ASEAN over Kampuchea. In effect, while Thailand, Malaysia, and Singapore enunciated the hard line in public and private, Indonesia was willing to hear Vietnam out.

Just prior to Nguyen Co Thach's arrival in Jakarta, Foreign Minister Mochtar Kusumaatmadja set the stage for a successful Vietnamese effort by stating publicly that new proposals were expected from Vietnam on the Cambodian problem. However, when President Suharto met with the Vietnamese foreign minister, it became apparent that Nguyen Co Thach had no new proposals and was not authorized to make concessions to keep the dialogue moving. In leaving the palace grounds, the visiting foreign minister added insult to injury by immediately and publicly rejecting Suharto's concept of inviting Vietnamese troops to participate in a peacekeeping force that would police Cambodia after the Vietnamese withdrew. If the proposal had become reality, this would have given Vietnam substantial direct influence over any electoral process to choose a permanent government for Cambodia. This was President Suharto's own initiative and went far beyond the authorized ASEAN line at the time.

The manner in which Hanoi treated President Suharto's proposal marked the beginning of a new, more negative trend in relations between Indonesia and Vietnam on the Cambodian issue.[18] The cynicism of high-level Indonesian officials was further stimulated when the Vietnamese foreign minister, in Canberra a few days later (March 14-19), constantly emphasized the theme of negotiations. Could it be possible that the same official, who was unauthorized to negotiate with President Suharto, could sincerely return to the negotiation theme once safely out of ASEAN? The depth of Indonesian disillusionment with Nguyen Co Thach is reflected in the explanation given to this author by a senior Indonesian foreign ministry official:

*To understand Nguyen Co Thach you must understand he is an actor
and a very good one. He speaks his lines upon the stage on a given
day and can deliver no less convincingly quite different lines even on
the same day. In the morning session he was forthcoming on several
issues; after lunch his position changed completely.*

Of course, it remains unclear whether Nguyen Co Thach's
moderate-sounding public statements were intentional obfuscation
or whether a factional struggle over Cambodia policy had been
taking place in Hanoi. The period of hope in 1983–84 came to a
final halt when the Vietnamese army's dry season offensive began
several days after Nguyen Co Thach flew home from Bangkok on
the last leg of his Bangkok-Jakarta-Canberra-Bangkok mission. To
many ASEAN officials, the indecent interval between the end of
his peace mission and Vietnam's return to arms along the Thai-
Cambodian border was reminiscent of similarly reassuring Vietnamese diplomatic tours of ASEAN just prior to the December
1978 invasion of Cambodia.

## The Vietnamese Return to Armed Struggle

In any case, the second half of 1984 was dominated by hostility.
The Vietnamese dry season offensive arrived late and was rather
limited in scope. The major feature was an intrusion into Thai
territory. The Vietnamese engaged in their annual ritual of over-
running camps from which the insurgents withdrew in the face of
superior fire power. On the diplomatic front, increasing harshness
was the order of the day on both sides. Nguyen Co Thach rejected
all suggestions of power sharing with the CGDK.[19] This was
paralleled by statements from the Heng Samrin government wel-
coming Sihanouk and Son Sann back to Cambodia on the condition
that they first break with the Khmer Rouge.[20]

From the ASEAN side the chill winds also blew. The July 1984
Joint Communiqué of the ASEAN foreign ministers denounced
Vietnam for its "illegal occupation of Kampuchea," "the recurrent
acts of Vietnamese aggression along the Thai-Kampuchean border," "intentionally made incursions into Thai territory," "annual
troop rotations which were meant to deceive the international
community, the Kampuchean people, and Vietnam's own citizens,"
and the presence of "at least half a million Vietnamese settlers in
Kampuchea."[21] The ASEAN proposal for settling the Kampuchean
problem reiterated earlier proposals for settlement on the basis of a
completely sovereign Kampuchea that was truly independent and
neutral with a government selected by the Cambodian people. It

also emphasized support for Sihanouk's concept of "national reconciliation among all Kampuchean factions," which envisions representation for Heng Samrin as well as for the CGDK in a reconstituted Cambodia. That the communiqué was issued in Jakarta with the full support of Indonesia served notice on Vietnam that its efforts to drive a wedge between Indonesia and Thailand on the Kampuchean problem had come to naught.

The depth of Indonesian alienation from the Vietnamese was manifest in the hard-line position taken by Foreign Minister Mochtar in June 1984. He stated that Vietnam must accept a Cambodia that is not a puppet of either Hanoi or Beijing:[22]

> *The solution to the Kampuchean problem (is one that) will result in the establishment of a sovereign—and I mean sovereign, not part of any federation, confederation, or anything—Kampuchea; independent, I mean headed by, a group of people who are really independent; neutral, that is, a status that will fully be able to negotiate with the great powers; and non-aligned in its foreign policy, not wedded to any bloc.*

If 1984 had begun with Hanoi's attempt to split ASEAN and Jakarta's attempt to turn events in the direction of genuine compromise, by mid-year both efforts were stillborn and would continue to be so until November 1984 when hostility became even more pronounced as Vietnam launched the largest military offensive since 1978.

The major change in late 1984 and the first half of 1985 was the military escalation on the Thai-Cambodian border. During a heightened military push against the guerrillas, featuring repeated large-scale violations of Thai territory, Vietnam's public pronouncements manifested confidence bordering upon hubris, with neither rhetorical nor substantive concessions to the fact that for the seventh consecutive year Vietnamese troops found themselves soldiering in the Cambodian quagmire.

The military offensive began early in November of 1984 and continued through March of 1985 with a greater expenditure of men and materiel than at any time since the December 1978 invasion of Cambodia. The Tenth Indochina Foreign Ministers Conference was held in Ho Chi Minh City on January 17–18, 1985. It "confirm[ed] the irreversibility of the Cambodian situation"[23] and reiterated their "willingness to enter negotiations,"[24] but in pursuit of a settlement similar to the ones achieved at "Geneva and Paris." That these earlier international conferences serve as Hanoi's model of "a political settlement"[25] supplies scant encouragement to proponents of Cambodian sovereignty and independence:

Geneva in 1954 marked the capitulation of the French, while the Paris Accords of 1973 set the stage for terminating the independent existence of the Republic of Vietnam. The Indochina foreign ministers blamed "the present tension prevailing on the Cambodian-Thai and the Lao-Thai borders" on "the Thai expansionist policy."[26] Vietnamese withdrawal would occur after "the exclusion of the genocidal Pol Pot clique," "respect for the Cambodian people's right to self-determination," and an "election in the presence of foreign observers."[27] While "the three Indochinese countries" would prefer such a negotiated outcome, the final communiqué of the conference expressed confidence "that within 5 to 10 years the so-called Cambodian problem will be settled even in the absence of a negotiated solution."[28] In such an event, according to Nguyen Co Thach, "the Kampuchean issue would cease to exist within a few years."[29]

The uncompromising nature of the position of the Indochinese countries was further enunciated by Hun Sen (foreign minister of the People's Republic of Kampuchea) during discussions with Australian Foreign Minister William Hayden in Ho Chi Minh City on March 8, 1985.[30] Hun Sen called for:

1. "The complete withdrawal of Vietnamese troops" following "the elimination of Pol Pot."
2. Immediate "free elections" under "the PRK Constitution" "with foreign observers." "A number of individuals" (possibly Sihanouk and Son Sann) could stand for election if they "dissociate themselves from Pol Pot and unite with the PRK against the Pol Pot gang." Only the ruling Communist Party, however, could participate legitimately in the elections under the PRK constitution.
3. Cessation of Thailand's use of its "territory against the Indochinese revolution." This would be achieved via "an international conference on Southeast Asia in Canberra."
4. "Cessation of all interference by countries outside the region" (read China and the United States).
5. An international guarantee of such a settlement of the Cambodian problem.

Barring such a negotiated settlement, Hun Sen allowed that the situation might be "resolved by itself—by this we mean the progress of the PRK, the crumbling of the Pol Pot forces and other Khmer reactionaries, and the withdrawal of all Vietnamese forces from Cambodia."[31] Heng Samrin's foreign minister can, perhaps, be excused for believing that everything was going his way; the Indonesian foreign minister was preparing to visit Hanoi (March

14–17) and the Australian foreign minister was parleying with him in Ho Chi Minh City at the precise moment when Vietnamese troops were storming the Sihanouk base at Tatum by penetrating 10 kilometers inside Thailand with a force of 800 to 1,000 PAVN troops.[32]

The ASEAN response to the Vietnamese dry season offensive was tendered at the extraordinary meeting of the ASEAN foreign ministers in Bangkok on February 11, 1985. ASEAN's formal negotiating position, like Vietnam's, did not vary greatly from previous formulations. ASEAN denounced Vietnam's "numerous . . . blatant violations of Thailand's sovereignty and territorial integrity" and called on Vietnam and the Coalition Government of Democratic Kampuchea to enter "a direct dialogue . . . to arrive at a political settlement." Although these positions had all been aired before, the last sentence of the Joint Communiqué broke entirely new public ground:[33]

> *The Foreign Ministers call upon the international community to increase support and assistance to the Kampuchean people* in their political and military struggle *to liberate their homeland from foreign occupation. (Emphasis added.)*

Several commentators immediately noted the none too subtle shift from primarily political to blatantly military pressure against Vietnam.[34] Even though various members of ASEAN had for some time been privately calling on Washington for military assistance, for the first time ASEAN put itself on record as favoring such assistance. In the decade since 1975, American foreign policy-makers at all levels had explained their unwillingness to assist the non-Communist factions by stating that the United States was "following ASEAN's lead" and that ASEAN had never made such a request, at least formally. At its February 1985 meeting, ASEAN apparently decided that Vietnam's attempted knock-out blow against the CGDK required a countermove from the ASEAN side. The pressure on the United States to act had become direct and public:[35]

> . . . *we think the time has come for the United States to support the non-Communist factions of the CGDK with arms and other aid.*

The most significant single advantage possessed by Hanoi in the conduct of its foreign policy over the last 40 years has been the ability of its foreign policy establishment to pursue both peace and war, conciliation and confrontation, simultaneously. The opening months of 1985 witnessed a Vietnamese military onslaught combined with unstinting negative rhetoric against the American role in supporting ASEAN and the CGDK. However, at the same time, Vietnamese policy planners put in motion an entire series of conciliatory gestures toward the United States. The most probable rationale for inviting National Security Council staff official Richard Childress to Hanoi in early March and for subsequent releases of MIA remains, and the talk of setting up a technical mission in Hanoi, was to entice the Americans toward normalization without offering any substantive concessions concerning Vietnam's occupation of Cambodia. President Reagan's personal commitment to a final accounting of the MIAs and the widespread emotional impact of the MIA issue made the United States peculiarly vulnerable to Vietnamese moves, even while Vietnamese troops were repeatedly violating Thailand's border. Not only did Vietnam raise the MIA issue but, in addition, as spring approached, Hanoi trotted out last year's new issue by renewing the prospect of releasing to the United States the remaining re-education camp inmates.[36]

As in earlier years, the late spring of 1985 witnessed diplomatic overtures by ASEAN toward Vietnam. Malaysia created the concept of proximity talks, indirect negotiations between Heng Samrin and the CGDK through an ASEAN intermediary. Indonesia's foreign minister, for his part, sought to advance the possibility of normalizing relations between Washington and Hanoi as an integral part of the overall peace process. Although neither of these proposals seemed likely to bear fruit, they provide further examples of a seemingly inexhaustible supply of diplomatic contrivances designed to bring Vietnam into meaningful negotiations. One suspects, however, that the ultimate function of the proposals is to maintain ASEAN unity by consistently demonstrating Hanoi's reluctance to negotiate. For instance, the July 9-12, 1985 communiqué of the annual ASEAN Foreign Ministers Meeting called for "indirect or proximity talks" with the CGDK, "which could be attended by representatives of Heng Samrin as part of the Vietnamese delegation."[37] This was the first time that Heng Samrin's name had ever been mentioned in an official ASEAN pronouncement, and altering the ASEAN lexicon was undoubtedly designed to show Hanoi that ASEAN accepts the fact that no settlement can be achieved without the active participation of what ASEAN originally viewed as a mere puppet government. The immediate reaction of the Heng Samrin government was to "categorically reject" the concept of proximity talks while describing it as "the perfidious policy of the reactionaries among the Thai ruling circles."[38] Hanoi, in turn, dismissed the proposal as "absurd" and claimed it did "not reflect the real stand of the ASEAN countries.

. . . It is an established fact that the Kampuchean situation is irreversible."[39]

In the end, the entire three-year period of diplomatic point and counterpoint led to naught. The brief period of hesitation in Hanoi in 1984 had been replaced almost immediately by an intensification of the rhetoric of "irreversibility." Only on the MIAs and possible normalization with the United States did there appear to be renewed interest in Hanoi—and these signs of flexibility may have been motivated by a warming trend in Sino-Soviet relations, which would probably weaken Soviet support for the Vietnamese, rather than by any real interest on Hanoi's part in resolving its differences with ASEAN. Indeed, these moves can be seen as motivated primarily by the desire to *weaken* ASEAN's position, through normalization with the United States in advance of a Vietnamese withdrawal from Cambodia and a decrease in American support for the CGDK. Normalization in advance of withdrawal of Vietnamese troops from Cambodia would be a direct repudiation of the U.S. policy that has been in place since the December 1978 invasion of Cambodia. Furthermore, the *quid pro quo* Vietnam had in mind may have been revealed by a Hungarian broadcast in which Nguyen Co Thach implicitly linked improvement of U.S.-Vietnam relations with decreased American political and military support for the CGDK.[40]

## The Coalition Government of Democratic Kampuchea

At the time of its establishment in June 1982, the CGDK's forte was almost entirely diplomatic representation. At the United Nations in 1983 Vietnam did not challenge the credentials of the CGDK because the margin of defeat would have been embarrassing. In 1982, the margin favoring CGDK retention of the Cambodian seat had already grown to 90 (62 percent) in favor, 29 (20 percent) against, with 26 (18 percent) abstentions. Furthermore, support for the CGDK seems to grow rather than decrease with time. The number of governments that have established formal diplomatic relations with the CGDK is small but increasing, and there is heightened willingness to provide humanitarian assistance to the displaced and struggling Khmer.

The military power of the non-communist factions in the resistance grew in 1983, although not nearly as rapidly as the Khmer Rouge. Vietnamese attacks on refugee camps along the Thai border during the 1983 dry season offensive destroyed infrastructure and inconvenienced the Son Sann and Sihanouk forces, but the attacks did not cripple the insurgencies. Just prior to the dry season offensive in November 1982, 4,000 armed soldiers were in the field representing Prince Sihanouk, while Son Sann's armed force consisted of approximately 11,000 men. One year later Sihanouk's arms equaled 4,500 and there were just under 13,000 KPNLF soldiers. In both instances the limiting factor has been the shortage of materiel, particularly small arms, uniforms, blasting material, and money—not a shortage of eager adherents. Knowledgeable observers think that the non-communist forces could double in a matter of months if significant assistance were provided to them.

Proof positive of the relationship between money, military supplies, and successful recruiting is provided by the record of the Khmer Rouge in 1983–84. Pol Pot's regime clearly ranks as one of history's most brutal and least successful; few governments in history have given more plentiful reasons for being deserted by their people. When Pol Pot was driven from Phnom Penh in January 1979, the Khmer Rouge should have disappeared; however with sanctuaries in the Cardamom Mountains and along the Thai border, and with sufficient supplies of money and materiel from China, the Khmer Rouge have survived and grown. In November 1982, Khmer Rouge strength was estimated to be 20,000 to 35,000; by early 1984 rapid expansion had brought them to between 40,000 and 50,000.[41]

Dr. Steven Morris, currently affiliated with the Indochina Project at the University of California, Berkeley, spent three weeks in Khmer Rouge, KPNLF, and ANS camps inside Cambodia in the summer of 1983. His film vividly conveys the disproportionate supply situation. The Khmer Rouge troops had uniforms, ammunition, and AK-47s; in addition, every sixth man carried a B-40 rocket. The Khmer Rouge had so much ammunition that they even put on a fire display for Morris. In contrast, the KPNLF officer trainees in Morris's film had guns but no rockets, and the ranks had neither guns nor complete uniforms. Sihanouk's officer candidate trainees had no guns whatsoever and trained for war with sticks, adding "bang, bang" to provide "realism" in the same way that American youngsters do when they play cops and robbers. With a plethora of Chinese aid, the Khmer Rouge have been the most attractive resistance organization because they, unlike the KPNLF and ANS, offer a serious Khmer recruit the food, weapons, and other resources necessary to do the job. Even though China in 1984 provided new weapons to the KPNLF and the ANS, the supply remained a trickle in comparison with the amounts made available to the Khmer Rouge. However, those U.S. government officials who are most resistant to any form of American involvement in supplying arms, contend that there are no shortages among the non-communist resistance fighters.[42]

## The Military Situation

After the dry season offensive of 1982–83, some observers might have supposed that the Khmer Rouge, KPNLF, and ANS had been badly hurt. The Vietnamese army of occupation had brought troops and tanks to western Cambodia in large quantities, and fighting reached proportions not seen in western Cambodia since the original Vietnamese invasion in 1979. Khmer Rouge, KPNLF, and ANS camps were demolished, and for the most part the forces of the CGDK did not distinguish themselves on the field of battle. At Phnom Chat, Vietnamese forces not only routed the Khmer Rouge defenders but entered several kilometers into Thailand where they dug in. They were dislodged by Thai air attacks but not without provoking international concern about yet another flagrant violation of Thailand's territorial integrity.

The Vietnamese 1981–82 dry season offensive was highly successful as a series of military engagements, but rebel ranks soon swelled with the creation of the CGDK coalition. Likewise, in the 1982–83 dry season offensive it is hard to imagine how much more successful it could have been in attaining military objectives: camps overrun, forces routed, tens of thousands of refugees displaced into Thailand.[43] However, with the rains came the most difficult time faced by the Vietnamese since their occupation of Kampuchea in 1979. Khmer Rouge forces spread out over wide sectors of western and northern Cambodia. They had a relatively free hand on the Tonle Sap and along Route 6 (north of the lake). The Khmer Rouge claim to have conducted numerous battalion-size operations, and journalists traveling with them affirmed the increasing scope of Khmer Rouge control over villages.[44]

For Vietnam the trouble did not cease with the rain. The early dry season offensive belonged largely to Pol Pot rather than to the People's Army of Vietnam (PAVN). In addition to the customary round of attacks on truck convoys and isolated detachments, the Khmer Rouge, sometimes in concert with the KPNLF, raided major urban areas: Kampong Thom (January 19); Siem Reap (January 27); Pursat (February 6); and Battambang (February 17).[45] In these attacks, damage was inflicted on Vietnamese military installations and ammunition dumps. More important, the attacks were indicative of the continuing insecurity that led to the deaths on August 23, 1983, of eight Soviet advisers at Kampong Thom.[46] It is important to recognize that we are not only describing raids in the border area, such as those against the outskirts of Battambang, but of operations well inland at Kampong Thom during the dry season and operations along almost the entire length of the Thai-Cambodia border (from Preah Vihear to Kampong Som) during the rainy season. Rail and road links to western Cambodia have been cut repeatedly, thereby compounding already difficult logistical problems for PAVN.

The dry season offensive of 1983–84 did not get underway until the last week of March. The 1984 offensive was smaller than its immediate predecessor and very much smaller than the 1984–85 offensive. Compared with the 1982–83 offensive, the 1983–84 effort involved smaller numbers of troops and armor. The first major attack of the 1983–84 offensive took place in the north. On March 24, 1984, PAVN crossed through Thai territory near Preah Vihear to destroy a Khmer Rouge base that had been used for attacking the Kampong Thom area of Central Cambodia. Thailand's reaction was no less swift than in 1983; airpower and troops were used to drive the Vietnamese back into Cambodia. In addition to Vietnamese troops captured and killed, the attack blunted much of the international impact of the Vietnamese peace offensive. Moreover, China retaliated almost immediately along its border with Vietnam by attacking several hills and shelling the Vietnamese side of the border. In mid-April, Vietnam attacked the KPNLF headquarters at Amphil. This was at best only partially successful because the non-communist resistance counterattacked vigorously following the initial Vietnamese assault. If anything, fighting between Vietnam and the forces of the CGDK in 1983–84 was inconclusive. The Vietnamese—with armor and artillery—can still take virtually any objective; but CGDK forces acquitted themselves well, withdrawing, as guerrillas should, to fight another day. Vietnam was unable to destroy more than a few dozen CGDK operatives, and there was no decline in troop morale.[47] The military situation at the end of 1984 was similar to what it had been previously: the number of armed insurgents was growing, but the non-communist elements did not yet have the wherewithal (in leadership or materiel) to operate deep inside Cambodia.

Gone in 1984–85 was any Vietnamese reluctance to resort to the sword. November 17, 1984 kicked off a round of heavy fighting that lasted until mid-March 1985. The Vietnamese began by attacking the KPNLF base at Nong Chan. Late December witnessed 60,000 residents being driven from Nong Samet (Rithisen) and the beginning of an attack that eventually overran KPNLF headquarters at Amphil in early January. Next came Sihanouk's base at Phum Thmey and the Khmer Rouge redoubt at Phnom Malai. Finally, attacks were initiated across the Thai border against Sihanouk's forces near Tatum in early March.[48]

The number of troops, tanks, and artillery that Hanoi threw into the dry season offensive of 1984–85 was much larger than in any previous year. The resistance of Kampuchean forces was formidable, but in the end firepower prevailed and the guerrillas withdrew into Thailand. Vietnamese forces occupied guerrilla bases along the entire length of the border. This prompted Vietnamese claims of a decisive victory. Speculation was heard even in quarters favoring the CGDK that the resistance might have suffered a decisive blow. Every year speculation of this type has been rife after each "successful" Vietnamese dry season offensive, in spite of the fact that the resources of the resistance in men and materiel grow after each Vietnamese "success."

Although Vietnam expended more resources in 1984–85 than ever before, there has been no change in the fundamental balance of forces. The CGDK border bases have been wrecked, but military hardware is more readily available from China than ever before,[49] and U.S. contributions, now mandated by the Congress, will undoubtedly grow. There is no evidence that large numbers of guerrillas were cornered and killed. The war, in fact, seems to have shifted to the Cambodian interior, with all three factions rather than just the Khmer Rouge waging attacks inside the country. Security, even in Phnom Penh, appears to be an increasing problem for the Vietnamese and PRK forces concentrated in western Cambodia, while the guerrillas have shifted inland.[50] The bottom line on the dry season offensive is that the forces of Son Sann and Sihanouk have been forced to operate as guerrillas, the United States and China are now providing more support, and the overall military strength of the coalition is probably greater than ever. Stalemate endures, albeit at a higher level of conflict.

## The Potential Impact of Sino-Soviet Negotiations on Vietnam

Outcomes in regional confrontations are heavily influenced by the major powers. Within Southeast Asia a predominant factor in the evolution of political events since the late 1960s has been the increasing tendency for the Vietnamese to become ever more dependent on the USSR. This dependency gave Vietnam the wherewithal to fight the Americans and to vanquish the Republic of Vietnam after the Americans withdrew. After 1975, dependence on the Soviet Union grew in direct proportion to Vietnam's economic woes and the extravagances of its post-1975 foreign policies toward Kampuchea and China. Nearly $10 billion worth of economic and military assistance, thousands of Soviet advisers and technicians, membership in CMEA, the November 3, 1979 Treaty of Friendship between Vietnam and the Soviet Union, and regular Soviet utilization of military installations at Da Nang and Cam Ranh Bay are the milestones illuminating the progression of Vietnamese dependency on the Soviet Union. Presently, neither Vietnam's economy nor its military establishment could be sustained in the absence of massive Soviet and Eastern European assistance.

The possibility, however remote, of a Sino-Soviet detente when combined with Vietnam's utter dependence on the Soviet Union gives Vietnam a vested interest in the endurance of the Sino-Soviet split. Anxieties over the possible scope of a Sino-Soviet settlement probably accounted for the flurry of behind-the-scenes diplomatic activity in which a variety of alternative proposals were being considered in late 1982 for settling the Kampuchean conflict. In addition, the new Soviet weapons deliveries in 1982 and 1983, the direct threats against ASEAN by the Soviet Deputy Foreign Minister in March 1983, and high-level Soviet statements in 1984 and 1985 indicate a desire to reassure a nervous ally who provides valuable base usage to Soviet naval and air forces. Also significant is the fact that no dramatic breakthrough has been achieved on Kampuchea in the opening rounds of the Sino-Soviet normalization talks.

For its part, Beijing has not disappointed its friends in ASEAN. In both 1982–83, 1983–84, and 1984–85, China has followed the same action plan. After an initial period of criticism of Vietnamese offensive moves, China in each case became more rhetorically assertive and the situation along the Sino-Vietnamese border deteriorated into artillery duels and minor contact between Chinese and Vietnamese troops.[51] Although neither China's verbiage nor troop movements indicate that "a second lesson" is in the offing, Vietnam undoubtedly feels the Chinese threat cannot be ignored. In 1978–79 Hanoi incorrectly gambled that Beijing would not intervene in response to a Vietnamese invasion of Kampuchea; Vietnam, chastened by the experience of 1979, now stations 700,000 combat troops in the northern portion of the country.

There are many scenarios for Sino-Soviet rapprochement, and several have the potential for diminishing Vietnam's resources and thereby impelling it toward a more flexible attitude regarding

Kampuchea. The most probable scenario is that Sino-Soviet talks will result in ad hoc agreements for mutually advantageous economic exchanges without any progress whatever on the Afghanistan and Kampuchean controversies, thereby ensuring no global improvement in Sino-Soviet relations. From Vietnam's vantage point, "no settlement" would be a positive outcome because continuation of a severe Sino-Soviet split underlines the practical importance for the Soviet Union of its alliance with Vietnam.

Even the partial normalization now apparent between China and the Soviet Union is disquieting to Hanoi because any dilution of Sino-Soviet hostility diminishes the practical (as opposed to the ideological) rationale for large-scale Soviet economic and military investment in Vietnam. If a decrease in Soviet support for Vietnam transpired in the absence of a Sino-Vietnamese detente, the resources of Vietnam would be severely stretched. It is probable that the resistance in Cambodia will continue almost indefinitely, and any decrease in Soviet support would raise the Vietnamese share of the occupation costs. If the Soviet cutback were sufficiently extensive, Hanoi would face unpleasant alternatives such as (1) taking the costs of the war out of the already inadequate Vietnamese development budget; (2) reducing the expense of the war effort by adopting an "enclave strategy" and rapidly pursuing "Cambodianization" of the war; (3) withdrawing to the Mekong and thereby partitioning the country; or (4) suing for a compromise, coalition peace that Vietnam might hope to dominate politically after a decent interval.

A more extreme, and hence much less probable, scenario might feature the Soviet Union paying the price for fundamental detente with China in Vietnamese *dong* by agreeing to accept China's position in Southeast Asia in a trade-off for a freer hand in Afghanistan and for Chinese support *vis-à-vis* the United States globally. Logically, this is not a very plausible scenario. China has very little to offer in Afghanistan or in the Third World in general that would begin to compensate the Soviets for the loss of Soviet military facilities that would almost certainly result from any deal between the USSR and the PRC harmful to Vietnamese interests. Bureaucracies being what they are, the Soviet bases in Vietnam have probably become sacrosanct among Moscow's military planners. Hence, the Soviet Union would not risk access to these facilities unless there were fundamental geopolitical gains to be attained such as the rebirth of the Sino-Soviet alliance of the early 1950s.

Given the vicissitudes of Chinese diplomacy over the last decade, all predictions are hazardous. However, if Vietnamese value preferences were assigned to various scenarios, continuation of the Sino-Soviet split is most advantageous to current Vietnamese policies. Partial detente is to be feared because of its potential for diminishing long-term Soviet assistance to Vietnam. And a complete Sino-Soviet rapprochement would pose almost unthinkable dilemmas for Vietnamese policymakers.

## Upgrading Soviet Military Access

When World War II ended, the era of *Pax Americana* dawned in the Pacific. Japan had been humbled, and the British and French empires were dissolving. For nearly two decades America had its way in the western Pacific. Not until the mid-1960s did the Soviet Union begin to build up major troop concentrations in Asia (directed against China) and, subsequently, naval forces in the Pacific (directed against the United States). Prior to the 1960s, the Soviet Pacific fleet was a coastal navy supplemented by submarines and constrained in its outreach by its dependence on isolated ports of the northern Pacific. Only the United States was a significant naval power with bases and aircraft carriers, marines, and naval aviation. In the 1970s, Soviet naval expansion became significant; carriers were built, and naval aviation expanded. At present, the Soviet Pacific fleet is now the largest of the four Soviet ocean fleets, although it is still not as powerful as the Baltic fleet. Furthermore, one-third of Soviet SS-20 intermediate-range missiles have been deployed to the Soviet Far East, which means that more than 1,000 nuclear warheads are targeted on East Asia and the Pacific.[52]

With Hanoi's victory over South Vietnam in 1975, Soviet naval vessels first visited Cam Ranh Bay, albeit for transit purposes only. In terms of arms deliveries, Vietnam received more in the period from 1979 to 1982 than other established Soviet clients such as Cuba, Ethiopia, Angola, and Mozambique. In 1979, at the time of China's invasion of Vietnam, the Soviets began to station their forces permanently in the former American naval and air facilities on the southern coast of Vietnam. The size of the Soviet military presence at Cam Ranh Bay has expanded inexorably from an initial presence of five to eight ships in 1979. By 1982 the deployment averaged 15 ships on a given day, and new pier construction had been started to service Soviet submarines and surface ships. In 1983, 22 to 28 ships and auxiliaries were based at Cam Ranh Bay.[53]

The most remarkable development in this buildup occurred in November 1983, when the Soviet Union for the first time stationed attack bombers at Cam Ranh Bay. By late 1984, 16 *Badgers* (10 with strike capabilities) were stationed at Cam Ranh along with 8 *Bear* bombers and a squadron of advanced fighters (MiG-23s). These *Badger* bombers can carry out missions along a 1,500-mile radius from Cam Ranh.[54] The wartime mission of the aircraft is probably to attack shipping in an arc from the Indian Ocean, through the Malacca Straits, to the Java Sea and the South China Sea and the southern coast of mainland China. These aircraft would probably be a poor match for sophisticated American air elements stationed at Clark Field and Subic Bay in the Philippines. In the event of direct war between the superpowers, these Soviet air elements would be extremely vulnerable. The most likely function of both the air and sea elements is *not* against the United States but to pressure other potential enemies in the region, especially China. An additional motivation for these deployments is probably to give practical meaning to the concept of parity by projecting Soviet military power into another region where American power had once predominated. This reasoning applies to both the Indian Ocean and the South China Sea, where Soviet naval and air elements can now operate much more readily because of their newfound facilities at Cam Ranh Bay. Access to these facilities reduces the Soviet Navy's transit time to the vital straits of Southeast Asia from two weeks (using Vladivostok) to three days (using Cam Ranh Bay).[55] Enhanced capability to project Soviet naval power into the Indian Ocean is probably the single most compelling motivation for increased ship and aircraft deployments.

The most germane questions about the new deployments at Cam Ranh Bay concern their portent for the future. Why would the Vietnamese agree to such a significant increase in the Soviet military presence on their territory, particularly at this time; and what do the new deployments imply for the future?

There are several interpretations of Vietnam's decision to allow the Soviets to bring the *Badgers* into Vietnam. First, the isolation of Vietnam may be such that the elite does not fully appreciate how the outside world will perceive this new deployment. The Vietnamese politburo may not see the deployment as a major change; the leadership may not be aware that such deployments, beyond areas directly contiguous to the Soviet Union, are rare. Although the deployment to Vietnam is the first of its kind by the Soviet Union since 1972, it is at least possible that Vietnam's leaders have incorrectly gauged international reaction to this development, in the same way that they failed to anticipate the adverse worldwide reaction to marching their forces into Cambodia to topple Pol Pot in 1978.

A second hypothetical explanation might be that Vietnam knew that China would take a very dim view of Soviet medium-range bombers near its southern border, but that the Soviets simply demanded this privilege in the name of past and future friendship and economic and military assistance.

A third and more likely explanation is that Vietnam may have felt that this concession would permanently foreclose any unilateral Soviet concessions on the Kampuchean question in future Sino-Soviet discussions. This concession to the Soviet Union might be the ultimate insurance policy for Vietnam. By giving the Soviets the potential capacity to extend their manned bomber coverage over the entire southwestern Pacific (assuming that *Badgers* will one day give way to *Backfires*), Vietnam will have made itself irreplaceable in the eyes of Soviet strategic and political planners. Just as Philippine security against external attack is guaranteed by the U.S.-Philippine Mutual Defense Treaty and the Military Bases Agreement, Vietnam may perceive the Treaty of Friendship and the Soviet base facilities as permanent assurances that the Soviets will never desert Vietnam in favor of China.

## The Future Is Past: Why the Doves Crashed

One possible interpretation of the somewhat softer rhetoric of the Eighth Indochina Foreign Ministers Conference in 1984, the partial absence of a PAVN dry season offensive in 1983–84, and the travels to Hanoi of General Murdani and the Indonesian Center for Strategic and International Studies delegation[56] was that there seemed to be a light at the end of the tunnel and that a satisfactory settlement of the Kampuchean problem was in the offing in early 1984. Indonesian informants indicated that at the time Vietnam had become amenable to serious negotiations. Specifically, Indonesians contended that Vietnam would have accepted the concept of a phased, but *eventually* total, withdrawal in return for cutting off supplies and withdrawing recognition from the Khmer Rouge. With regard to policing the withdrawal, Vietnam indicated a willingness to accept an international peacekeeping force comprised of nations such as India, Britain, France, and Vietnam, but *not* under the auspices of the United Nations.

On the political front, in February 1984 there may have been some willingness to accept Sihanouk as head of the coalition and to subordinate Heng Samrin. According to the Indonesian interpretation current in February 1984, no decisions had been taken on how to define "Khmer Rouge." Many of the Heng Samrin regime's highest officials, including Heng Samrin himself, are former Khmer Rouge, and Indonesian observers thought the Vietnamese might be willing to accept many Khmer Rouge functionaries while refusing to include the leadership in plans for the future of Kampuchea. According to this optimistic view, Hanoi might accept Son Sann and the non-communists (albeit without top leadership). While the makeup of a coalition government could be negotiated, for Vietnam there must be a fundamental understanding that any Cambodian government must recognize the "primacy" of Hanoi within Indochina and have a relationship of "special solidarity" with Vietnam.

What happened to these optimistic prognostications that were current in January-February 1984? Why did the doves of peace fail to land safely? This author believes that the long-awaited Cambodia settlement failed to mature because of Hanoi's long-term intentions, the relative military balance inside Cambodia, and the interests of China and the Soviet Union.

First, in discussions in Hanoi, Indonesians were told that any government sitting in Phnom Penh must recognize the "primacy" of Hanoi and accept a relationship of "special solidarity" with the SRV. Given the meaning attached to these phrases by Vietnam in the past, there was no reason to assume that the Vietnamese were saying anything different from the January 5, 1978 statement of the Vietnamese ambassador to Beijing who, in response to the Pol Pot government's charge that Vietnam had invaded Cambodia, stated that Vietnam had full respect for the sovereignty and independence of Democratic Kampuchea and that Vietnam wanted only the same relationship of "special solidarity" that it then enjoyed with Laos. Since at that time Vietnam had stationed 20,000 to 40,000 troops in Laos and had a commanding position from which to influence all important decisions, this statement could hardly have been very reassuring to Pol Pot and his associates. In fact, in 1977–78 the term "special solidarity" entailed a fundamental diminution of Khmer national sovereignty. After all the diplomatic maneuvering of 1984 and 1985, it should be clear that Vietnam continues to attach the same operational meaning to the term "special solidarity," and that no meaningful restoration of Khmer sovereignty is actually being contemplated. It became increasingly apparent in 1985 that Hanoi's model for a negotiated settlement is Geneva 1954 or Paris 1973—that is, a venue for the capitulation of its enemies rather than a locale for genuine compromise and accommodation.

When Vietnam speaks of "eventual" total withdrawal, how should this be interpreted? Surely it does not mean a withdrawal that would be disadvantageous to Vietnam. Vietnam certainly knows that Heng Samrin's army could not police the country at present if Vietnam withdrew. Without either total capitulation to Vietnam's design or national reconciliation of a type that Vietnam deems unacceptable, total withdrawal would clearly be impossible in less than five or ten years, even if outside supplies evaporate for Pol Pot.[57] After the experiences of 1984 and 1985, it should be clear that "eventual" withdrawal implies a very long time frame rather than any compromise of Vietnamese long-term goals.

Second, the constellation of military forces fighting inside Kampuchea does not favor an early settlement. No settlement can be considered by Vietnam if it raises the possibility that Pol Pot's ultra-nationalists might rule again in Phnom Penh. Any meaningful settlement demands, not a coalition of voters, but a coalition of armies that is capable of ruling the land and keeping the peace with Thailand and Vietnam. Any government that expects to rule without resort to foreign armies at minimum must integrate the armies of Son Sann, Sihanouk, and Heng Samrin, while attracting as many as possible of the Khmer Rouge rank and file and harrying the remainder out of the land. Creating a state with the power to rule Cambodia requires rapid growth of the ANS, KPNLF, and the forces of the PRK to a point where they become superior in number and quality to the Khmer Rouge. Unfortunately, the trends of the last two years have not favored this outcome. PRK forces remain largely impotent, and the stalwarts of Son Sann and Sihanouk remain relatively poorly armed, underprovisioned, and gravely lacking in basic leadership. In contrast, the resources provided to the Khmer Rouge by China are sufficient to facilitate rapid expansion. As a result of burgeoning anti-Vietnamese sentiments as well as a favorable supply situation, the quantum of military power at the disposal of the Khmer Rouge today is greater than at any time since early 1979, and this bodes ill for any coalition-style solution to the fighting in Cambodia.

The third factor weighing against a settlement is the position of China. The goal of China is to neutralize a combined Soviet/Vietnamese threat from the south by continuing to paralyze Vietnam and drain Soviet resources through (1) military pressure on the Sino-Vietnamese border and (2) guerrilla activity inside Cambodia. Ensuring the security of Thailand and the independence of Cambodia remains an important but secondary concern of China. Unless Vietnam becomes willing to diminish the Soviet presence in Indochina and move toward recognizing Chinese interests in the region, compromise solutions are largely irrelevant. For instance, a national reconciliation government in Cambodia, even if it produced a state with which Vietnam and Thailand could coexist, would be disadvantageous to China if (1) the Soviets retain use of the facilities at Cam Ranh Bay and (2) Vietnam remains hostile to China. Hence, China's military aid policies to the Khmer resistance are more closely attuned to "bleeding Vietnam" than to building up armed forces that, in concert with Heng Samrin, might be capable of ruling Cambodia and establishing a peaceful relationship with both Vietnam and Thailand. For China, the present situation is relatively attractive: the continuing conflict is costly to the Soviet Union and precludes the economic modernization of Vietnam, thereby guaranteeing its ultimate decline as a power if China achieves a modicum of modernization. The cost of this policy, however, is sustaining Vietnamese dependence on the Soviets—and thus Moscow's military presence on China's southern frontier.

Fourth, the Soviet position also militates against a settlement. The Soviet Union, from bases in Vietnam, can now project power readily throughout Southeast Asia and into the Indian Ocean. Giving up these facilities would not end the ability of Soviet naval aviation to threaten the vital supply lines to Japan, but doing so from bases in the Soviet Union would require more modern, long-range weapons. The Soviets are stepping up their military presence in Indochina rather than decreasing it, and this, in and of itself, provides a sufficient motivation for China to continue to block a settlement. This remains true even though Chinese leaders, for tactical reasons, have indicated that they would not object to the Soviets maintaining themselves in Cam Ranh Bay if they first convinced the Vietnamese to restore Cambodian sovereignty and true independence.[58] China's concession, in this instance, is not unlike the Heng Samrin government's willingness to contemplate the return of Sihanouk to Cambodia if he were first to break totally with the Khmer Rouge. Deng Xiaoping and Heng Samrin are both offering a concession that they know the opposite side cannot accept. The Soviets know that undercutting Vietnam's design for hegemony in Indochina would be seen as treachery and would lead to their expulsion from military facilities in Vietnam. It remains unlikely that Soviet planners would be willing to assume the very substantial risks required to take up China on its offer.

Rather than peace being "just around the corner," in retrospect it is clear that Hanoi in early 1984 was mounting a peace offensive with the maximum goal of dividing ASEAN and the minimum goal of decreasing Vietnam's diplomatic isolation. Rather than being on the verge of a genuine settlement, the events of early 1984 should be understood as a "bombing pause." During the American war in

Indochina, bombing pauses were the product of political pressures and bureaucratic infighting; they were oversold to the leadership by holding out the prospect that the enemy, if only given an opportunity, would acquiesce to basic U.S. terms, or at least that they would convince our increasingly restive public of the administration's sincere desire for peace. After peace "had had its turn," however, military efforts were redoubled. The same logic applied to Indochina in 1984 when ASEAN and China did not prove amenable to Vietnam's "peace offensive." Under these circumstances, Vietnam energetically returned to military forms of struggle and the "pause" of 1984, like its American predecessors in the 1960s and early 1970s, turned out to be a prelude to more war in 1985 rather than a pathway to peace. Stalemate, set on ever-ascending levels of violence, continues to be a more likely outcome for Indochina than either a negotiated settlement or a successful Vietnamese conquest of Cambodia.

## Endnotes

1. See "Belgium May Find Role to Play Among Actors on Khmer Stage," *Asia Record*, February 1983, p. 12; Nayan Chanda, "Fueling New Hopes," *Far Eastern Economic Review*, March 3, 1983, pp. 10–13; and Nayan Chanda, "Romanian Rendezvous," *Far Eastern Economic Review*, March 17, 1983, pp. 22–23.
2. Sixth Conference of Foreign Ministers of Laos, Kampuchea, and Vietnam, Hanoi Domestic Service, 7 July 1982, *Daily Report: Asia and Pacific*, Foreign Broadcast Information Service (FBIS), 7 July 1982, pp. A2–6.
3. Letter dated September 15, 1982, from H. E. Mr. Phoune Sipaseuth, Vice President of the Council of Ministers, Minister of Foreign Affairs of Lao People's Democratic Republic, addressed to their Excellencies the Ministers for Foreign Affairs of the Five Member Countries of ASEAN, Embassy of the Lao People's Democratic Republic, Washington, D.C., Press Release No. 002/WT. 04182.
4. "Kaysone Phomivhan Opens Session," *Daily Report: Asia and Pacific*, FBIS, 23 February 1983, p. I4.
5. "Final Statement of the Indochinese Summit," *Daily Report: Asia and Pacific*, FBIS, 23 February 1983, p. I7.
6. "Statement on the Presence of Volunteers of the Vietnamese Army in Kampuchea, *Daily Report: Asia and Pacific*, FBIS, 24 February 1983, p. I7.
7. "Further Reportage on Indochina Foreign Ministers Meeting," *Daily Report: Asia and Pacific*, FBIS, 20 July 1983, p. H4.
8. "Further Reportage on Indochinese Ministers Conference," *Daily Report: Asia and Pacific*, FBIS, 20 July 1983, p. H2.
9. "PRK Agrees Not to Attend ASEAN, Indochina Talks," *Daily Report: Asia and Pacific*, FBIS, 20 July 1983, p. H4.

10. On further indications of an incipient but partial thaw between China and Vietnam, see Willy van Damme, "Closer to Compromise?" *Far Eastern Economic Review*, December 15, 1983, p. 18.

11. Contrast the constant repetition of the border problem formulation in the 21 July 1983 proposal with its virtual absence six months later.

12. "VNA: Indochinese Foreign Ministers Communique," *Daily Report: Asia and Pacific*, FBIS, 31 January 1984, pp. K10-11.

13. "Nhan Dan Praises Results of Vietnamese Conference," *Daily Report: Asia and Pacific*, FBIS, 31 January 1984, p. K6.

14. "Sitthi Comments on SRV's Troop Withdrawal," *Daily Report: Asia and Pacific*, FBIS, 3 May 1983, p. J2; "Further Response to SRV Troop Withdrawal," *Daily Report: Asia and Pacific*, FBIS, 5 May 1983, p. J1.

15. See "Foreign Minister Addresses UN on Kampuchea's Plight," *Daily Report: Asia and Pacific*, FBIS, 4 October 1983, pp. J1-4.

16. See Nayan Chanda, "ASEAN's Odd Man Out," and Susumu Awanohara, "Where There's a Will . . . ," *Far Eastern Economic Review*, March 1, 1984, pp. 8-10. For Murdani's most controversial statement, see "Further Reportage on Indonesian General's Visit," *Daily Report: Asia and Pacific*, FBIS, 16 February 1984, p. K5.

17. "Further Reportage on Indonesia General's Visit," *Daily Report: Asia and Pacific*, FBIS, 16 February 1984, p. K5.

18. Rodney Tasker, "ASEAN Toughs It Up," *Far Eastern Economic Review*, July 26, 1984.

19. See "Nguyen Co Thach Interview on PRC, Indochina," *Daily Report: Asia and Pacific*, FBIS, 9 April 1984, pp. K3-6, and "Nhan Dan Marks Kampuchean Liberation Day," *Daily Report: Asia and Pacific*, FBIS, 26 April 1984, pp. K5-6.

20. "Svenska Dagbadet Interview with Kong Korm," *Daily Report: Asia and Pacific*, FBIS, 27 April 1984, pp. H2-3.

21. "Reportage on ASEAN Foreign Ministers Meeting," *Daily Report: Asia and Pacific*, FBIS, 10 July 1984, pp. A1-5; "ASEAN Ministers Issue Communique After Meeting," *Daily Report: Asia and Pacific*, FBIS, 12 July 1984, pp. A1-2; and Tasker, "ASEAN Toughs It Up."

22. Raphael Pura, "Jakarta's Frustrated Wooing of Hanoi," *Asian Wall Street Journal*, June 4, 1984, p. 14.

23. "Indochinese Foreign Ministers Issue Communiqué," *Daily Report: Asia and Pacific*, FBIS, 23 January 1985, p. K1.

24. *Ibid.*, p. K3.

25. "Nguyen Co Thach Opens Foreign Ministers' Meeting," *Daily Report: Asia and Pacific*, FBIS, 18 January 1985, p. K1.

26. "Indochinese Foreign Ministers Issue Communiqué," p. K2.

27. *Ibid.*, p. K3.

28. *Ibid.*, p. K3.

29. "Nguyen Co Thach Opens Foreign Ministers' Meeting," p. K1.

30. "Hun Sen Interview on Meeting with Hayden," *Daily Report: Asia and Pacific*, FBIS, 14 March 1985, pp. H4-7; and "Australian Foreign Minister Hayden on SRV Visit," *Daily Report: Asia and Pacific*, FBIS, 14 March 1985, pp. J2-4.

31. "Hun Sen Interview on Meeting with Hayden," p. H6.
32. "Army Commander on Border Situation, SRV Tactics," *Daily Report: Asia and Pacific*, FBIS, 14 March 1985, pp. J4–5.
33. Joint Statement on Kampuchea by ASEAN Foreign Ministers issued in Bangkok on February 11, 1985, *Daily Report: Asia and Pacific*, FBIS, 14 February 1985, pp. A1–2.
34. See "ASEAN Conference Communiqué Criticized," *Daily Report: USSR*, FBIS, 19 February 1985, p. E1; and "Papers View ASEAN Foreign Ministers' Statement," *Joint Publications Research Service: Southeast Asia*, 85-052, 26 March 1985.
35. "U.S. Urged to Supply Arms, Other aid to CGDK," *Daily Report: Asia and Pacific*, FBIS, 12 February 1985, p. J1.
36. Nayan Chanda, "A Clear Link," *Far Eastern Economic Review*, 14 March 1985, p. 30.
37. Eighteenth ASEAN Ministerial Meeting Joint Communiqué," Paragraph 44.
38. "Radio Condemns Thai Proximity Talks Idea," *Daily Report: Asia and Pacific*, FBIS, 11 July 1985, p. H1.
39. "Hanoi English Comments on ASEAN's Proposal," *Daily Report: Asia and Pacific*, FBIS, 12 July 1985, p. K1.
40. "Nguyen Co Thach Interviewed on Southeast Asia," *Daily Report: Asia and Pacific*, FBIS, 12 July 1985, p. K2.
41. "Cambodia: A Growing Threat From Within," *Asiaweek*, October 14, 1983.
42. For a description of this viewpoint, see Donald K. Emmerson, "Benefits of Deadlock, Hints of Accommodation: Kampuchea and the Interests of the Outside Powers," unpublished paper, May 1985.
43. On the 1982-83 dry season offensive see Karl D. Jackson, "Indochina: War Without End" in Karl D. Jackson and Hadi Soesastro (eds.), *ASEAN Security and Economic Development* (Berkeley, Calif.: Institute of East Asian Studies, 1984).
44. See Naoki Mabuchi, "Focus on the War Inside Kampuchea," *Bangkok Post*, June 26, 1983; *Indochina Chronology*, vol. II, no. 4, pp. 11–12 (Berkeley: Institute of East Asian Studies, 1983) and Paul Quinn-Judge, "A Harvest of Death," *Far Eastern Economic Review*, October 13, 1983.
45. See John McBeth, "Jumping the Gun: Khmer Rouge Claims That It Attacked the Vietnamese Deep Inside Cambodia Are Confirmed by U.S. Satellite Pictures," *Far Eastern Economic Review*, February 16, 1984, p. 22, and "Cambodian Insurgents Report Raid on City," *New York Times*, February 17, 1984.
46. "VONADK (Voice of the National Army of Democratic Kampuchea) Reports Guerrillas Kill Eight Soviet Advisors," *Daily Report: Asia and Pacific*, FBIS, 1 September 1983, p. H2.
47. On the 1984 dry season offensive see: William Branigin, "Vietnamese Seized Across Thai Border as Rebel War in Cambodia Intensifies," *Washington Post*, March 30, 1984, pp. A21–22; William Branigin, "Cambodia Border Fight Spurs Conflicting Claims," *Washington Post*, April 5, 1984, p. A20; Michael Weisskopf, "Vietnam Reports Border Attack," *Washington Post*, April 8, 1984, pp. A21, A24; William Branigin, "Vietnamese Drive 70,000 Out of Cambodia," *Washington Post*, April 17, 1984, p. A13.

48. On the dry season offensive, see Douglas Pike (ed.), *Indochina Chronology*, vol. 3, no. 4 (October-December 1984), vol. 4, no. 1 (January-March 1985), vol. 4, no. 2 (April-June 1985).

49. Paul Quinn-Judge and Rodney Tasker, "Victory for All," *Far Eastern Economic Review*, March 14, 1985, p. 26.

50. Rodney Tasker, "The War Continues," *Far Eastern Economic Review*, May 9, 1985, pp. 28–30.

51. "Chinese Artillery Shells Vietnamese on Second Front," *Washington Post*, April 18, 1983, p. 16; Michael Wilkinson, "China's Border Clash with Vietnam Linked to Kampuchean Offensive," *Christian Science Monitor*, April 18, 1983; "China Reports Shelling Vietnam," *New York Times*, April 3, 1984, p. A3; Serge Schmemann, "Chinese Said to Finish Talks in Soviet Union with No Major Gain," *New York Times*, March 27, 1984.

52. See John C. Dorrance, "United States Security Interests in the Pacific Islands," (Office of Australia and New Zealand Affairs, Department of State, February 1984), p. 3. Also, see Chapter 3 by Harry Gelman and Chapter 4 by J. J. Martin in this volume.

53. See Office of the Secretary of Defense, *Soviet Military Power 1982*, *Soviet Military Power 1983*, *Soviet Military Power 1984*, and *Soviet Military Power 1985* (Washington, D.C.: U.S. Government Printing Office). See also, "Build-Up on the Bay," *Far Eastern Economic Review*, December 29, 1983, p. 16.

54. See John W. R. Taylor (ed.), *Jane's All the World's Aircraft 1980-81* (London: Jane's Publishing Company, 1981), pp. 206-209.

55. Karen De Young, "New Arms, Troops Expand Soviet Military Role in Southeast Asia," *Washington Post*, December 21, 1983, p. 1, and Drew Middleton, "Soviet Buildup in Far East Causing U.S. Concern," *New York Times*, January 30, 1984.

56. See Jusuf Wanandi, "Seeking Peace Amid Cambodia's Conflict," *Far Eastern Economic Review*, March 8, 1984, and Susumu Awanohara, "Up Against the Wall: A Hoped-For Breakthrough on Cambodia Runs into Trouble," *Far Eastern Economic Review*, March 22, 1984, pp. 12–13.

57. For speculation on when the armed forces of the PRK might be ready to assume full authority for policing Kampuchea, see Paul M. Kattenburg, " 'So Many Enemies': The View From Hanoi," *Indochina Issues*, no. 38 (June 1983), p. 6.

58. "Cambodian Incursion: China Asks Russia to Rein in Vietnam," *San Francisco Chronicle*, April 18, 1985, p. 18. Private conversations with PRC academics confirm the brief that China will not require Vietnam to expel the USSR from its bases; however, the Chinese privately admit that Soviet complicity in a Kampuchean settlement would probably result in decreasing levels of Soviet access to its important bases in Indochina.

For statements by Deng Xiaoping and senior political adviser Huan Xiang on the Soviet bases in Vietnam, see, respectively: *New York Times*, April 18, 1985; "Huan Xiang Reviews World Situation and Foreign Policy," in Hong Kong *Wen Hui Bao*, June 22, 1985, as translated in FBIS, *China*, June 24, 1985, p. W1.

*Part Four*

# THE EUROPEAN EXPERIENCE WITH THE SOVIET NUCLEAR THREAT: IMPLICATIONS FOR ASIAN SECURITY

*Chapter 12*

# DISTANT RELATIONS: LINKS BETWEEN ASIAN AND EUROPEAN SECURITY

*by Henry S. Rowen*

The members of collective security alliances have often been geographically separated by common enemies. The countries of Western Europe, together with several in East Asia, are in such a situation today vis-à-vis the Soviet Union, although the most immediately threatened countries (the Federal Republic of Germany and the People's Republic of China, for example) have not expressed their shared security interests in the form of treaties that span Europe and East Asia.

This chapter assesses the shared vulnerabilities of the United States and its allies in both Europe and Asia to the growing Soviet military threat. It also considers ways in which European and Asian defense activities, loosely coordinated through the central role of the United States in countering the Soviet threat, could strengthen constraints on expansionist moves by the USSR.

## Intertheater Linkages

From the perspective of Washington, Asian security and European security have long been seen as interconnected. For instance, the attack by North Korea, with Soviet complicity, on South Korea in June of 1950 was interpreted in the United States as an initial move in a Soviet strategy of global expansion. It triggered a large-scale strengthening of American strategic nuclear and general purpose forces, and resulted in U.S. reinforcements being sent to Europe as well as to Asia. The war in Korea was seen as possibly setting the context for a follow-on Soviet attack in Europe. With American forces committed in the Far East, Soviet planners may have calculated, it would be easier to make a move in Europe, which both Moscow and Washington have judged to be the most vulnerable, vital area at stake in their ongoing and global geopolitical rivalry.

One consequence of this viewpoint has been the famous—or infamous—"swing strategy," in which U.S. defense planners have held open the possibility of transferring naval units in the Pacific to the Atlantic in the event of a major U.S.-Soviet conflict. Whether or not such a shift would actually occur would depend on events and judgments at the time. Moreover, there was an intertheater symmetry to "swinging." For instance, during the Vietnam War the United States moved forces from Europe to Southeast Asia—to the displeasure of the European allies.

A basic strategic problem facing the United States is the difficulty of dealing simultaneously with Soviet threats in Europe and Asia; or to be more precise, with threats in some combination in Europe, Southwest Asia, and East Asia. In contrast, the Soviet Union has been credited with a capacity to operate in each theater more or less independently—that is, without reinforcements from other areas.[1] Such an asymmetry in defense posture, if it exists, puts the West in a decidedly inferior position. The Soviets, masters of chess, know how to exploit such a disparity on the "board" of global politico-military rivalry.

The Soviet Union, in fact, has large forces in each of its geographical regions that are more numerous—or at least stronger— than those immediately opposing them. But some of these force dispositions also reflect geostrategic weaknesses. This is most obvious with its navy, which has difficult access to the seas from each of its four base areas. On land, communications between Europe and the Far East Maritime Provinces remain largely dependent on a rail system that is long and vulnerable to disruption. (This vulnerability was an important reason for the construction of the BAM railroad, which parallels to the north the Trans-Siberian line.) Only Soviet air units are reliably mobile among widely separated theaters of military operation.

The Soviet Union faces another strategic disadvantage: For each additional theater in which it is involved in military operations, it engages more adversaries. Although strong in each area, Soviet

planners cannot be enthusiastic about the prospect of being involved in conflict, at the limit, with nearly the entire industrialized
world plus China and other developing nations. This is the well-
known two-front security problem faced by the Soviet Union,
although in reality it could face more than two fronts. Not only are
there three major regions of potential conflict around its periphery, but there are possibly some "fronts" internal to the Soviet
Empire (discussed below). At most, the Soviets want to be faced
with conflict on only one (external) front at any given time.

Therefore, it has long been to the advantage of the West to try to
convince Moscow that it would face a multifront problem if it
attacks anywhere along its extensive Eurasian periphery. We do
not know how Soviet planners estimate this prospect; they might
reasonably be skeptical that they would today confront the difficulties of a multinational war on two or more fronts. Any rational
government has an incentive not to take its people to war with the
Soviet Union; they will do so only if they believe their country's
fate will be worse if it doesn't support other beleaguered states.
Even though Soviet planners may rate as low the probability that
widely separated and nonallied countries may act jointly against
the USSR if it undertakes to attack any single country—and they
may even have some doubts about the response of those that are
members of alliances—with so many hostile states around it, even
the modest probability of a grand intertheater coalition may weigh
heavily on their minds. (The Soviet attack on Afghanistan is one
case, however, in which Moscow was not deterred by the fear of
multiple and coordinated responses by its adversaries.)

The Soviet strategic situation is potentially worse. It also faces
adversaries from *within* its empire. This is evident in Eastern
Europe, a region whose peoples have repeatedly demonstrated a
desire to unburden themselves of Soviet rule. This rejection has
implications for the military balance in the West. With normal
peacetime deployments, approximately one-half of the Warsaw
Pact ground forces and one-third of the air forces in the Central
Region in Europe are non-Soviet. To Moscow, the East European
forces and peoples are of uncertain reliability. Moreover, the
logistic line of supply from the Soviet Union to Western Europe
extends over 1,000 km through countries with hostile populations.
In a conflict with NATO, the non-Soviet Warsaw Pact soldiers and
civilians may or may not behave according to Moscow's directives,
and uncertainty concerning their behavior has to weigh heavily in
the thinking of Soviet military planners. One conclusion that they
may draw is that massive reinforcement with Soviet troops would
be necessary before the start of any conflict to try to ensure against

trouble within Eastern Europe. From the perspective of intertheater linkages, such reinforcements would not be available to be sent elsewhere, as to Southwest Asia, or the Far East. And under some circumstances, Moscow might even find it necessary to pull back some troops from its Far Eastern military districts to hold down the "rear" in Europe. If this were to happen, it would amount to a kind of Soviet "swing" response.

Moscow's potential internal problems do not end with its Warsaw Pact allies. For instance, the peoples of the Baltic states clearly resent Soviet domination. During World War II, they quickly went over to the German side. In terms of numbers, the defections by the peoples of the Ukraine and North Caucausus were more significant. These events may seem too remote in time to be pertinent today, but the memory of these defections is probably fresh in the minds of Soviet leaders. Reports of desertions among Moslem Soviet soldiers in Afghanistan suggest that there may be a substantial potential for such dissidence.

## Similarities and Differences Along the Soviet Periphery

Overall, the Soviet military posture is intended to prevent or correct threatening developments within the Soviet empire (e.g., as in Hungary in 1956, Czechoslovakia in 1968, or Poland in 1980–81), to deter hostile moves against Soviet allies (e.g., by China against Vietnam), to extend power abroad (e.g., to Syria, Cuba, and Vietnam), to induce more compliant behavior by other states (in all regions), to control important "buffer" territories (e.g., Afghanistan), and to be prepared to fight adversaries wherever necessary.

These are general missions of the Soviet military establishment, but the conditions it faces in the varied regions of concern to Moscow differ widely. In Europe, the Soviet Union confronts a coalition, which has weaknesses, with its own coalition—which also has weaknesses. This fact sets important limits to Soviet options in that region.

In contrast, in Southwest Asia the USSR faces inherently unstable states that might in the future (as in centuries past) provide opportunities for the extension of Moscow's power. The United States has taken on Great Britain's historical role in opposing the tendency of Moscow to expand in this direction; but unlike Britain in times past, the United States does not have the incentive of protecting colonial holdings on the Indian subcontinent. Instead, the United States has an interest in the security of Turkey,

Pakistan, and other states in the area, and an interest in protecting access to the oil of the Persian Gulf; but this latter interest is no greater than that of Japan or Europe, and is arguably less. Yet the United States receives only modest help from these other countries in this region.

In East Asia, the Soviet Union faces an opponent, China, which appears to be a long-term menace—one that might be coerced in the short run from acting strongly against Soviet interests (e.g., in Vietnam), but which holds the promise of gaining strength over time. It also faces Japan, which although not as hostile as China, is not friendly and which has an industrial capacity as great or greater than that of the Soviet Union itself.

In Europe, the Soviet Union faces a coalition whose erosion and fragmentation is seen as an important task for Moscow; in East Asia the main Soviet concern has been to prevent the formation of a Chinese-Japanese-U.S. coalition directed against it. Through a combination of good luck and management by the Soviets, this coalition has not come into existence; but the potential for its formation remains. This possibility sets important limits to Soviet options in this region. While it seeks to extend its power there (e.g., into and beyond Vietnam and Afghanistan and at sea), the Soviet Union must do so without acting so as to provoke into existence a superior coalition in opposition. There is some Soviet maneuvering room, but Moscow must be uncertain as to its precise limits.

## What Have Soviet Investments Achieved?

To many in the West, it may appear that the Soviet Union has engaged in a form of strategic "overkill" in the Far East in the form of massively increased military forces assigned to Siberia and the Maritime Provinces since the mid-1960s. What have more than 50 divisions along the Chinese border, the reinforcing of islands in the southern Kuriles claimed by Japan, a major expansion of naval units in the Pacific, and a dramatic increase in theater nuclear forces bought? They clearly have been costly.

It is plausible to assume that Soviet leaders see these investments as having produced a China that is less threatening to Soviet interests, one that has not forged an alliance with the United States, and one that has held back from moving decisively against Vietnam. They may also attribute the fact that Japan continues to present no serious threat to the Soviet Union to coercive activities directed against it.

They might do more. Edward Luttwak has suggested that

Moscow might try to create a buffer against China and weaken it by occupying the lightly populated Western provinces of China, notably Xinjiang (Sinkiang).[2] Moscow's attack on Afghanistan suggests that this possibility should not be dismissed out of hand; but China must appear a formidable adversary in a protracted conventional conflict (a la Afghanistan), and it also possesses nuclear weapons. It is more reasonable to attribute to Moscow a continued game of maneuver—although an invasion of China is a possibility to be kept in mind.

From a longer time perspective, the trend of several important parameters is moving against Soviet security and influence in East Asia. The region has the most dynamic economies in the world, and if these countries continue on their present path, they will be a powerful group industrially—and therefore potentially militarily— by the year 2000. They also display a good deal of political stability (with the principal exception of the Philippines). Perhaps worst of all from the Soviet standpoint is the possibility that China's moves, thus far tentative, toward adopting a market economy might produce rapid, sustained growth, while the Soviet Union remains burdened with a sluggish and backward economy. For Marxist-Leninists, people who are supposed to take the long view, this should be a distressing prospect. It also may be doubted that Vietnam will remain indefinitely a poverty-stricken state dependent on the Soviet Union, surrounded by countries that are becoming increasingly strong economically.

On a shorter time scale, that of the 1980s, the Soviet Union no doubt believes that it has made good, indeed necessary, security investments in the Far East. China is still a poor country with only modest military capabilities (although its nuclear forces present the Soviet Union with problems). Above all, Moscow has put in place enough military power to feel confident that adversaries in Asia will be deterred from moving against it in all but the most dire circumstances.

## The Extension of the Soviet Military Reach

Perhaps the most striking change in the Soviet military posture in the past 20 years is the increase in its ability to apply military power at a distance. This change became most dramatically evident with its large buildup of ICBM and SLBM forces beginning in the mid-1960s. The Soviet navy is being transformed from a coastal defense force to one of "blue water" capabilities; the Soviet airlift capacity has expanded enormously; and medium- and long-range reconnaissance aircraft and bombers now reach areas remote from Soviet territory. The Soviet Union has put in place an intelligence and command and control system of worldwide scope. The magnitude of Soviet space programs implies even greater ambitions for global activities in the future.

This extension of "reach" entails the growing use of foreign territory. There are now extensive intelligence facilities around the world in Vietnam, Cuba, and elsewhere. Air and naval bases are available for various purposes in Vietnam, Cuba, South Yemen, Ethiopia, and elsewhere. Soviet combat forces are on the ground in Syria, Cuba, Afghanistan, and Mongolia—as well as in Eastern Europe. These overseas deployments and facilities serve several functions: they provide peacetime intelligence both on local activities and on American forces; they can be used to support friends in conflicts within the region (e.g., Vietnam vs. Cambodia and China, Ethiopia vs. Somalia, the MPLA vs. UNITA in Angola); and they could be used for attacks on U.S. and other Western forward deployments in case of a larger war. Although the Soviet and other forces that the West would have to neutralize at the outset of a war in Cuba, Vietnam, Syria, etc., are not likely to be large, it could be an important diversion to have to deal with them during a period in which rapid access to threatened areas could be crucial to success in combat. In effect, these overseas Soviet stations and forces could exact a form of attrition on Western forces by tying them down when they are needed urgently elsewhere.

In Asia, the two most important places where Soviet military reach is being extended are Vietnam and Afghanistan. As Harry Gelman points out in Chapter 3, Afghanistan can be expected to be used by aircraft whose range into the Indian Ocean and over the Arabian Peninsula will be greatly extended. Vietnam is already being used as a staging base by Soviet aircraft and naval units. The Soviet Union will make more use of these forward bases; and it will try to gain access to new ones, although at the present time the prospect for facilities in other countries in the Pacific and East and South Asia are not good.[3]

## The Significance of the SS-20 "Theater" Missile

Wide concern has been aroused in the last several years, in East Asia as well as in Western Europe, about the growing threat from Soviet SS-20 intermediate-range or "theater" ballistic missiles. Analyses of the exact character of this threat, and how it differs from preceding ones, however, have been scarce. The chief dis-

tinctive characteristics of the SS-20, by comparison with its predecessors, are three: high mobility, multiple warheads, and accuracy
of delivery. Mobility makes the SS-20 difficult to attack; multiple
warheads increase the number of targets that can be attacked with
each missile; and higher accuracy increases weapon effectiveness
against blast-resistant targets and enables a given target to be
damaged with less "spillover" or collateral damage to the surround-
ings.

Although these are militarily desirable attributes for weapons, in
the aggregate it is difficult to believe that they significantly affect
the power balance in Europe or East Asia. Other nuclear systems
already in place or coming along have these same attributes in
various combinations. Short-range land-based missiles are mobile
and accurate. Sea-based cruise missiles are mobile and will be
increasingly accurate, as will the ground-launched cruise missiles
(GLCMs) the Soviet Union is developing. Soviet submarine-based
ballistic missiles (SLBMs) are mobile, and although not very
accurate at present they are improving in this respect. Intercontinental ballistic missiles (ICBMs) can be used at less-than-intercon-
tinental range, many have multiple warheads, and their accuracy
can be very high.

Therefore, why the stir about the SS-20s? Much of it is the result
of Western politicians deciding to make an issue of the missile
when it was first deployed.[4] West German Chancellor Helmut
Schmidt intensified the concern about this weapon in 1977 by
pointing to the asymmetry that existed with the SS-20s in Soviet
hands and no parallel weapon on the ground in Europe able to
reach the Soviet Union. He argued that something should be done
to avert the possibility of a nuclear exchange limited to the two
halves of Europe (i.e., excluding the territory of the Great Powers)
and, therefore, to the need to strengthen the nuclear "coupling"
between Europe and the United States.[5] There followed discussions within NATO leading to the "two-track" INF decision in
December 1979, which in turn led to the INF negotiations with
the Soviet Union to limit these weapons (see Chapter 13 for a
detailed account of this history). With all of this attention, it was
inevitable that the SS-20 would be represented as being of vital
*political* importance, whatever the military significance of the
missile might be.

What, then, should be done about the SS-20? In Europe, given
the history of this issue, politically necessary steps are being taken
with the deployment of the *Pershing IIs* and GLCMs. In addition,
we should go on with our efforts to have a better protected,

controlled, and discriminate nuclear posture while paying more attention to the deficiencies in our capabilities for nonnuclear conflict. For nuclear forces this implies primarily improving our forces at sea (with more accurate *Trident II* missiles, sea-launched cruise missiles, and carrier-based air). With respect to nonnuclear forces, it means modernizing our ground forces in Korea, our air forces there and in Japan, Guam, and elsewhere in the region, and our ability to reinforce the area from the United States rapidly. It does *not* imply putting *Pershing* missiles or GLCMs into the area. In Europe, their deployment was primarily a response to political needs; in Asia there is no obvious political or military case for such a deployment.

## Prospects for the U.S.-China Relationship

The now-normal relationship between China and the United States is important in itself as it has freed American military resources for deployment elsewhere and has given Washington enhanced political flexibility. It is also important because of its influence on the Soviet Union and, in the more distant future, on the military potential of China.

Those who have held extreme views on the evolution of the Sino-American relationship have been wrong in several respects. Predictions that China's vulnerability to the Soviet Union, in combination with an American desire to offset growing Soviet power, would impel Beijing and Washington to seek a close defense relationship have been as much in error as predictions that a continuing U.S. arms supply program for Taiwan would lead to a major retrogression in the relationship. It turns out that the present leadership in Beijing is dominated by practical people who have been willing and able, thus far, to steer a middle course, including active cultural and economic dealings with the United States, while showing reserve in matters of political and defense cooperation. They have done so in part because they have chosen as highest priority the goal of turning China into an economically modernized state. For this to happen within a reasonable period of time, say 50 years, they need a high level of interaction with Western societies (to train scientists and managers) and markets (to gain access to capital and advanced technology). That need, to date, has had higher priority than other goals, such as bringing Taiwan under control or building a much more enhanced military capability with which to counter the Soviet threat.

The Chinese face several difficult problems in achieving their economic objectives. One is the ability of the regime to stay the course in its decentralizing strategy of achieving some form of market socialism. No one, including China's present leaders, can be confident that the country will persist in its present policies. But if it remains dedicated to this goal, it will have important implications for China's foreign policy and for relations with the United States, Japan, and the Soviet Union.

If the Chinese leadership wants rapid economic development, Japan and the newly industrialized Asian states have shown the way: give scope to market forces; hold down the size of government; provide strong incentives for savings; import technology (and possibly, as South Korea has done, import capital); and actively promote exports while gradually reducing restrictions on imports. In combination with a disciplined work force, the Confucian ethic, and a large reserve pool of labor still in agriculture and available for industry, this formula can sustain rapid growth at a rate up to 10 percent a year.

These conditions are far from being met in China today, and they may not be met in the future. But approximations to them should produce respectable results—for instance, 5 to 6 percent growth a year—and China ought to be capable of at least that rate. But active dealings with the West are probably crucial for the success of a high-growth strategy: it is the main source of technology, markets, and—depending on Beijing's willingness and the response of Western markets—of capital. The United States produces 25 percent of the world's GNP and 40 percent of the economic output of the industrial countries; Japan and the United States together produce 40 percent of world output and 60 percent of the industrialized countries' total. It is fair to say that if the Chinese leadership really wants to develop rapidly, it must remain on reasonably good terms with these two countries. This factor sets limits to China's foreign policy.

The development of economic relationships does not bear directly on military cooperation; but it does indirectly. Access to Western technology will inevitably increase China's military potential even if restrictions on certain high technologies are sustained (itself no small task for the West). Although it is easy to imagine the Chinese Communist Party and other bureaucracies resisting such a development strategy, or political instability in Beijing disrupting it, if China is able to get on a path of rapid and sustained growth, one that implies a doubling of real GNP every seven to ten years, the Soviet Union will have much to worry about in terms of a future political and military challenge.

## Soviet Economic Stagnation and
## Future Military Strength

The Soviet Union has carried out a military buildup over the past three decades on a scale previously unknown in history for a country not in a major war (although in Leninist terms, existing world circumstances are not properly regarded as those of peace). Over the same period it has experienced a progressive slowing in its economic growth to a rate that is now only about 1 percent greater than population growth. There is a fair chance that output, at least in per capita terms, will cease to grow in the absence of substantial changes in its economic (and, therefore, political) system.

This prospect has important implications for future Soviet military strength. How deeply the military sector might be affected depends on a number of uncertain factors: the likelihood that fundamental economic changes will be introduced (low, for at least the next several years); the possibility that the regime will reduce the share of consumption or investment in order to increase the military share (also low); and the importation of large amounts of additional capital goods from the West (uncertain, but probably also low).

Moreover, the present situation in the Soviet Union may be worse than is recognized in the West, for one reason: the burden of the Soviet military system on the economy may be much greater than is estimated by most Western analysts. This is partly because the Soviet military system inflicts costs on the economy that are indirect and difficult to assess; but they are real costs nonetheless. It may also be that the size of the total Soviet economy—itself very difficult to measure—may be a good deal smaller than is generally estimated. If this view is correct, Moscow's new leadership under the relatively youthful Party Secretary-General Mikhail Gorbachev is facing considerably more difficult choices than the West has recognized to date.

Faced with difficult trade-off choices, the Soviet Union seems least likely to cut back substantially the military sector given the values that dominate its political system. Even so, it appears that there has been some reduction in the rate of growth of military output since the mid-1970s. Given the nearly static economic performance that is likely to be experienced, military output may grow very slowly. Despite this, large existing stocks of weapons means that the present regional and other military imbalances favoring the Soviet Union will be preserved for some years to come.

Within such a slowly growing military sector, some components might grow more rapidly while others are absolutely reduced. Which components might be the winners and which the losers? This depends on Soviet grand strategy as well as on political influences at the top among the major claimants to economic resources. Those who would argue for giving priority to high-technology arms (space, rocket forces, aviation, naval forces, intelligence) and cutting back on the others (largely ground forces) would have a powerful argument that would be reinforced by the leveling off in the growth in draft-age manpower. This is not a prediction that such a shift will occur, for such a prediction depends on knowledge we do not have; but if it were to occur, there could be important implications for Asian security as well as for that of other regions. It might imply a reversal, at least to a modest extent, of the ground force deployments in the Far East, with resulting greater relative dependence on air and naval power and on nuclear arms. Ground force cuts in the Western USSR seem less likely, given the high priority the leadership attaches to this region in combination with its need for reliable troops.

The other members of the Warsaw Pact also face similar economic problems and, therefore, difficult choices. Their governments are more disposed, however, than is Moscow to holding back on military spending. This preference is a subject of contention within the Pact.

Such a military leveling off is not certain. By some means Moscow might eke out enough economic growth to sustain a growing military establishment, or it might simply squeeze consumption harder in favor of the military. By such means the present system might manage for another decade or so. And during this time, the anticipated political returns from its large military investment might be large.

## The Requirements for Effective Defense of the West

The West faces two major dangers from the Soviet Union: one is that Soviet involvements in the Third World, especially Southwest Asia and the Middle East, will extend the reach of Soviet power well beyond its present boundaries into other regions of high importance to the West. Most important under this heading would be Soviet control over the oil of the Persian Gulf. The other danger is that the Western alliance system will progressively weaken, with a consequent growth in Soviet influence in Europe and Asia, possibly leading to a direct Soviet military move into some vulnerable, important country (e.g., Iran). The essentials of effective Western defense are to sustain alliance systems and to strengthen them, while helping friends in the competition for influence in Third World countries.

In the latter, with limited exceptions, the United States is bearing the burden—with uneven results—and enjoying this role less and less. Congress, which of course reflects an important element in American popular opinion, puts important obstacles in the way of the executive branch's ability to compete in such areas as the Middle East, southern Africa, and Central America. And there are growing signs of restiveness in the public and among elites even with regard to major alliance ties. At the moment, a substantial rebuilding of American military power is taking place, but the domestic political underpinnings necessary for sustaining the post–World War role of the United States around the world is being eroded.

This slow change in attitudes within the United States need not produce dramatic changes in alliance ties or in the U.S. role in the Third World competition. But it implies at least changes at the margin. Actually, adjustments have been going on for a long time as the military forces of the European countries, Japan, Korea, and others have been built up and modernized. In any case, it seems likely that the United States will continue to shift toward providing air and naval support for allies and less support on the ground.

Although the Soviet Union is encumbered by the disadvantages described above, it has been working hard to overcome them and it may succeed. Central to its strategy has been to pose so great a threat in *capabilities* at both the nonnuclear and nuclear levels that its neighbors in Asia and Europe are intimidated while it limits its military *operations* to peripheral regions (Afghanistan, and more recently Pakistan). These areas are not seen—so far—as vital by the United States and the major European and Asian powers. The Soviets apply pressure to vulnerable nations while inducing, through threats and promises, other nations to remain relatively passive. For this Soviet strategy of differentiated pressure to be frustrated, either the separate "target" nations must be strong enough individually to withstand the Soviet Union—a condition that none can meet, although China comes the closest—or they must band together. The common factor today for these countries (with the exception of China) is their ties to the United States. The United States is both the strongest member of the Western camp and the one least directly exposed to Soviet power. Our incentive to gain security through collective action is arguably not as intense as it would be were we more directly vulnerable. Nonetheless, since the late 1940s we have taken the lead in constructing a set of alliances to limit the extension of Soviet power; and despite the strains in our alliance system it continues to play a constraining role.

The present situation can be viewed as meta-stable. It has averted direct Soviet action against U.S. allies. But it has not prevented Soviet-supported successes elsewhere (Cuba, Vietnam, and others), and there are other relatively "soft" targets against which the Soviets might move—especially in Southwest Asia. There are also vulnerable areas not contiguous to the Soviet Union; for example, we are in increased danger of losing our important position in the Philippines. If this happens, no matter what Moscow's role in supporting the insurgency in that country, the Soviet Union will be a clear beneficiary.

The second main danger is a shift toward neutralism by some countries in part in response to the growth of Soviet power. This seems unlikely in much of East Asia—although China's recent efforts to reduce tensions with Moscow despite the lack of any reduction in the Soviet military encirclement of the PRC have some quality of accommodation—but such a shift is discernible in Europe. Given the Europe-Asian connections discussed earlier, a Europe that tilts noticeably in a more neutral direction would have implications for the security of the East Asians as well.

No bold new formula emerges from this analysis. A substantially changed role for the United States does not seem in order. The political basis does not now exist for formal security ties between any of the nations of East Asia and those of Europe. There is no adequate basis at present for formalizing ties among the East Asian countries exposed to the Soviet (and North Korean and Vietnamese) threat. Nor is there sufficient political basis for establishing explicit security ties between the United States and China. All of these relationships will have to continue to be pursued at an informal level—unless, of course, the Soviet Union upsets the present meta-stability. This being so, we need to stay our present course. This is not a course without risks, but there seems to be no more workable approach available in current circumstances.

## Endnotes

1. This point is developed in Chapter 3 by Harry Gelman.
2. Edward N. Luttwak, *The Grand Strategy of the Soviet Union* (London: Weidenfeld & Nicolson, 1983), pp. 104–05.

3. The Soviets have been making determined, but thus far unsuccessful, efforts in recent years to establish friendly relations and gain naval access to the newly independent island countries of the South Pacific (especially Tonga, Vanuatu, and Kiribati). And growing instability in the Philippines could present Moscow a major strategic windfall in the next few years, either in the form of a loss to the United States of its forward naval and air bases at Subic Bay and Clark Field (which would "uncover" the Soviet military presence in Indochina), or— less likely—an opportunity to supplant the United States in the Philippines, as it did in the Vietnamese bases at Cam Ranh Bay.
4. See the analysis of this issue in Chapter 13 by James A. Thomson.
5. Helmut Schmidt, *Survival* (London: International Institute for Strategic Studies, January-February 1978), p. 4.

*Chapter 13*

# THE EUROPEAN THEATER NUCLEAR FORCE DEPLOYMENT DECISION, 1975–1979: IMPLICATIONS FOR U.S.-ALLIANCE RELATIONS

*by James A. Thomson*

## Background

The deployment of American intermediate-range nuclear force (INF*) missiles in Western Europe in December 1983 marked the culmination of a decision process largely completed four years earlier. From 1975 to 1979, the United States, together with its NATO allies, fundamentally changed alliance policy toward theater nuclear forces (TNF). Although the European allies played a strong role in initiating this process, the change in policy was ultimately one for the United States to make as the chief nuclear power of the alliance.

In 1975, when the Soviet SS-20 missile first appeared, the

---

*The terms intermediate-range nuclear forces (INF) and long-range theater nuclear forces (LRTNF) are used interchangeably in this chapter. LRTNF was the term in vogue at the time of the 1979 decision. President Reagan subsequently adopted the term INF.

United States did not possess nuclear missile forces capable of striking Soviet territory from the continent of Europe, nor had it had such a capability since the early 1960s. On December 12, 1979, the United States and its allies decided to deploy such missile forces on the continent of Europe. The process by which the change in policy occurred is the subject of this chapter. The history of this process may be instructive for future decisionmaking and the conduct of nuclear diplomacy, especially for America's relations with its allies. It emphasizes the U.S. policymaking process and the conduct of U.S. diplomacy; hence the lessons are most relevant to the United States, although the experience is clearly of concern to America's allies (and to Soviet observers of Western alliance politics).

By its very nature, such a process is political, and many observers have overlooked the nonpolitical motivations that lay behind it. The LRTNF decision has often been described as purely politically motivated. This description contains elements of truth, but in fact there was a fundamental strategic motive to the decision.

A lengthy analysis of the strategic foundations of the LRTNF decision is not included here. The debate within the United States and the alliance over LRTNF was a complex one that saw many different analyses and points of view. To oversimplify, the decision was a response to two changes that occurred in the strategic balance between the early 1960s, when U.S. missiles were withdrawn from Europe, and the mid-1970s, when the SS-20 first appeared.

The 1970s was a period in which the Soviet Union attained strategic parity with the United States. This had been foreseen for some time; it had led to the formal adoption by NATO in 1967 of the "flexible response" strategy. Western strategic analysts believed that *in Soviet eyes* Soviet strategic parity would reduce U.S. willingness to use its strategic nuclear forces in contingencies short of nuclear attack on the United States itself, thereby sharply reducing the credibility of the American nuclear umbrella over Europe. The flexible response strategy sought to give NATO leaders a range of nuclear employment options below the level of massive strategic nuclear strikes. These options were believed to strengthen deterrence because they would provide an unbroken chain from theater conventional war to strategic nuclear war. Although NATO had enunciated this doctrine in 1967, by 1975 there had been no important changes in the structure of NATO's nuclear forces in Europe to give reality to the doctrine.

The second strategic change was a broad modernization of all weapons in the Soviet nuclear arsenal, not just strategic nuclear forces. During the early 1970s, the Soviet Union began deploying a new family of nuclear-capable fighter-bombers and medium bombers, including the *Backfire*. In 1975, it was expected in the West that Moscow would begin to deploy by the late 1970s a new family of theater nuclear missiles—the SS-21, SS-22, and SS-23— as well as nuclear artillery shells. Finally, in 1975 testing began of a new Soviet intermediate-range ballistic missile (IRBM)—the SS-20—apparently intended as a replacement for the older SS-4s, and SS-5s. Across the board, these capabilities gave the Soviet Union major improvements in employment flexibility of its nuclear forces and put it in a position to counter NATO's nuclear employment options at every level of conflict. Most importantly, the SS-20, which was also a major improvement over its predecessors, reminded Western strategists that NATO had no employment options to speak of at the LRTNF level. Soviet nuclear deployments thus exploited strategic nuclear parity and sought to undermine NATO's flexible response strategy.

These strategic changes led to growing concern about the state of NATO's deterrent capabilities among both American and European defense experts. On the whole, however, these concerns were rarely enunciated in public.[1]

By 1975, the United States was embarked on development programs to field air-launched and sea-launched cruise missiles in nuclear roles. Cruise missiles have long been a matter of interest and dispute within the United States, especially between Department of Defense civilians and the U.S. Air Force, because of the inevitable suggestion that such weapons could substitute for manned aircraft. But there was also considerable interest in the potential application of cruise missile technology for NATO defense problems, chiefly in the conventional role. Because cruise missile technology was moving forward rapidly and appeared extremely promising, it is hardly surprising that a link was drawn between the technology and the emerging strategic problem that the SS-20 symbolized. As early as 1975–76, analysts in the Pentagon began to speak of cruise missiles as the U.S. "counter" to the SS-20 and its medium bomber counterpart, the *Backfire*.

## Phase I: American Foot-Dragging

It remained for political forces to combine with strategic and technological motivations to push the LRTNF issue forward. The political forces centered on SALT—in particular, the agreement reached between the United States and Soviet Union in Vladivostok in November 1974. This "framework" agreement was expected to be turned quickly into a formal SALT II treaty, but it became hung up on two major problems: (1) The United States wanted to see the *Backfire* bomber limited, and (2) the Soviet Union desired to sharply constrain U.S. cruise missile programs, including a ban on long-range ground- and sea-launched cruise missiles (GLCMs and SLCMs).

The Pentagon fought hard against the latter proposed restrictions. While attempting to justify the U.S. right to deploy a long-range GLCM, civilian analysts within the Pentagon posited a theater nuclear mission for the system, which at that time was not even under development. They pointed out that a GLCM force would give the Supreme Allied Commander Europe (SACEUR) the capability to hold targets in the Soviet Union at risk and also to provide a political and strategic counter to the SS-20. They also argued that cruise missiles could substitute for tactical air forces in nuclear strike roles. Defense Department insistence that SALT II preserve the right to deploy GLCM and SLCM systems led to serious frictions within the government, which became readily apparent to European observers.

As they watched the internal American debate, European strategic analysts became concerned that the United States might bargain away capabilities that would be important for Europe's defense—both conventional and nuclear-armed cruise missiles— or for negotiating limits to the Soviet nuclear threat to Europe. Many of the SALT negotiating options under consideration in Washington during 1975 and early 1976 included bans on long-range (greater than 600 km) GLCMs and SLCMs, but no limits on the Soviet nuclear forces arrayed against Europe. Some West German officials began to express worries about the imbalance of "Eurostrategic forces," underscored by the SS-20, and suggested that cruise missiles might help to redress the imbalance.

The American response to such European concerns was a reminder that U.S. strategic forces provided ample target coverage of the Western USSR, and that was the reason the alliance had long foregone a capability to strike at Soviet territory from the European continent. In the face of growing European worries about the meaning of strategic parity and the SS-20, this response was hardly reassuring. European concerns about U.S. SALT policy were transformed into outright suspicions when it was learned that the United States had included a ban on long-range SLCMs and GLCMs in its SALT proposal to the Soviets of February 1976. The

Soviet Union did not accept this proposal, however, and soon thereafter the SALT negotiations went into hiatus as the United States entered the 1976 presidential election campaign.

The Carter administration thus inherited a looming strategic and political problem. By its initial policy inclinations and personnel makeup, the administration hoped to make this problem go away. Yet it pursued policies that deepened rather than alleviated European concerns and thereby increased the political pressures on the United States from its alliance partners to move forward with cruise missiles. The more the United States displayed its reluctance to pursue cruise missiles for NATO, the more its allies wanted them.

The first policy area that intensified the political problem was the Carter administration's emphasis on improving NATO's conventional defenses. At a summit of NATO leaders in May 1977, President Carter called for a comprehensive, long-term conventional defense improvement plan. Immediately thereafter, the United States mounted a major push to put together what came to be known as the Long-Term Defense Plan (LTDP). Although this was not the first such effort within NATO, it was mounted with unusual vigor and involved all levels of the Defense Department, as well as the State Department and the White House. When coupled with the President's own well-known aversion to nuclear weapons (exemplified by his call for complete nuclear disarmament in his inaugural address), this enthusiasm led many Europeans to suspect that the administration intended to shift NATO strategy away from nuclear deterrence and toward conventional defense. This was anathema in Europe, especially in the Federal Republic of Germany.

The administration's SALT policy raised even greater difficulties. The initial Carter negotiating position collapsed during Secretary Vance's March 1977 trip to Moscow. Because a major Soviet objection to the March proposals was their failure to substantially restrict cruise missiles, these weapons now loomed as an obstacle to President Carter's highest priority, a SALT II agreement. Consequently, the administration fashioned a new proposal in May, including a three-year ban on the deployment of long-range GLCMs and SLCMs; in this respect, the proposal did not differ greatly from the February 1976 American proposal.

Nevertheless, when news of this proposal reached Europe, it combined with suspicions about President Carter's antinuclear preferences to produce a strong and negative reaction. The United States appeared to be more concerned about limiting the nuclear threat to the United States than the nuclear threat to Europe, and it seemed to be willing to bargain away weapons important to Europe to obtain limits on Soviet strategic forces. The British and the Germans expressed European concerns most vocally.[2] Allied governments intensified earlier requests to have technical and operational American analyses of the cruise missile issue, which the Carter administration had refused to supply for fear that they would whet the European appetite for cruise missiles.

After a good deal of internal wrangling between the State and Defense Departments, the United States finally decided to answer these requests. In a typical bureaucratic compromise, it decided to discuss cruise missiles more in policy than in technical terms, and to do so in an "evenhanded" way. From the point of view of the Carter administration, the effect of this policy of evenhandedness on the Europeans was disastrous, for those aspects of the U.S. paper that described, especially, the implications of potential cruise missile deployments for arms control, deepened European worries about American intentions. The paper suggested that cruise missiles might have negative arms control implications, for example, by posing verification problems, and raised the possibility of a vigorous and negative Soviet reaction.

The paper went even further to imply that cruise missile deployments might be unwise because of a "decoupling" effect—they would suggest a Eurostrategic balance independent of U.S. strategic forces and thus reduce the credibility of the U.S. strategic nuclear commitment to Europe's defense. Furthermore, the Europeans were not satisfied with the repeated explanation that because U.S. strategic forces provided ample coverage of targets in the USSR, NATO did not need long-range cruise missiles. This episode led the West German government to suggest that the United States alter its SALT position to permit the deployment of long-range GLCMs and SLCMs. The suggestion was peremptorily rejected by the Carter administration.

Soon thereafter, Chancellor Schmidt made his concerns public in the Alastair Buchan memorial lecture, sponsored by the International Institute for Strategic Studies (IISS) in London.[3] Contrary to a now popular myth, Schmidt did not actually call for the deployment of cruise missiles or anything else in the speech. But he did go quite far in outlining his analysis of the implications of strategic parity for the Americans and their allies. In particular, he suggested the need to establish a balance of forces in categories of capability below the strategic level. These remarks could only have been interpreted, and were, both in Europe and the United

States, as meaning that Schmidt was advocating the establishment of a Eurostrategic balance through the deployment of cruise missiles in Europe as a counter to the Soviet SS-20.

The first opportunity to test the true meaning of Schmidt's words came in the initial meetings of NATO's High Level Group (HLG).[4] In these meetings in late 1977 and early 1978, British and German officials pushed hard for the adoption of a consensus that there should be an "evolutionary upward adjustment" in the long-range portion of NATO's TNF. U.S. Defense Department (DoD) officials initially agreed to this formulation, which implied that GLCMs should be deployed. The State Department and the National Security Council (NSC) staff were angry that the DoD could have permitted the United States to become committed to such a position in the absence of a U.S. policy on cruise missile deployments. The NSC staff directed that the consensus be watered down and that formal interagency procedures be established within the government to manage American participation within the HLG. However, U.S. attempts to back away from the HLG consensus again deepened European concerns about American policy and whet even further their appetite for cruise missiles.[5]

In sum, by the spring of 1978, Carter administration policies had increased European pressure for a forthcoming American policy on potential cruise missile deployments and on theater nuclear arms control, although exactly what the Europeans had in mind was by no means clear.

## Phase II: American Policy Shifts

This period of American reluctance and foot dragging on the cruise missile issue ended with the denouement of the "neutron bomb" affair in April 1978. Thereafter, a policy review process was set in motion inside the government that sharply shifted the U.S. stance on LRTNF issues in general, and on cruise missiles in particular. This process took approximately 6 to 8 months and was finally completed during the preparation for President Carter's meeting with the leaders of Britain, West Germany, and France at Guadeloupe on New Year's Day 1979.

This is not the place to recount the neutron bomb affair. Suffice it to say that the American officials who participated in it drew lessons from the experience that they then applied to the LRTNF issue. Among them were the following:

1. *The importance of a unified American position on politically*

*sensitive issues*. The lack of an internal U.S. government consensus during the early phases of the neutron bomb affair in the summer of 1977 had contributed substantially to administration dithering over whether it was for or against the neutron bomb. While Washington dithered, the public debate over the weapon careened out of control.

2. *The importance of American leadership on nuclear issues within the alliance*. Partly as a consequence of internal divisions, in the fall of 1977 the administration had requested that its allies provide the United States with a pro or con decision on the neutron bomb. Used to following the American lead on such matters, the allies did not know how to respond and instead asked for U.S. views; these, of course, were not forthcoming. While this "Alfonse-Gaston" act was underway, the neutron bomb debate spread to Europe and got further out of control, spurred on by Soviet propaganda efforts.

3. *The importance of keeping the President closely involved in day-to-day diplomatic activities*. President Carter adopted a position more or less in favor of the neutron bomb in November 1977. Because the President had set broad policy, U.S. officials approached the subsequent allied consultations as though they were simply a matter of diplomatic detail. Unfortunately, the details of the proposed alliance position changed in the course of consultations, and the President remained largely unaware of these changes. U.S. officials viewed these alterations as nuances. When the President learned of them, however, he viewed them as critically important and disapproved. He ultimately withdrew American support for the alliance neutron bomb decision, precipitating a political disaster for the alliance, and ultimately for himself.

In addition, the neutron bomb affair changed the view of NSC officials about whether it would be wise to conduct a full-scale policy review of the LRTNF issue within the government. Up to that time, the NSC staff had agreed with the State Department that such a review was bound to generate leaks (suggesting impending cruise missile decisions) that could harm U.S. efforts to negotiate a SALT II agreement. However, NSC officials now became convinced that the LRTNF issue could boil over, as had the neutron bomb debate, with far more disastrous consequences for America's strategic position, not to say for the prospective SALT II Treaty. Accordingly, the President ordered an internal policy study, which was known as Presidential Review Memorandum 38 (PRM-38).

An interagency study group chaired by NSC staff completed the study in August 1978. (The NSC chaired this study effort, and all subsequent activities on LRTNF, so as to adjudicate policy disputes between the State and Defense departments and ensure a unified U.S. position.) In essence, the study offered decisionmakers two options: (1) to support the HLG consensus on the "evolutionary upward adjustment" and determine the hardware that would be involved in such an adjustment, and (2) to seek to set the issue aside by offering the allies political solutions such as procedures for assigning more U.S. strategic forces to SACEUR.

A cabinet-level meeting recommended the first option to the President. In supporting the so-called hardware solution, senior officials stressed that the purpose of any new LRTNF deployments would be linkage—that is, filling the perceived gap in NATO's nuclear options at the level of LRTNF and thus forging the link between theater and American central strategic forces. They saw the hardware as a "gap filler" that was not intended to match Soviet LRTNF capabilities on a one-for-one basis and that therefore would not be decoupling. This hardware solution was to be incorporated into an integrated approach that foresaw LRTNF deployments and negotiation over LRTNF limits in SALT III.

Immediately following this presidential decision, the internal U.S. LRTNF working group prepared an initial analysis of potential hardware options, including the GLCM, the SLCM, a new medium-range ballistic missile (MRBM), the *Pershing II XR*, and a new bomber force equipped with ALCMs. The HLG then discussed the analysis. The procedure of internal U.S. analysis, followed by a discussion within the alliance, followed by a further refinement of U.S. analysis, then alliance discussion, and so on, was followed throughout the remainder of alliance discussions over LRTNF.

By January 1, 1979, President Carter was in a position to tell the three allied leaders at Guadeloupe that the United States supported new LRTNF deployments and was prepared to take the lead in forging an alliance consensus around them.

The U.S. position had shifted dramatically in a few months. It would be naive to suppose that the reasons for this shift had to do entirely with the strategic analysis contained in PRM-38, which was similar to that described in the introduction of this chapter. The strategic factors would ultimately have led to a decision of this sort, but political considerations were probably more important immediate determinants of the shift: Specifically, political actors and institutions, namely the State Department, that would normally opt for political solutions and oppose hardware solutions (and had done so previously) did not do so in the summer of 1978. This abnormal behavior was a consequence of two factors. First, the neutron bomb affair had left both the alliance and the image of the United States as its leader badly tattered. Many American officials believed that something had to be done to demonstrate that the United States and the alliance could successfully manage nuclear defense affairs. Second, growing European concerns about U.S. defense policy in general, and LRTNF policy in particular, appeared to threaten ratification of the SALT Treaty. Although European leaders publicly supported the SALT II Treaty, private criticisms—especially from German leaders—had become well known in the U.S. Senate. Offering the Europeans a hardware solution was seen as a way of increasing the prospects for ratification of SALT II.

## Phase III: American "Pressure"

The Guadeloupe summit kicked off a year of intense alliance activity. There was much to be done to put flesh on the bones of the HLG's "evolutionary upward adjustment"—a deployment program was needed, an arms control policy, a public information approach, and so forth. The United States believed that the deployment program should be agreed on within the alliance.

The U.S. decision to seek alliance agreement was subsequently criticized on the grounds that it abrogated American responsibility for nuclear matters in the alliance and placed heavy political burdens on weak European governments, exposing them to domestic turmoil and Soviet pressure. Although these are important considerations, they are unfortunately antiquated in the political context of the Western Alliance. The shifts in political and economic power that have occurred within the alliance mean that it is impossible, both in the United States and in Europe, for the United States to have sole responsibility for the deployment of nuclear weapons in Europe. European nations, especially West Germany, are unwilling to surrender territorial sovereignty on such important matters, existing status-of-forces agreements notwithstanding. The American political scene has led Washington to become disinclined to shoulder major defense responsibilities alone. And, in the case of LRTNF, U.S. officials believed, justifiably, that Congress would not fund weapons production if the allies were uncertain in their support for deployment arrangements. More to the point, President Carter refused to be left standing politically alone as the nuclear "ogre of the world."

The United States therefore sought to build an alliance consensus during 1979 on LRTNF deployments. American strategy was guided by several considerations, among them the following:

1. Many officials believed that the European allies were likely to shift from enthusiasm to resistance as the LRTNF debate shifted from the abstract guideline of "evolutionary upward adjustment" to specific weapons deployed in specific numbers in specific countries. The State Department and the NSC, in particular, believed that the allies ultimately would be unable to muster the political strength to support such deployments, especially after the neutron bomb fiasco. Such concerns had been behind the reluctant attitude of many Carter administration officials toward LRTNF during 1977 and 1978. These concerns continued to heavily influence American diplomatic strategy. The United States sought to tie its allies as tightly as possible to a deployment program that specified locations, numbers, and types of weapons, and to do this by the end of 1979. Only by firmly anchoring the allied position in concrete arrangements would it be possible to weather the political storms that would blow up over the LRTNF issue, according to this view.

2. U.S. strategy was complicated by the German government's so-called "nonsingularity" principle. Chancellor Schmidt held that Germany should not be the sole "host" for the deployment of LRTNF, but that at least one other country on the European continent should also host deployments. This nonsingularity condition could not be met by deployments in Britain. In addition, the German view of nonsingularity was that it was not enough to obtain the agreement of the host countries to deployments. Rather, the entire alliance should join a consensus, thereby spreading the political burden of LRTNF even more broadly. The United States could not possibly object to such a principle, but it made the diplomatic problem all the more difficult. Bases would have to be found in Italy, Belgium, or the Netherlands—the possibilities for which appeared remote in early 1979—and Norway and Denmark would have to be persuaded to endorse a nuclear program for the first time.

3. In seeking firm deployment commitments from Britain, Germany, Italy, Belgium, and the Netherlands, American officials believed it was important to include the leaders of those countries in the decision process at an early stage. Otherwise, it would be too easy for allied leaders to let work proceed in NATO committees only to disown the results politically at a later date. By the same token, following the neutron bomb affair, it was necessary to show

European leaders that the American President was firmly behind the U.S. diplomatic effort. Accordingly, the United States established two diplomatic tracks: one, in the HLG and later in the Special Group (see below), developed the details of the forthcoming alliance position. The other track involved periodic contacts between President Carter (through his designated emissary, David Aaron) and allied leaders. In this latter channel, Aaron usually previewed American positions on the emerging LRTNF program before they were introduced into the HLG and Special Group.

The United States thus set in motion a broad and carefully coordinated diplomatic and decisionmaking process, involving the NSC staff and the State and Defense Departments, which was designed to draw the allies steadily deeper into commitments to a deployment program that would culminate in a NATO agreement in December 1979. To guide diplomatic planning and action, an "analysis/decision track" paper was regularly updated at NSC meetings. This effort was to lead to subsequent charges in Europe that the United States had put pressure on its allies to agree to missile deployments.

The first step in 1979 was to narrow the range of hardware options. In a series of U.S. and HLG studies during the spring of 1979, the *Pershing II* and GLCM emerged as the sole contenders. The United States and its allies eliminated SLCM on numerous grounds, the most prominent of which was that, as a sea-based system, it was not strategically different from existing alliance SLBM forces. The ALCM-equipped bomber force was eliminated because it would be as vulnerable as the existing dual-capable tactical air forces. The new MRBM was eliminated as it would probably not be ready for deployment until the mid- to late 1980s. In addition, the HLG recommended that the deployment numbers be in the range of 200 to 600 LRTNF warheads. Finally, the HLG recommended a mix of ballistic and cruise missile systems on the standard military grounds that a mixed force would complicate enemy planning.[6]

In the course of initial consultations with allied leaders during the spring of 1979, the Germans and Dutch expressed concern that the definition of the hardware program was moving quite rapidly in the HLG, whereas there was no parallel effort to develop a counterpart arms control policy. In adopting the "integrated" approach in 1978, the United States believed that LRTNF would be covered in SALT III. SALT II was not yet complete; therefore there seemed to be plenty of time. However, these allies believed it was politically necessary to have a concrete arms control policy in place when the deployment decision was made. They therefore requested that the United States help form a second group within NATO to develop an arms control policy. This proposal became a matter of some dispute within the U.S. government. Opponents argued either that the development of a separate arms control policy might indicate that arms control could substitute for hardware and that the deployment program could consequently be avoided, or that the arms control program should also be developed by the HLG after the deployment program had been agreed upon. Nevertheless, the United States finally did agree to form the Special Group (SG) to develop an arms control strategy as a counterpart to the LRTNF development.[7]

U.S. strategy in the SG was to reach a consensus on the broad objectives and principles that might guide the United States in the conduct of negotiations over LRTNF in SALT III. To this end, a so-called "objectives and principles" paper formed the basis of evolving internal U.S. government decisions and SG discussions. From an American perspective, the most important of these principles was that "arms control should be viewed as a *complement to and not a substitute for* force modernization."

All the progress of the HLG and SG notwithstanding, the most important development of the spring consultations was the appearance of Italy as a strong contender for basing LRTNF. This took American officials by surprise, for they had reckoned that their only hope of finding a second continental basing country was in Belgium or the Netherlands. Indeed, some American diplomats initially suggested that Italy be ruled out altogether as a potential basing candidate on the grounds that it was politically too frail to withstand the domestic storms that would probably break over the LRTNF issue. However, for a series of complex internal political reasons, as well as their determination to bring Italy back to the "top table" in the alliance, the Italian leaders were determined to push through with deployments on their territory. This development substantially eased America's diplomatic tasks by making success less dependent on unpredictable Belgian politics and on the ability of Dutch leaders to overcome mounting antinuclear sentiment in their country.

By summer 1979, the United States was in a position to formally propose a deployment program to its allies. This was the now well-known plan to deploy 572 warheads on *Pershing II* ballistic missiles and on GLCMs in five European countries. In the end, the United States decided to suggest small deployments in Belgium and the

Netherlands, despite the uncertain political situation in those countries.

The 572 figure was the result of various considerations. In the fall of 1978, the HLG had already narrowed the choice to the 200 to 600 warhead range simply by "eyeballing" several options. Options with fewer than 200 warheads seemed too puny to be viewed as anything but a token response to the Soviet SS-20 deployment. Options with more than 600 suggested an attempt to establish a "Eurostrategic balance" and thus to decouple the U.S. strategic deterrent from Europe. Options in the 200 to 600 range seemed large enough to support the selective nuclear employment options called for by NATO strategy. Subsequent U.S. and HLG analysis of selective employment options and force survivability arrangements pointed toward the higher end of the HLG's range, as did the fact that the forces would be spread around five countries. An additional consideration that argued for the higher end of the range was the view of senior U.S. officials that the program should be large enough to avoid degradation either by arms control cuts or as a consequence of one or more countries dropping out of the program.

Following established procedure, the plan for a 572 warhead deployment was previewed by allied leaders in July 1979, before it was formally introduced into the HLG in late August 1979. By this time, it was clear that the two-track U.S. diplomatic strategy was working well with Britain, Germany, and Italy. All three countries addressed the program seriously, indicating their acceptance or suggesting minor changes, and discussing political strategy needed to bring about an alliance agreement by December.[8] However, the strategy was having no effect in Belgium and was failing in the Netherlands. Belgian leaders reassured the Americans that they understood well how to handle their internal political situation and would be able to manage it successfully by springing the issue late in the autumn. They did not seem to want American help, nor to address the deployment program in any detail.

This strategy precipitated a government crisis in Belgium in December and led to the adoption of an ambiguous position on deployment. Dutch leaders, by contrast, adopted an ostrichlike attitude, saying that it was premature to address the deployment program because the NATO "experts"—the HLG—had not yet reached a conclusion. Only after the HLG had pronounced their position would Dutch leaders consider the program. This proved to be a fatal mistake. When Dutch leaders did address the program in October, the political debate in their country had already gone out of control. Meanwhile, Dutch ability to affect the NATO

deployment program had been sharply reduced because the program had become set in political concrete. They had missed their
chance.

On the basis of the summer consultations, the HLG and SG
finished their work in September 1979. The combined work of
these two groups outlined policy recommendations that have since
remained unchanged: The HLG recommended the deployment
program that is being implemented today. The SG recommended a
series of objectives and principles for arms control that have since
guided American behavior in the INF talks. Although these became more detailed than the United States had initially hoped—
pointing toward the goal of equal global levels of warheads on land-
based long-range theater missiles for both the United States and
the Soviet Union—the SG report continued to contain the admon-
ishment that arms control should not substitute for force modernization. By the end of September, all that was required was formal
NATO endorsement of the positions outlined in the HLG and SG
reports. Achieving this would be the agenda of the next two
months.

As 1979 proceeded, the Americans felt growing disquiet about a
dog that didn't bark. The U.S. diplomatic strategy was working far
better than anyone had expected. Although the allies showed
growing political nervousness, they were responding to American
leadership and rallied round the U.S.-proposed deployment program. Yet there was little public discussion of the issue. American
officials attempted to stimulate press interest in the subject but had
little success. They were fearful that, unless a public consensus
were built behind the program, the Soviet Union would make a
political or diplomatic maneuver that would precipitate a negative
political reaction in Europe and destroy the NATO consensus
behind the deployment program. They kept waiting for the Soviet
dog to bark.

It did so on October 6, when President Brezhnev proposed what
amounted to a freeze on the number of launchers for LRTNF
missiles, which would have permitted the Soviet SS-20 program to
proceed unabated while blocking the emerging U.S. program.
Contrary to American fears, this speech proved quite helpful to
American efforts. The Soviet Union was too late and offered too
little, for by now allied governments were more or less behind the
deployment program. The key governments responded to the
Brezhnev proposals quickly, negatively, and in similar terms.
Ironically, the Brezhnev speech stimulated the press interest that
Western governments could not. The press quickly picked up the
government reactions, especially information on the SS-20 deploy-

ments, thereby setting a favorable political stage for the December decision.

The diplomatic calendar for October and November was full, but most of the activity was not decisively important. However, there was one important shift in the American and allied positions. As allied governments grew increasingly worried about how they would handle negative domestic political reactions to the deployment decision, they began making a series of proposals, the net effect of which would be to insert a second decision on deployment after December 1979 and before the scheduled initial deployments in 1983. For example, the Danish government suggested the decision be delayed for six months to give additional time to assess the results of American arms control initiatives with the Soviet Union. The Norwegian government suggested the decision should be reviewed in the light of arms control progress in two years, to see if deployments were still necessary. Other governments were attracted to similar ideas. But the United States opposed them on the grounds that to introduce a second decision would effectively nullify the validity of the first one, leaving the United States with no bargaining leverage in arms control and no ability to convince the Congress that its allies intended to follow through with the deployments.

Although the United States ultimately beat back many of these "second decision" proposals with the help of some of its allies, or found that it could accommodate to others, the basic idea was subtly reintroduced in the form of Chancellor Schmidt's request to the United States that he be allowed to explain to the West German Social Democratic Party (SPD) at its Berlin convention in December that it would be "theoretically possible" for arms control results to do away with the need for the deployments altogether. Up to this point, it had been the American and German position that some deployments would be needed regardless of the outcome of arms control negotiations, although the negotiations might affect the overall size and shape of the deployment program. This was the essence of the Special Group's principle of "a complement to and not a substitute for." However, in view of his mounting political problems within the SPD, the United States acceded to the Chancellor's request, which at the time seemed harmless enough.

This was a blunder. It was compounded two years later when President Reagan transformed the "theoretical possible" into a formal American arms control proposal—the so-called zero option. By suggesting that zero U.S. deployments were a possible outcome of Soviet-American arms control talks, these steps had the effect of making the implementation of the deployment program hostage to the INF negotiations in Geneva.

## Aftermath and Lessons

The NATO LRTNF decision, reached by a joint meeting of NATO's defense and foreign ministers on December 12, 1979, was viewed at the time as a success. The alliance had managed a sensitive and vitally important issue and did so in the face of Soviet opposition and mounting political nervousness within Europe.

In the four years since that decision, the gleam of success has been tarnished. The European political weakness that was already apparent in the latter stages of the decision process grew during 1980: European pressure for some move on the arms control front induced the Carter administration to open LRTNF negotiations with the Soviets separate from SALT III, the originally planned venue. Of course, the failure of SALT II ratification had made SALT III a distant prospect at best. The Reagan administration, with its widely perceived anti-arms control attitudes and rhetoric about limited nuclear wars and the use of enhanced radiation weapons—the "neutron bomb"—contributed substantially to the growth of the "peace movement" in Europe. While European governments clamored for the reopening of a Soviet-American arms control dialogue to stem the peace movement's tide, the Reagan administration delayed a decision to return to the bargaining table until November 1981. At that point, as noted above, President Reagan decided to propose the zero option, which European governments had advocated as a way to counter the demands of the peace movement.

In the following two years, while European political leaders "waited for Geneva to give the answer" as to whether deployments would proceed, the antinuclear movement grew in strength and gained broad political appeal. The impression grew in Europe that a final decision on deployment would not be reached until the very last minute, thus creating the appearance of a deadline and heightening political tension. By the time the deployments actually occurred, the alliance had paid a heavy political price for the 1979 decision.

The LRTNF story is thus one of both success and failure—a success in pulling together a difficult, but needed, decision—a failure in not avoiding serious alliance political tensions. In the causes for both are political, bureaucratic, and diplomatic lessons that may be instructive in more effectively managing future episodes on such policy issues. From the element of success are these important lessons:

1. Internal U.S. government agreement on policy direction is necessary before the United States seriously enters a diplomatic process with its allies that might substantially alter U.S. nuclear weapon deployments overseas. An unclear policy line from Washington, or signs of internal political or bureaucratic strife, may well doom any initiative. This happened in the case of the "neutron bomb" issue and threatened to occur in the LRTNF case until PRM-38 provided a catalyst for internal agreement.

2. Close alliance consultations—to the point of including allies directly in the U.S. analytic and decisionmaking process—will be extremely valuable to building a policy consensus. To the extent that allies understand and feel a part of U.S. decisions, they are more willing and better able to support those positions. Until the fall of 1978, American unwillingness to consult openly about cruise missiles became a source of U.S.-European friction and contributed to a growing allied appetite for the weapon. The subsequent close consultations smoothed the way to the December 1979 decision.

3. Leaders must be involved in the consultation process at an early stage. If they are, the decision can be shaped to meet their political needs, as was the case with LRTNF. If they are not, they may later disown the bureaucratically shaped decision, as President Carter did in the case of the neutron bomb. (This lesson naturally depends on the style of the leader, especially his willingness to delegate.)

4. American leadership must be firm. This is a cliché, but it should not be overlooked. In the Atlantic Alliance, it is all too easy to find reasons for delay or obfuscation of difficult issues. If decisions on sensitive matters are needed, only the United States has the political wherewithal to join them and define their terms.

From the element of failure there are no less important lessons:

1. Officials must prepare the public for difficult decisions, through debate that includes a clearly articulated and easily understood public rationale for forthcoming decisions. This is easy to say but hard to do. In the LRTNF case, Carter administration officials wanted a debate during 1979 but were unable to stimulate one, perhaps because they didn't try hard enough. When the debate did break out during the early days of the Reagan administration, the United States was not ready to lead it. The Reagan administra-

tion included officials who either did not enthusiastically support INF (and said so) or who, in supporting INF, caused more political problems than they solved.

2. Firm links between the implementation of arms programs and the success of arms control negotiations should be avoided. This may be the most important lesson of all; and it is hardly new that a decision about security should not be placed in the hands of an adversary through his ability to control highly visible arms control negotiations. In its insistence that arms control should complement, not substitute, for modernization and its desire to avoid a second decision-point, the United States recognized this lesson. Yet political forces steadily eroded these positions. It is not clear that these forces could have been resisted at the time. But perhaps if the lesson is now more widely recognized, it will be better heeded in the future.

In drawing these conclusions from the LRTNF experience, it is tempting to say "if only these lessons had been followed, there would have been no problems during 1980–1983." The problems stemmed from far more sources than the organization and procedures of the American government. Streamlining such processes of decisionmaking and implementation would not have made the problems go away. The most that can be said is that their impact might have been lessened.

### Endnotes

1. A notable exception was a speech by Fred Iklé, then director of the Arms Control and Disarmament Agency, to the Los Angeles World Affairs Council on August 31, 1976. Iklé described the SS-20 as a "dark cloud towering over Europe and Asia." Although Secretary of Defense Schlesinger had informed the press about the SS-20 a year earlier, this speech marked the first notable public discussion about the system and its implications.
2. The British, of course, had two axes to grind—their NATO one, which they shared with the Germans, and their unilateral one, in which they were beginning to consider options for the follow-on to their *Polaris* SSBN force, including cruise missile options.
3. See Helmut Schmidt, *Survival* (London: International Institute for Strategic Studies, January-February 1978), p. 4.
4. This group had been established as an afterthought as part of the LTDP program. Fearing that the allies would interpret the LTDP as a shift away from nuclear deterrence, the United States decided to add a so-called tenth task force to the LTDP work program. This became the HLG, which was chaired

by U.S. Assistant Secretary of Defense David McGiffert and included partici-
pants from the defense and foreign ministries of other NATO capitals.

5. Up to this point, the debate was entirely about cruise missiles. However, about this time the prime contractor—Martin Marietta—suggested that the range of the *Pershing II* missile, then in development, could be extended from 750 km to 1800 km, giving it a capability to attack Soviet territory. Many American officials, especially in the State Department, began advocating the *Pershing II XR* (for extended range) as an alternative to the GLCM.

6. There was also a more practical justification for this conclusion. GLCM was judged to be far less expensive than *Pershing II*, especially if new bases for the LRTNF had to be constructed. However, bases already existed for the *Pershing* in Germany, so it made sense to simply replace the existing *Pershing I* with *Pershing II* on those bases and to deploy the GLCM on new bases.

7. This group was chaired by the director of the Bureau of Politico-Military Affairs in the Department of State, first Leslie Gelb, then Reginald Bartholo-mew.

8. It was at this juncture that Chancellor Schmidt ruminated about the possibility of including the SLCM in the deployment program in the hope that Denmark and Norway would participate in the program more directly by hosting port calls by SLCM-carrying ships. However, this idea was clearly a nonstarter and was quickly dropped by the German government.

*Chapter 14*

# EUROPEAN AND JAPANESE PUBLIC DEBATE OVER INF MODERNIZATION: LESSONS FOR THE FUTURE OF WESTERN SECURITY COOPERATION

*by John Roper and Yukio Satoh*

The security of the United States and its allies in Europe and in the Asia-Pacific region depends, in substantial measure, on the extended deterrence provided by U.S. nuclear forces. In the last decade the debate over the attempt to reassure the NATO allies of the U.S. nuclear commitment to Europe by the deployment of a new generation of land-based "theater" or intermediate-range nuclear weapons has, in the view of many, had the unintended consequence of breaking the consensus on security matters in a number of the NATO countries. Instead of reassuring the Europeans, the attempt to reinforce deterrence has had the paradoxical effect of raising even more doubts about the credibility of nuclear deterrence.

In Japan, nuclear strategy has been much less debated in public despite (and, to a certain extent, because of) a pronounced public abhorrence of nuclear weapons; and on the INF question, despite the increased public interest which was influenced by U.S.-European debates, confidence in the security relationship with the United States has, in contrast to Europe, increased rather than diminished.

This chapter examines the different contexts of the public INF debate in Western Europe and Japan with particular reference to the question of how the United States and its allies should respond to the major Soviet buildup of SS-20 intermediate-range missiles, and the U.S.-European arms control negotiations with the Soviet Union designed to reverse the threat posed by Moscow's intermediate-range nuclear forces (INF). In this debate, American extended nuclear deterrence was for the first time considered in a global context rather than in terms of the security interests of the Atlantic Alliance alone.

## The European Debate: 1977–1984

Helmut Schmidt's lecture at the International Institute for Strategic Studies (IISS) in October 1977 is frequently cited as the genesis of NATO's theater nuclear force modernization program and was indeed the beginning of the public debate on this issue. However, Schmidt himself made clear in his lecture that he had already raised the implications for Europe of the institutionalization of strategic nuclear parity through the SALT process at the May 1977 Summit in London.[1] The need for modernization of theater nuclear forces had, in fact, first been raised at the 1976 Hamburg meeting of the NATO Nuclear Planning Group (NPG). The High Level Group set up by the NPG indeed began its work in the autumn of 1977 with the specific purpose of examining the role of theater nuclear forces (TNF) in NATO strategy, the implications of recent Soviet TNF deployments, the need for TNF modernization, and the technical and political implications of alternative NATO TNF postures.

It is important to note that the guidelines under which the HLG was established in 1977 made it clear that TNF modernization was to be evolutionary, was not intended to increase the number of NATO nuclear weapons in Europe, was not designed to match the Soviet SS-20, but merely to have an offsetting capacity to provide a credible response. It was not initially clear that the new systems should be land-based. Indeed, Harold Brown, the U.S. Secretary of Defense, in the summer of 1977 advocated that an augmentation of the submarine-launched *Poseidon* missiles assigned to SACEUR would provide an adequate enhancement of NATO's theater nuclear forces. This view was refuted by the British Labour Defence

Minister, Fred Mulley, in a letter of August 1977, which argued that as much of NATO's existing capability was in increasingly vulnerable land-based aircraft, the new force should be land-based in order to maintain an essential component in the range of flexible response. There were additional arguments of command and control in favor of land-basing and, in view of the need to reassure the Europeans of the American commitment, it was agreed that in order to achieve greater credibility in terms of public perceptions, the systems should have as much visibility as possible.[2]

The justification for the decision, therefore, was the need to maintain an intermediate rung in NATO's ladder of deterrence between the incredible strategic nuclear level and the increasingly inadequate level of nonnuclear forces in Europe. Theater nuclear forces were seen as making deterrence more credible and, therefore, more effective by giving the alliance evident and credible options for resisting levels of aggression—conventional or nuclear—too high for nonnuclear resistance to meet but not high enough to warrant strategic nuclear action. The case for modernization in 1977 was that existing TNF—the United States F-111 aircraft and the British *Vulcan* bomber force—were becoming vulnerable on the ground, as a result of the replacement of Soviet SS-5 missiles by SS-20s, and were less certain of penetrating improved Soviet air defenses.

It is important to note that although the increased accuracy of the SS-20 missile was one of the reasons for this NATO modernization effort, it was not originally seen as a "tit for tat" response to Moscow's SS-20 deployment; nor was it part of a concept of Eurostrategic balance. Nothing in the doctrine of flexible response requires NATO to have the same numbers of the same sorts of weapons as the other side. The initial case for TNF modernization, therefore, was to give NATO the capability to do what its own strategy required, not to give it the capability to match precisely the weapons that its opponents have acquired to do whatever their strategy suggests that they should do.

This case for TNF modernization—to enhance NATO's capacity for flexible response—was a case for the defense elite; it was not even the case argued by many European politicians when the NATO decision (termed the "dual-track" decision) was made in December 1979. Then the argument was made on the need to match the SS-20s—a case that was effectively demolished by Professor Michael Howard in his letter to the *London Times* of November 3, 1981:

> *There is no consensus in the European defence community, and no sense among the European peoples as a whole, that the SS-20s*

*present a threat of a new order of magnitude. They are more accurate than the old SS-4s and -5s, but, with warheads of such destructive powers, accuracy is of little significance. They remain a very small proportion of the enormous nuclear force that the Soviet Union is capable of launching against Western Europe if it so wished.*

*The belief of some strategic analysts that the Russians can only be deterred from attacking us by the installation of precisely matching systems—"ground-launched missiles must be matched by ground-launched missiles"—is politically naive to the point of absurdity. The United States is "coupled" to Europe, not by one delivery system rather than another, but by a vast web of military installations and personnel, to say nothing of the innumerable economic, social and financial links that tie us together into a single coherent system. To satisfy those pedantic analysts who require still further guarantees, the Americans, whose patience seems inexhaustible, have already allocated to NATO a submarine-based nuclear force of immense destructive power.*

*If all this is insufficient to deter the Soviet Union from a course that they are in any case likely to contemplate only in the very direst of extremities, what difference will be made by the installation of* Pershings *and cruise missiles, particularly if these remain under sole American control?*

The problem of public attitudes became more acute as some sections of European public opinion were more concerned about overbelligerence by the United States rather than by fears of a "decoupling" of the U.S. defense commitment from Europe. Over the last six years in Europe there has been, with the exception of France, a significant decline in public confidence in the United States. Although this has crystallized on occasion around demonstrations over NATO INF deployments, they have been the focus of concern rather than the underlying cause. There have been a number of developments since 1979 that have led to a cumulative strain on the alliance.

In September 1979, before the NATO dual-track decision was taken, Henry Kissinger had warned Europeans in a speech at Brussels not to rely on the United States' strategic deterrent. The European press reported him as saying "deterrence is dead." Although his speech in full was intended to support the case for INF deployment, its effect on European opinion-formers was unsettling. Europeans were further concerned by the failure of the United States to ratify SALT II; and although President Carter's final withdrawal of the treaty arose from the Soviet invasion of Afghanistan, the responsibility for the failure in strategic arms control was not all laid at the Soviet door. The nonratification of

SALT II had the consequences of preventing the arms control "track" of the NATO INF decision from being pursued within SALT III, and stimulating the establishment late in 1980 of separate INF negotiations in Geneva.

While presidential candidate Ronald Reagan's hard-line campaign rhetoric in 1980, and his subsequent speeches in office, did much to erode popular support in Europe for American security policy, it must be mentioned that the publication of Presidential Directive 59 (PD-59) by the Carter administration in July 1980—which, to the lay reader, appeared to stress a warfighting rather than a deterrent approach to nuclear strategy—caused considerable alarm to Europeans. The concept of limited nuclear options was, of course, not new; but the publicity given to it by PD-59 disturbed those in Europe who thought that this might mean nuclear war restricted to the European continent.

President Reagan's political rhetoric was ably exploited by European critics of NATO strategy who argued that the United States was no longer prepared to accept parity between the superpowers and was striving for superiority. Such a goal was criticized by some in Europe as unrealistic; but many saw it as increasing the risk of war. Over the three years 1980 to 1983, many on the political left in Europe who had accepted the 1979 NATO decision on theater nuclear force modernization in the context of prospects for political detente and arms control felt that their shift to opposition was justified by what they considered to be the change in the international political environment produced by President Reagan.

It can be further argued that some Europeans were equally disturbed by the behavior of American "doves" as well as by President Reagan and his "hawks." Certainly Robert McNamara's 1983 *Foreign Affairs* article[3] was seen as suggesting that in practice nuclear weapons would not be used; and the remarkably "dovish" pastoral letter from the U.S. Catholic bishops could be pointed to as making U.S. behavior all the more difficult for Europeans to predict.

During the four years between the INF decision of December 1979 and December 1983 there were, of course, other differences between Western Europe and the United States. As the IISS states in *Strategic Survey 1982-83,* "some commentators hyperbolized the tension (of 1982) as NATO's worst ever confrontation."[4] There was not only spectacular disagreement over the Siberian pipeline, over monetary policies, and over steel and food protectionism, there was also a significant divergence in perceptions of the Soviet Union and, therefore, also in policies for dealing with the Soviet leadership.

In spite of all the arguments and demonstrations, however, the initial deployment of cruise missiles in Britain and of *Pershing II* missiles in West Germany took place on time at the end of 1983. The first Italian cruise missiles became operational in early 1984, and the Belgian missiles in the first half of 1985. In Britain and Germany the right-of-center governments of Mrs. Thatcher and Chancellor Kohl were successful in general elections in the first half of 1983. In both of these campaigns the NATO INF deployments were one of the main issues. In Italy, the coalition government led by Socialist Prime Minister Craxi had a substantial parliamentary majority in favor of deployment. Although there was widespread opposition to the deployment in the Netherlands, the government's commitment to the "dual-track" decision remained firm.

This apparent success tells only one side of the story. The process of decisionmaking over INF in the last six years has put very considerable strains on the security consensus in most European countries; and in some it has caused political divisions on defense questions which, while not yet strong enough to challenge NATO membership, certainly challenge the nuclear component of its strategy.

Although there have been variations in the debate among the different European members of NATO, there have been similar strands in the debate in most countries, whether among defense specialists, in political parties, within the churches, and among public opinion at large. The one main exception has been the position of France,[5] which is, of course, not directly involved either as a host country or as a member of NATO's Nuclear Planning Group.

Among defense specialists, both inside and outside of government, the general debate has forced a reexamination of NATO's doctrine of flexible response. While some authors[6] have provided a statement in defense of NATO's existing nuclear doctrine and opposed proposals for a shift to a "no first use" of nuclear weapons, others have suggested that NATO's nuclear strategy "is incredible to those who are supposed to be protected by this strategy."[7] Within European governments there has been a hesitation to reveal doubts either to the United States or to domestic public opinion; but there are considerable doubts as to whether the deployment process has either significantly strengthened deterrence or reassured public opinion. The debate among specialists has spilled over into the public debate to a much greater extent than in the 1960s or the 1970s. As a leading British official wrote, governments "will have to take every opportunity to explain the rationale behind NATO's dependence on nuclear weapons as an essential element in its deterrent strategy."[8]

The most significant change has been among the political parties belonging to the Socialist International—the SPD in Germany, the Labour Party in Britain, the Belgian Socialist Party, the Dutch Labour Party, and the Danish Social Democratic and the Norwegian Labour Parties—all of whom had been in government during some of the period from 1977 to 1983. They all found themselves in opposition to deployment as the moment for implementation arrived at the end of 1983. The Dutch Labour Party was opposed to the original dual-track decision in 1979; and there was little enthusiasm in the Belgian, Danish, or Norwegian parties. The British Labour Party took an anti-INF decision in the course of 1980, and this was one of the factors leading to the creation in Britain of the Social Democratic Party. With the loss of power by the West German SPD in 1982, the Party moved in 1983 into opposition to the actual deployment of the weapons system whose introduction was to some extent seen as a response to the concerns of their former leader Helmut Schmidt.

While all of these parties have insisted that they see no inconsistency between their opposition to INF deployment and continued support for NATO, they have almost all paralleled their opposition to INF with calls for a "no first use" nuclear strategy and, in the case of the British Labour Party, with a call for a "nonnuclear strategy." They have not indicated how such a policy, which would involve much greater expenditures for conventional forces, is to be financed. There is concern that the return of a Labour government in Britain or an SPD government in West Germany could present problems for the alliance. The French and Italian Socialist Parties, which are both in government, have supported the deployment decision. The French Party has had very few qualms about nuclear policy, and the Italian Party has had only limited ones.

The views of the other political parties in Western Europe have been more predictable and more consistent on the INF issues. The communist parties have been unanimous in opposition; the parties of the center and right have been more or less enthusiastic in their support. In the Netherlands and in Denmark some center parties opposed deployment.

The focus on nuclear strategy resulting from INF deployment has led to a debate in the churches of most northern European countries on the ethics of nuclear war. This had led in the Netherlands to the churches playing a leading role in the "peace movement" and to critical debates taking place in British, German, and Danish churches. Although the ethics of nuclear strategy have been discussed previously by church bodies, the recent debates have been the most substantial and have, as with the U.S. Catholic bishops, provided a greater challenge to the traditional nuclear strategy of the alliance.

It is more difficult to assess the attitudes of public opinion in general to the INF deployments. The majority of Europeans have very little everyday concern with defense questions. A recent study[9] suggests that less than 10 percent of the electorate concern themselves personally with the prospects for international peace. It is, therefore, difficult to place too much weight on the answers to questions in opinion polls dealing with particular weapon systems. This study suggests that in spite of a "decline in the image of the United States in Western Europe," "public support for NATO remains high in all the European member states."[10] It concludes that even on the issue of nuclear weapons, public opinion is not as hostile as is commonly assumed. It nonetheless found in an analysis of poll data from all the NATO countries that the issue of nuclear force modernization was the most divisive of all defense issues. The survey of polls indicated that nuclear weapons as such are not generally rejected, and even on the question of intermediate-range nuclear force modernization public opinion is about evenly divided.[11] It may be, however, that public opinion lags behind the views of political leaders. If this is the case, the debate about INF modernization and the divergencies between European and American interests expressed by political leaders may soon be reflected more widely in public attitudes.

## Some Distinctions Between Europe and Japan

Japan, like Europe, has been buffeted in recent years by the debate over SS-20 deployments and the U.S.-Soviet INF negotiations. The Japanese government, a wide range of political parties and the press, together with a number of increasingly vocal defense specialists, have expressed grave concern over the increased Soviet SS-20 deployment in the Far East, particularly since the Soviet government in January 1983 began to suggest that Japan was a target of these missiles. As a consequence, the Japanese government strongly supported the Reagan administration's so-called "zero option" in the INF negotiations, calling for the withdrawal of Soviet SS-20s in return for an American agreement to forego new INF deployments in Europe.

Moreover, Japanese concern that the West European governments might press for a separate agreement on SS-20 missiles capable of reaching Europe, without providing for limits on the SS-20s deployed in the Far East, led the government to insist on the need to establish "global limits" on SS-20 deployments in the INF negotiations. It was against this background that Prime Minister Nakasone joined American and European leaders at the Williamsburg Summit in May 1983 in endorsing a statement underlining the global approach to INF and supporting deployment of U.S. *Pershing II* and cruise missiles in Europe in the absence of a U.S.-Soviet agreement on INF limits.

There are important differences, however, between the situations in which Europe and Japan find themselves with regard to the SS-20 question. First, Japanese perceptions regarding the military threat posed by Soviet intermediate-range missiles are different from those held by Europeans. The Japanese are concerned over what they see as a rapid increase in Soviet nuclear forces in the Asian region, and the consequent shift of the U.S.-Soviet nuclear force balance from one of perceived American superiority to one of perceived parity. The Soviet announcements that Japan will be the target of Soviet nuclear attack heightened their concern. Nonetheless, the Japanese (except for a limited number of defense specialists) remain less sensitive than Europeans to the increased threat posed by the deployment of the SS-20s. With so many Soviet nuclear systems already in Asia, the addition of the SS-20s to Moscow's Far Eastern arsenal does not appear, to many Japanese, to make a fundamental difference in an already dangerous situation. Moreover, the SS-20 deployment has been seen largely as a move directed at China. And although U.S. forces in Japan could be a target of the SS-20s, it has been generally regarded that a nuclear attack on U.S. forces (no matter whether with the SS-20s or not) could be deterred by the effect of mutual strategic nuclear deterrence between the two superpowers. Many Japanese are unfamiliar with the concept of flexible response and believe—intuitively rather than in terms of military theory—that a limited nuclear war (battlefield or theater in scope) between the two superpowers is not a practical option for either Washington or Moscow.

Second, the Japanese are less concerned about the impact of the SS-20s on the American nuclear guarantee to their security than are the Europeans—at least in the view expressed by Helmut Schmidt. On this question, Japan has for a long time opted simply to trust the American commitment to defend Japan under the terms of the U.S.-Japan Mutual Security Treaty. The clearest expression of this commitment in recent years was made in the

1975 joint announcement between President Gerald Ford and Prime Minister Takeo Miki, which stated that "the United States would continue to abide by its defense commitment to Japan under the Treaty of Mutual Cooperation and Security in the event of armed attack against Japan, whether by nuclear or conventional forces." From the viewpoint of guaranteeing American strategic nuclear deterrence, the Japanese approach of simply trusting the general American commitment to the defense of Japan may be less reassuring than the European option of participating in American nuclear planning and of having American nuclear weapons deployed on their own territory. Given their deep abhorrence of nuclear weapons, however, the Japanese have preferred not to be involved in American nuclear strategy development, much less in joint defense operations. The Japanese have been less persistent than the West Europeans in questioning the credibility of the American security guarantee.

Underlying this position is a conviction (although one not often made explicit) that the deployment of U.S. forces in Japan is viewed by the Soviet Union as a "tripwire" linked to America's nuclear systems. At the same time, Japanese public sentiment holds that Japan is safer from nuclear attack if it has no nuclear weapons deployed on its territory.

These differences between Japanese and European approaches toward the question of the credibility of the American defense commitment are, however, not attributable solely to the differences in perception regarding the role of nuclear weapons. More fundamentally, they arise from the different geostrategic situations. In Europe, nuclear weapons have long been regarded as necessary to counterbalance the overwhelming conventional force superiority of the Warsaw Pact, while in the Pacific the need for the tactical or theater use of American nuclear weapons has been little discussed because of the absence of a perception of a conventional imbalance.

Third, there are fewer anti-American overtones in the Japanese public debate on INF than in Europe. This is because in Europe the deployment of American intermediate-range and battlefield nuclear weapons generated public concern that Europe alone would become the battleground for limited nuclear war between the two superpowers. In Japan, where government policy prohibits the deployment of American nuclear weapons, public sentiment against nuclear weapons is leveled at *all* nuclear weapons rather than those of the United States alone. On the basis of a strong public abhorrence of nuclear weapons deriving from Japan's wartime experience as a target of nuclear attack, the Japanese government holds firmly to its so-called three Non-Nuclear Principles—of not possessing, not producing, and not allowing the introduction of nuclear weapons into Japan. The United States, for its part, has been attentive to Japanese sentiment against nuclear weapons. Under the Security Treaty and its related agreements, the two governments understand that the introduction of American nuclear weapons into Japan would require prior consultation, and Japanese leaders have assured their public that an American request to introduce nuclear weapons into Japan would be refused in accordance with these three principles.

Fourth, there is a difference in the foreign policy environment surrounding the INF debate in Japan as compared with Europe. While West European nations hold a firm defense posture against the Soviet military threat, pressure for continued and, if possible, closer contacts with the Soviet Union and Eastern Europe is a firmly entrenched aspect of political, economic, and social life in Western Europe, particularly in West Germany. The prevailing economic recession makes West European countries even more reluctant to reduce trade with Eastern Europe. More fundamentally, many Europeans also consider that managing East-West relations requires a long-term approach of building political and economic ties. Accordingly, they consider American military and economic pressures on the Soviet Union, and even more American anti-communist political rhetoric, to be counterproductive in reducing East-West tensions. This has become conspicuous in recent years as a tendency to question American leadership in foreign policy has become more prevalent in the West European community.

The picture differs in Japan. Although the Japanese used to be more reluctant than the West Europeans in taking a confrontational attitude toward the Soviet Union, the increasingly antagonistic attitude of the Soviet Union toward Japan in recent years (particularly the fortification of several islands in the Northern Territories, despite the absence of a threat from Japan) and the Soviet invasion of Afghanistan have changed quite markedly Japanese perceptions of the Soviet Union. Soviet military activities have created a political atmosphere in Japan that has led to public recognition that the "potential" threat to Japan's security comes from the Soviet Union. And the natural response to this threat, most Japanese believe, is to increase defense efforts, strengthen support for the American alliance within the framework of the Japan-U.S. Mutual Security Treaty, and participate together with other Western countries in political and economic actions against the Soviet Union. Accordingly, the gap between Japanese and American perceptions of the Soviet Union has narrowed, while that between West Europeans and the United States has widened.

And finally, recent changes in West European attitudes contrast with those of the Japanese in the important dimension of alliance relations with the United States. As described earlier, a mood of cynicism and distrust toward the Atlantic Alliance can be found in some sections of public and political opinion in Europe. Skeptical attitudes toward the United States are particularly strong among the younger generation. The pacifist and antinuclear sentiments that prevail among a significant segment of European public opinion have in some cases been translated into outright anti-Americanism. The perception that America lacks a coherent and consistent foreign policy has led many European intellectuals and politicians to question the wisdom of automatically following American leadership. This trend in European attitudes toward the United States affected the European approach to the INF question, although the extent to which Western Europe is distancing itself from the United States should not be exaggerated.

There is a trend, however, that appears to be running in the opposite direction in the Japan-U.S. relationship. The Japanese, too, have become increasingly self-assertive vis-à-vis the United States. Like the Europeans, they seek political independence and react emotionally against too much pressure from Washington. Overt American pressure on Japan in matters of national defense is particularly counterproductive. Yet, understanding their lack of a national capability to defend themselves, and their consequent heavy dependence upon American military protection, the Japanese are more diffident than the West Europeans in asserting themselves on security questions. Anti-American sentiment was once vocal in public criticism of Japan-U.S. security arrangements, which were regarded as a symbol of Japan's postwar subjugation. But this attitude has subsided, and Japanese public opinion has shifted to positive support for the alliance with the United States.

A growing national mood of self-confidence stemming from economic success, which has visibly affected Japan's position on the international scene, is perhaps helping the Japanese to become more pragmatic about dependence on American military support. Furthermore, since the late 1970s Japan has come to act with increasing self-assuredness as a member of the Western community in the international political arena, particularly regarding issues affecting East-West relations—especially since the Soviet invasion of Afghanistan. And Prime Minister Nakasone's unequivocal commitment to strengthening the Japan-U.S. alliance has established a relationship of unprecedentedly close rapport between Tokyo and Washington despite the ever-growing trade imbalance between the two countries. In sum, therefore, the political imperative to strengthen the alliance relationship with the United States has weighed more heavily than tactical military considerations in the Japanese approach to the INF question. Needless to say, given the Japanese strategic position, strengthening the alliance relationship with the United States is the most important requirement for Japanese security.

## Concluding Remarks

The experience of INF underlines, among other things, the increasing importance of public opinion in the setting of Western nuclear strategy, and a growing need for the United States and its allies to develop a policy consensus in global terms rather than separately for the Atlantic and Pacific alliances.

With regard to public opinion, it should be remembered that although the INF deployment in Europe was carried out despite public protests, popular support for the concept of nuclear deterrence based on the ultimate threat of nuclear retaliation has been shaken in most European countries. There is no simple method of restoring confidence in the offensive defense concept of deterrence through mutually assured destruction in the minds of an already anxious and skeptical public; and ironically, debate about President Reagan's Strategic Defense Initiative (SDI) seems to be heightening public anxieties about a new cycle of arms competition between the superpowers. Carefully coordinated efforts by the United States and its allies on the public presentation of policies with respect to nuclear deterrence are therefore more than ever necessary to ensure popular support—especially in circumstances in which the Soviet Union will try to influence Western defense policies by encouraging opposition to nuclear modernization by various peace groups in countries allied to the United States. For the U.S. government to consult fully with allied governments before announcing policy initiatives is particularly important in this regard. From this viewpoint, the initial presentation of President Reagan's Strategic Defense Initiative in a speech from the White House—a major change in security policy made without prior notification of allied governments—is a precedent that should not be followed.

Although security conditions in Japan differ from those in Europe, it should also be remembered that the consensus in favor of defense policy based on the concept of nuclear deterrence depends in most West European countries and in Japan on the United States and its allied governments being seen to take arms control negotiations seriously. The governments should be most careful not to allow a situation to develop in which the Soviet Union can undermine the unity of the relationship between the United States and its allies through public disillusionment with their governments' performance in arms control negotiations.

With regard to the need to develop a security policy consensus among the tripartite partners of the Western industrialized democracies, it is important to recognize the fact that although INF, together with other issues such as the Soviet invasion of Afghanistan, prompted tripartite consultations on security questions, more opportunities must be arranged for ensuring that all three parties are properly informed of the security interests of the others. That the Western summit meetings now regularly include discussion of security matters is a welcomed trend. Yet more regular tripartite consultations at the ministerial and expert levels need to be held to promote mutual understanding of the varying national interests involved.

Improving the quality of Japanese-European dialogues on security questions is particularly important to this end. Such discussions, to date, remain inchoate. And, as the analysis in this chapter points out, there are important distinctions between Japan and Europe on security questions, both in substance and in perception. Furthermore, skepticism persists in European and Japanese perceptions of each other's security policies. On the INF question, for example, the Japanese have been concerned that European governments, preoccupied with the management of their domestic constituencies, might be content with a reduction in the number of missiles capable of reaching Western Europe at the expense of the security interests of Asian countries. This concern, evident in the initial stage of the INF negotiations, has now been alleviated considerably as a result of American and European assurances that they will not consent to any arrangement that would permit the Soviet theater nuclear threat to be transferred to Asia. Nevertheless, the Japanese public remains concerned that some European governments might seek to redistribute rather than to reduce the SS-20 risk.

In the light of prevailing views among Western security specialists on alliance defense strategy, it is plausible to assume that for the foreseeable future the concept of nuclear deterrence through mutually assured destruction will remain the mainstay of the defense policy of the Western industrialized democracies. As Paul

H. Nitze pointed out, "for the immediate future, at least the next ten years, we will continue to base deterrence on the ultimate threat of nuclear retaliation."[12] On the other hand, public antinuclear sentiment in the Western nations will persist. It could even grow stronger. The need for tripartite policy coordination regarding Western defense strategy will therefore increase, particularly given the growing interaction between formulation of defense policy and public debate in the Western industrialized democracies. Such policy-coordination will no doubt be complicated and difficult, as the analysis of the INF experience in the preceding pages suggests. Yet, if we draw the right lessons from the experience of the INF debates on security questions, cooperation and the development of common policies among the United States, Japan, and the NATO states of Western Europe can only be enhanced.

## Endnotes

1. Helmut Schmidt, *Survival* (January/February 1978), p. 4.
2. International Institute of Strategic Studies, *Strategic Survey* (1979), p. 101.
3. Robert S. McNamara, "The Military Role of Nuclear Weapons," *Foreign Affairs* vol. 62, no. 1 (Fall 1983), pp. 59–80.
4. The International Institute of Strategic Studies, *Strategic Survey 1982–83*, 1983.
5. Pierre Lellouche, "France and the Euromissiles," *Foreign Affairs*, vol. 62, no. 2 (Winter 1983/84), pp. 318–34.
6. J. Michael Legge, *Theater Nuclear Weapons and the NATO Strategy of Flexible Response*, R-2964-FF (Santa Monica: The Rand Corporation, April 1983).
7. Laurence Freedman, *Nuclear War and Nuclear Peace* (London: Macmillan, 1983).
8. J. Michael Legge, *Theater Nuclear Weapons*, p. 76.
9. David Capitanchik and Richard C. Eichenberg, "Defence and Public Opinion," *Chatham House Papers*, no. 20, 1983.
10. *Ibid*, pp. 80–82.
11. *Ibid*, p. 82.
12. Paul H. Nitze, "Towards a Nuclear Free World," Speech to the Los Angeles World Affairs Council, February 28, 1985.

*Appendix*

# NUCLEAR FORCES IN THE FAR EAST-ASIA/PACIFIC THEATER

Table A–1 displays Soviet nuclear forces that are deployed for use in a theaterwide conflict in the Asia-Pacific region. The table includes forces based in the Siberian, Transbaykal, and Far East military districts of the Soviet Far East theater, and ballistic missile submarines of the Soviet Pacific fleet. Additional nuclear forces of the Soviet Far East theater are deployed in the Central Asian military district, where they can be used against China, South Asia, Southwest Asia, or Europe. For example, in addition to the 135 SS-20 launchers in the theater shown in Table A–1 for 1985, there are another 36 SS-20 launchers in the Central Asian military district that can reach targets in both Europe and Asia. As of October 1985, U.S. Department of Defense and public sources assumed that 171 SS-20s were deployed so as to target U.S., allied, and Chinese territory in the Asia-Pacific region.[1]

The data in Table A–1 do not conform exactly to the categories used by the Department of Defense in discussing theater nuclear forces. The DoD categories were developed with the U.S.-Soviet intermediate-range nuclear force (INF) negotiations in mind, and were heavily influenced by nuclear forces deployed in Europe. They are not totally satisfactory categories for assessment of the nuclear balance in Asia. For example, elements of sea-based nuclear forces make important contributions to the balance of nuclear forces for theaterwide conflict in Asia, but are not classed as INF by DoD—U.S. and Soviet SLBMs, U.S. sea-launched cruise missiles for land attack, and U.S. carrier-based tactical aircraft.

---

*Note:* The editors are indebted to Dr. J. J. Martin for the preparation of this appendix.

271

Table A–1   Soviet Nuclear Forces for Theaterwide Conflict, 1985 (Far East Theater)[a]

|  | 1965 | 1970 | 1975 | 1980 | 1985 |
|---|---|---|---|---|---|
| MR/IRBM Launchers | | | | | |
| SS-4/SS-5 | 100 | 100 | 100 | 100 | 0 |
| SS-20[b] | 0 | 0 | 0 | 40 | 135–171 |
| Total | 100 | 100 | 100 | 140 | 135–171 |
| Medium-Range Bombers | | | | | |
| Strategic Air Armies | | | | | |
| *Badger/Blinder* | c | 175 | 160 | 145 | 80 |
| *Backfire* | 0 | 0 | 0 | 15 | 40 |
| Total | c | 175 | 160 | 160 | 120 |
| Soviet Naval Aviation | | | | | |
| *Badger/Blinder* | 55 | 70 | 85 | 95 | 90 |
| *Backfire* | 0 | 0 | 0 | 5 | 40 |
| Total | 55 | 70 | 85 | 100 | 130 |
| Submarine-Launched Ballistic Missiles (SLBMs)[d] | | | | | |
| Submarines (SSBN/SSB) | c | c | c | c | 31 |
| SLBM Launchers | c | c | c | c | 405 |

*Sources:* Department of Defense, *Soviet Military Power;* The International Institute for Strategic Studies (IISS), *The Military Balance.*

[a]Forces deployed in the Siberian, Transbaykal, and Far East military districts, and at sea.

[b]Each SS-20 missile is MIRVed with three warheads. Each launcher is assessed to have one missile on launcher, plus one refire missile. The upper range of numbers for 1985 includes launchers that can target both Europe and Asia.

[c]Data not available.

[d]SS-11 ICBMs deployed north of China could also be used to attack U.S., allied, and Chinese targets in the Asia-Pacific region.

The Department of Defense publishes information on Soviet theater nuclear forces in terms of four categories:[2]

1. Intermediate-range nuclear forces. These forces are further divided into:
   a. Longer-range INF missiles (LRINF), consisting of ballistic missiles with ranges between 1,800 and 5,500 km. Included are Soviet SS-4 medium-range ballistic missiles (MRBMs) and Soviet SS-5 and SS-20 intermediate-range ballistic missiles (IRBMs), which organizationally are part of the Strategic Rocket Forces.

b. Shorter-range INF missiles (SRINF), consisting of ballistic missiles with ranges less than 1,800 km. These include SS-22 missiles deployed with Soviet ground forces; there are approximately 40 SS-22 launchers deployed in the Far East theater.[3]

c. INF aircraft, including the medium bombers of the Strategic Air Armies and Soviet Naval Aviation, and dual-capable tactical aircraft.

2. Short-range nuclear forces, including battlefield nuclear missile and rocket systems (*Frog, Scud,* and SS-21) and nuclear artillery deployed with Soviet ground forces. Over 200 *Frog* launchers are deployed in the Far East; these are being replaced with SS-21 launchers. There are over 100 *Scud* launchers with forces on the Sino-Soviet border; these launchers are expected to be replaced with the SS-23 SRINF system. Soviet divisions in the Far East are equipped with nuclear artillery.[4]

3. Land-based defensive nuclear forces, consisting of nuclear-capable surface-to-air missiles (SAMs). No information on Soviet nuclear SAMs is publicly available.

4. Sea-based nuclear forces, including submarine-launched ballistic missiles (SLBMs), sea-launched cruise missiles (SLCMs) for land attack, and a variety of nuclear weapon systems for antisurface ship warfare (ASuW), antisubmarine warfare (ASW), and antiair warfare (AAW). The Soviet Pacific Fleet includes 103 general purpose submarines, many of which reportedly carry SS-N-15 or SS-N-16 nuclear ASW weapons and nuclear antiship missiles. Land-attack SLCMs are deployed on the new *Yankee* SSN.[5] Soviet surface ships carry nuclear antiship and ASW weapons.[6]

Table A–2 displays U.S. nuclear forces that could be used for theaterwide conflict in the Asia-Pacific region in 1985.

U.S. cruisers, destroyers, and attack submarines are being equipped with TLAM/N land-attack cruise missiles. The Pacific fleet currently has 14 cruisers, 31 destroyers, and 44 nuclear-powered attack submarines. Some of these ships and submarines carry nuclear-capable *Terrier* SAMs, the nuclear antisubmarine rocket ASROC, and the submarine-launched ASW rocket SUBROC. U.S. P-3 and S-3 ASW aircraft are capable of employing nuclear depth bombs.[7]

Table A–3 shows China's nuclear forces in 1985.

**Table A–2    U.S. Nuclear Forces for Theaterwide Conflict, 1985 (U.S. Pacific Command)**

| | |
|---|---|
| MR/IRBM Launchers | 0 |
| **Long-Range/Medium-Range Bombers** | |
| B-52 (Land-Based)[a] | 14 |
| **Nuclear-Capable Tactical Aircraft** | |
| A-6/A-7 (Carrier-Based) | 204 |
| F-4/F-16 (Land-Based) | 120 |
| Total | 324 |
| **Submarine-Launched Ballistic Missiles (SLBMs) and Cruise Missiles (SLCMs)[b]** | |
| Submarines (SSBN) | 5 |
| SLBM Launchers | 120 |
| TLAM/N | c |

*Sources:* Department of Defense, *Soviet Military Power;* International Institute for Strategic Studies, *The Military Balance; Armed Forces Journal International* (November 1983); *Air Force Magazine* (August 1985); Congressional Research Service, *U.S.-Soviet Military Balance, 1980-1985*, Report No. B5-B95.

[a]Based on Guam. In addition, a SAC wing of B-52s is based at March Air Force Base, California.

[b]Minuteman ICBMs could also be used to attack targets in the eastern USSR.

[c]Data not available.

**Table A–3    Chinese Nuclear Forces, 1985**

| | |
|---|---|
| **ICBM Launchers** | |
| DF-5 | 2 |
| **IRBM Launchers** | |
| DF-3 | 60 |
| **MRBM Launchers** | |
| DF-2 | 50 |
| **Medium Bombers** | |
| H-6/*Badgers* | 120 |
| ***Submarine-Launched Ballistic Missiles (SLBMs)*** | |
| *Submarines (SSBN)* | 1 |
| *SLBM Launchers[b]* | 12 |

*Source:* The International Institute for Strategic Studies, *The Military Balance*
[a]The CSS-NX-3 SLBM is being tested, but has not been deployed.

# Endnotes

1. *The Military Balance, 1984–1985* (London: The International Institute for Strategic Studies, 1984), p. 17; *New York Times,* October 4, 1985, p. 7.
2. Secretary of Defense Caspar W. Weinberger, *Annual Report to the Congress, Fiscal Year 1983,* Washington, D.C. (February 8, 1982), pp. III–71 to III–74.
3. *Soviet Military Power: 1985* (Washington, D.C.: Department of Defense, April 1985), p. 38.
4. *Ibid.*
5. *Ibid.,* pp. 96, 107; *The Military Balance, 1984-1985,* p. 19.
6. Gordon H. McCormick, "Nuclear Weapons, Sea Power and Theater War," in G. McCormick and J. Maurer, eds., *Doctrine, Technology, and Sea Power,* Annapolis: Naval Institute Press (1986).
7. *Soviet Military Power, 1985,* pp. 104–05; McCormick, "Nuclear Weapons, Sea Power and Theater War"; Anthony H. Cordesman, "The Military Balance in Northeast Asia: The Challenge to Japan and Korea," *Armed Forces Journal International* (November 1983), p. 98.

# ABOUT THE CONTRIBUTORS

**Harry Gelman** is a Senior Staff Member of the Political Science Department of The Rand Corporation, and a former Assistant National Intelligence Officer for the Soviet Union and Eastern Europe. He retired from the CIA in 1979 after many years of participation in the U.S. intelligence community's political and strategic analysis of Soviet affairs. He is the author of *The Brezhnev Politburo and the Decline of Detente* (Ithaca: Cornell University Press, 1984). He was educated at Cornell University, Brooklyn College, and the School of Slavonic and East European Studies of London University. In 1963-1964 he was a senior Fellow at Columbia University's Research Institute on International Change, and in 1972-1973 he was a Fellow of the Hoover Institution, Stanford University. He has published many articles on Sino-Soviet matters and Soviet policy toward Asia, including the SeCAP March 1983 study, *Soviet Expansionism in Asia and the Sino-Soviet-U.S. Triangle*.

**Young-Sun Ha** is Associate Professor of International Relations at Seoul National University. He received his B.A. and M.A. degrees in political science from Seoul National University and his Ph.D. in political science from the University of Washington. He was a Compton Fellow at the Center of International Studies, Princeton University (1978-1979). Dr. Ha is the author of *Nuclear Proliferation, World Order, and Korea* and has contributed numerous articles to journals and books published in Korea and the United States.

**Karl D. Jackson** is Associate Professor of Political Science at the University of California, Berkeley. He received his Ph.D. from the Massachusetts Institute of Technology and began teaching at Berkeley in 1972. His research efforts focus on Southeast Asia, with special emphasis on Indonesia, Cambodia, Vietnam, Thailand, and the Philippines. His publications include: *Traditional Authority, Islam, and Rebellion: A Study of Indonesian Political Behavior; Political Power and Communications in Indonesia* (co-edited with Lucian Pye); *ASEAN Security and Economic Development* (co-edited with Hadi Soesastro); and *Rendezvous with Death: Democratic Kampuchea 1975-1978*. During 1982-1984 Professor Jackson was attached to the Office of the Secretary of Defense.

**Euji Kamiya** has been a professor at Keio University, Japan, since 1970. He received his Ph.D. from Kyoto University in 1963 and has been a visiting professor at the University of Chicago and Columbia University. An expert on the Korean War and Japan-U.S. relations, he is the author of *Chōsen Sensō* [The Korean War], Chūō Kōron Sha, 1966; and "The Korean Peninsula after Park Chung Hee," *Asian Survey*, vol. 20, no. 7 (July 1980). He edited *Hokutō Ajia no kinkō to dōyō* [Balance and Change in Northeast Asia], Keio University Press, 1984, and *20-Seiki no sensō* [Wars in the Twentieth Century], Kōdan Sha, 1985 and co-edited *The Security of Korea: U.S. and Japanese Perspectives on the 1980s*, Westview Press, 1980.

**Hiroshi Kimura** has been a professor at Hokkaido University, Japan, for 15 years and currently serves as Director of the University's Slavic Studies Center. He received his B.A. and M.A. from Kyoto University and his Ph.D. in political science from Columbia University in 1968. From 1977 to 1979 he served as a visiting professor at Georgetown University and from 1982 to 1983 as a visiting fellow at Stanford University. Mr. Kimura has published numerous articles on Soviet foreign policy, including "The Soviet Proposal on Confidence-Building Measures and the Japanese Response," *Journal on International Affairs* (New York), Summer 1983; "The Soviet Threat and the Security of Japan," in Roger E. Kanet (ed.), *Soviet Foreign Policy in the 1980s*, Praeger, 1982; and "The Conclusion of the Sino-Japanese Peace Treaty (1978): Soviet Coercive Strategy and Its Limit," *Studies in Comparative Communism* (Summer/ Autumn 1985).

**Masataka Kosaka** has been professor of International Relations at Kyoto University since 1972. From 1983 to 1984 he was Chairman of Prime Minister Nakasone's Peace Problems Study Group, which in December 1984 produced a report on Japan's national security problems. From 1979 to 1980 he also served as rapporteur in Prime Minister Ohira's Comprehensive National Security Study Group. Dr. Kosaka's major publications include *Saishō Yoshida Shigeru* [Chancellor Shigeru Yoshida], Chūō Kōron Sha, 1968; *Koten Gaikō no seijuku to hōkai* (The Rise and Collapse of Classic Diplomacy], Chūō Kōron Sha, 1978; *Bunmei ga suibō suru toki* [When Civilizations Decline], Shincho Sha, 1981; and *Gaikō kankaku* [Diplomatic Senses], Chūō Kōron Sha, 1985.

**James J. Martin** is a Senior Vice President of Science Applications International Corporation (SAIC) and Director of its Theater Warfare Program Office. He is also Project Director for the Target Damage Requirements Study for DNA and SHAPE. He was educated at the University of Wisconsin and received his Ph.D. in Operations Research from the Massachusetts Institute of Technology. Formerly he served with the U.S. Navy for 20 years, where he directed a study of national intelligence for the National Security Council and served as a Special Assistant to the Assistant to the Secretary of Defense. He authored many OSD studies on the survivability, security, and operational effectiveness of theater nuclear forces.

**Tom Millar** has been a Professorial Fellow in the Department of International Relations at the Australian National University since 1968, but is currently seconded for three years to the University of London where he is Head of the Australian Studies Centre in the Institute of Commonwealth Studies. Professor Millar is a graduate of the Royal Military College in Canberra. He served in the Australian Army during and after World War II, retiring in 1950, two days before North Korea invaded South Korea. He graduated in Economics and History from the University of Western Australia (1953), did a Master's in History from the University of Melbourne (1958) and a Ph.D. in International Relations at the London School of Economics and Political Science (1960). In 1961-62 he was a Visiting Research Fellow in International Organization at Columbia University, and joined the Australian National University in July of 1962. He established the Strategic and Defence Studies Centre at ANU and headed it from 1966 to 1970. He then served as Director of the Australian Institute of International Affairs from 1969 to 1976. Professor Millar's publications include *Australia's Defence*, Melbourne University Press, 1965 and 1969; *The Commonwealth and the United Nations*, Sydney University Press, 1967; *Foreign Policy*, Melbourne: Georgian House, 1972; *Australia in Peace and War*, Canberra: Australian National University Press, 1978; *The East-West Strategic Balance*, London: George Allen and Unwin, 1981; and *Current International Treaties*, London: Croom Helm, 1984.

**John Roper** is currently Editor of *International Affairs*, the quarterly journal of the Royal Institute of International Affairs in London and is in charge of the Atlantic and Security Programs at the Institute. He has served as a special advisor to the House of Lords Sub-Committee on the Future Financing of the European Community and as consultant to the European Media Institute, University of Manchester. Mr. Roper first ran for Parliament in 1964 and was elected Member of Parliament for Farnsworth in June 1970, and was reelected in 1974 and 1979. During the 1970s he served on a number of committees and delegations including, from 1977 to 1979, as Chairman of the Committee on Defence Questions and Armaments, Western European Union Assembly. From 1974 to 1979 he was a member of the House of Commons Select Committee on Expenditure: Defence and External Affairs Sub-Committee. Mr. Roper took his undergraduate degree in social sciences from Magdalen College,

Oxford. He held a Harkness Fellowship in international economics at the University of Chicago (1959-1961) and a research fellowship in economic statistics at the University of Manchester from 1961 to 1962.

**Henry S. Rowen** is professor of Public Management at Stanford University's Graduate School of Business, and a Senior Research Fellow at the Hoover Institution. He was educated at the Massachusetts Institute of Technology and at Oxford University. From 1961 to 1964 he served as Deputy Assistant Secretary of Defense for International Security Affairs and was responsible principally for European policy issues. He was president of The Rand Corporation (1967-1972) and served as Chairman of the National Intelligence Council from 1981 to 1983.

**Yukio Satoh** is currently Director of the Policy Coordination Division of the Ministry of Foreign Affairs in Japan. He has been in the Japanese Foreign Service since 1961 and has served in Washington, D.C. and, as the Japanese Consul General, in London. During the latter assignment he co-authored, with John Roper, the paper that appears in this volume. From 1976 to 1977, Mr. Satoh was Director of Security Affairs Division, American Affairs Bureau, and two years thereafter, he served as Private Secretary to Foreign Minister Sunao Sonoda. Mr. Satoh received a degree in Law from the University of Tokyo and a degree in History from the University of Edinburgh. He has been a Fellow of the International Institute for Strategic Studies (IISS) and has written extensively on issues of Japanese and Western security, defense, and cooperation. Among his major publications are "The Evolution of Japanese Security Policy," *Adelphi Paper No. 178*, IISS (London), 1982; "Opportunities for Broader Co-operation," in Loukas Tsoukalis and Maureen White, eds., *Japan and Western Europe*, published by Frances Pinter, Great Britain, 1982; "Western Security: A Japanese Point of View," U.S. Naval War College, *Naval War College Review* (September-October 1983); "Security Cooper-ation between Western Europe and Japan: The Ignored Dimension of Western Security," *Japan and Europe: Towards Closer Cooperation*, Japan Center for International Exchange, Tokyo, 1983; "Le Japon et sa Défense," *Politique Etrangère*, IFRI (Paris), 4, 1985.

**Robert A. Scalapino** is currently Robson Research Professor of Gov-ernment at the University of California at Berkeley and also Director of the University's Institute of East Asian Studies. As well, he is editor of *Asian Survey*, a scholarly publication. Professor Scalapino has written over 200 articles and 15 books or monographs on Asian politics and U.S. Asian policy. His most recent works include *Asia and the Major Powers* (1972); *American-Japanese Relations in a Changing Era* (1972); *Commu-nism in Korea* (two volumes, with Chong-Sik Lee, 1972, for which they received the Woodrow Wilson Award for the best book published in 1973 on government, politics or international affairs); *Asia and the Road Ahead* (1975); *The Foreign Policy of Modern Japan* (editor and contributor, 1977); *The United States and Korea—Looking Ahead* (1979); "Asia," in *The United States in the 1980s* (1980); "China and Northeast Asia," in *The China Factor* (1981); "The Political Influence of the USSR in Asia," in *Soviet Policy in East Asia* (1982); and *Modern China and its Revolutionary Process* (co-authored with George T. Yu, 1985).

**Richard H. Solomon** was for a decade head of The Rand Corporation's Political Science Department, and Associate Director of Rand's research program on International Security and Defense Policy in the National Security Research Division. From 1971 to 1976 he served as Senior Staff Member for Asian Affairs on the National Security Council, having previously been Professor of Political Science at the University of Michigan. Dr. Solomon received his Ph.D. from the Massachusetts Institute of Technology in 1966, where he specialized in Political Science and Chinese politics. He has contributed articles to a variety of professional journals, including *Foreign Affairs* and *The China Quarterly*, and has published four books: *The China Factor* (1981); *Asian Security in the 1980s* (1979); *A Revolution Is Not a Dinner Party* (1976); and *Mao's Revolution and the Chinese Political Culture* (1971).

**James A. Thomson** is Vice President of Project AIR FORCE at The Rand Corporation. In addition, he directs two research programs at Rand—the National Security Strategies program for Rand's Project AIR FORCE and the International Security and Defense Policy program for Rand's other national security clients. In these roles, he oversees Rand's research agenda in national strategy, foreign policy, defense policy, and arms control. He also conducts research on nuclear deterrence and European security. Prior to joining Rand in 1981, he served on the National Security Council staff and in the Office of the Secretary of Defense.

**Yao Wenbin** was born in China's Sichuan Province in 1930. He attended Sichuan University, where he majored in history. In 1950 Mr. Yao joined the People's Liberation Army, in which his assignments have included staff work in the Ministry of Defense. Since 1979 he has been a researcher and council member of the Beijing Institute of International Strategic Studies. His writings, as presented in papers to various professional conferences in China and abroad, include: "Some Problems of Soviet Military Strategy"; "On Soviet Foreign Policy"; "Soviet Foreign Policy in a Transitional Period"; and "An Assessment of the U.S. Strategic Defense Initiative."

# GLOSSARY OF ACRONYMS

| | | | |
|---|---|---|---|
| AAW | Antiair warfare | DPO | Defense Program Outline |
| ABM | Antiballistic missile | GATT-IMF | General Agreement on |
| ALCM | Air-launched cruise | | Tariffs and Trade— |
| | missile | | International Monetary |
| ANS | National Sihanouk Army | | Fund |
| ANZAC | Australia-New Zealand | GLCM | Ground-launched cruise |
| | Army Corps | | missile |
| ANZUS | Australia, New Zealand, | GNP | Gross national product |
| | and United States | HLG | High Level Group, of |
| | Security Treaty | | NATO |
| | Organization | ICBM | Intercontinental ballistic |
| ASAT | Antisatellite (weapon | | missile |
| | system) | ICK | International Conference |
| ASEAN | Association of Southeast | | on Kampuchea |
| | Asian Nations | IISS | The International Institute |
| ASM | Air-to-surface missile | | of Strategic Studies |
| ASuW | Antisurface ship warfare | | (London) |
| ASW | Antisubmarine warfare | INF | Intermediate-range |
| BAM | Baykal-Amur Mainline | | nuclear forces |
| | Railroad | IPU | Inter-Parliamentary Union |
| C³ | Command, control and | IRBM | Intermediate-range |
| | communications | | ballistic missile |
| C³I | Command, control, | JSP | Japan Socialist Party |
| | communications, and | KAL | Korean Air Lines |
| | intelligence | KPNLF | Khmer People's National |
| CIA | Central Intelligence | | Liberation Front |
| | Agency | LPDR | Lao People's Democratic |
| CGDK | Coalition Government of | | Republic |
| | Democratic Kampuchea | LRTNF | Long-range theatre |
| CPSU | Communist Party of the | | nuclear forces |
| | Soviet Union | LTDP | Long-term defense plan |
| CONUS | Continental United States | MIAs | Servicemen missing in |
| CVBG | Carrier Battle Group | | action |
| DJP | Democratic Justice Party | MIRV | Multiple, independently |
| DKP | Democratic Korea Party | | targetable reentry |
| DoD | Department of Defense | | vehicle |

| | | | |
|---|---|---|---|
| MLF | Multilateral Nuclear Force | SDI | Strategic Defense Initiative |
| MPLA | Popular Movement for the Liberation of Angola | SEATO | Southeast Asia Treaty Organization |
| MRBM | Medium-range ballistic missile | SG | Special Group, of NATO |
| MR/IRBM | Medium-range/intermediate-range ballistic missiles | SLBM | Submarine-launched ballistic missile |
| NATO | North Atlantic Treaty Organization | SLCM | Sea-launched cruise missile |
| NKDP | New Korea Democratic Party | SLOC | Sea lines of communication |
| NPG | Nuclear Planning Group, of NATO | SNA | Soviet naval aviation |
| | | SPD | The Social Democratic Party of West Germany |
| NPT | Non-Proliferation Treaty | SRAM | Short-range attack missile |
| NSC | National Security Council | SRV | Socialist Republic of Vietnam |
| OECD | Organization for Economic Cooperation and Development | SSBN | Ballistic missile firing submarine, nuclear powered |
| PAVN | People's Army of Vietnam | | |
| PD-59 | Presidential Directive 59 | SSM | Surface-to-surface missile |
| PLA | People's Liberation Army | SSN | Submarine, nuclear powered |
| PRM-38 | Presidential Review Memorandum 38 | TLAM/N | Tomahawk land attack missile/nuclear |
| PRK | People's Republic of Kampuchea | TNF | Theater nuclear forces |
| ROK | Republic of Korea | TVD | Theater of military operations, of the USSR |
| SACEUR | Supreme Allied Commander, Europe | | |
| SALT | Strategic Arms Limitation Talks | UNGA | United Nations General Assembly |
| SALT | Strategic Arms Limitation Treaty | UNITA | National Union for the Total Independence of Angola |
| SAM | Surface-to-air missile | | |
| SDF | Self-Defense Forces, of Japan | ZOPFAN | Zone of Peace, Freedom, and Neutrality |

# INDEX

# INDEX